Women in STEM on Television

ALSO EDITED BY ASHLEY LYNN CARLSON

Genius on Television: Essays on Small Screen Depictions of Big Minds (McFarland, 2015)

Women in STEM on Television

Critical Essays

Edited by
ASHLEY LYNN CARLSON

McFarland & Company, Inc., Publishers
Jefferson, North Carolina

ISBN (print) 978-1-4766-6941-0
ISBN (ebook) 978-1-4766-3280-3

LIBRARY OF CONGRESS CATALOGUING DATA ARE AVAILABLE

BRITISH LIBRARY CATALOGUING DATA ARE AVAILABLE

© 2018 Ashley Lynn Carlson. All rights reserved

No part of this book may be reproduced or transmitted in any form or by any means, electronic or mechanical, including photocopying or recording, or by any information storage and retrieval system, without permission in writing from the publisher.

Front cover images *clockwise from top left* Jill Hennessy in *Crossing Jordan* (NBC/Photofest); Louise Brealey as Molly in *Sherlock* (PBS/Photofest); Tatiana Maslany in *Orphan Black* (BBC America/Photofest)

Printed in the United States of America

McFarland & Company, Inc., Publishers
 Box 611, Jefferson, North Carolina 28640
  www.mcfarlandpub.com

For Charlotte

Table of Contents

Acknowledgments   ix

Introduction
    Ashley Lynn Carlson   1

Achievements, Gaps and the "Achievement Gap":
STEM in Children's Programming
    Ashley Lynn Carlson *and* Hope J. Crowell   7

The Doctors Who Waited: The Lonely Woman Scientist Trope
in Geek TV
    Bridget M. Blodgett *and* Anastasia Salter   20

Girl Geniuses: Anti-Intellectual Stereotypes of Women in STEM
Careers in Contemporary Televisual Culture
    JZ Long   36

"One of the Guys": Female Engineers on Television
    Ashley Lynn Carlson   56

STEM and Diversity on Primetime Television: The Representation
of Gender and Race in *The 100*
    Natalie Krikowa   71

"We have to know our biology": Power, Patriarchy and the Body
in *Orphan Black*
    Lauren Riccelli Zwicky   86

"Not everyone's cut out for Hollywood": "The Iron Ceiling"
in Marvel's *Agent Carter*
    Lisa K. Perdigao   102

A Bad Case of the Feels: Emotion Versus Reason on *Blindspot*
  ERIN NICHOLES   120

Femininity and Forensics: *Silent Witness* and the Representation of the Female Pathologist
  LAURA FOSTER *and* HELEN MCKENZIE   134

When the Woman Cuts: The Figure of the Female Medical on *CSI: Miami* and *Crossing Jordan*
  CARY M.J. ELZA   152

A Woman in a Man's (Fictional) World: Considering the Importance of Dr. Molly Hooper in the BBC's Modern Adaptation of *Sherlock*
  JENNIFER PHILLIPS   170

The River, the Rock, the Relative and the Returned: Depictions of Women Scientists in *Doctor Who*'s Moffat Era
  KRISTINE LARSEN   187

About the Contributors   207

Index   209

Acknowledgments

Many thanks, first and foremost, to the contributors for this project, who went through multiple rounds of revisions to produce a collection of essays of which we can all be proud. I'm also grateful for the support of my wonderful colleagues at Montana Western, especially Michelle Anderson, Jed Berry, Bethany Blankenship, Shane Borrowman, Eric Dyerson, Brenden Kennedy, Laura Strauss, Alan Weltzien, and Erin Zavitz. Thanks also to Hope J. Crowell who assisted with some of the copy-editing and coauthored an essay with me, as well as all of my students, who inspire me every day. Finally, my deepest love and gratitude to my wonderful family, especially my husband, Daniel.

Introduction

ASHLEY LYNN CARLSON

The term "STEM," an acronym for Science, Technology, Engineering, and Math, has been showing up everywhere recently, from the local parent-teacher association meeting to the White House briefing room.[1] Educators, policy makers, and even celebrities have rallied to encourage young people in STEM. A large part of this interest is in response to the United States' slipping rankings in math and science compared to other countries (27th and 20th, respectively).[2] The National Math + Science Initiative describes the situation as a "STEM Crisis," stating, "the United States is losing its competitive edge in math and science while the rest of the world soars ahead. Our knowledge capital, which fuels innovation and economic growth, is at risk."[3] In the midst of this general frenzy over STEM, the subject of women in STEM has been particularly prominent. To understand why, one only needs to look at the numbers. Despite huge gains in the representation of women in a wide range of careers, they remain extremely underrepresented in many STEM fields. If the U.S. is going to regain its competitive edge, it needs participation from more than just the male population.

In the 20th century, the number of women to graduate from U.S. colleges and universities each year grew not only to rival, but also to actually surpass the number of men. In 1979–80, 49 percent of bachelor's degrees were awarded to women, by 1989–90 that number was 53 percent, and by 1999–2000 it was 57 percent.[4] Between 2000 and 2014, the percentage of college degrees awarded to women each year remained steady at about 57 percent.[5] Given these numbers, one might expect that women today would be well represented across all fields of study, but they lag significantly in many STEM fields. Women accounted for an astonishingly low 35 percent of all STEM undergraduate degree recipients in 2013–2014.[6] Worse yet, the percentage of women graduating with degrees in certain fields is downright abysmal. For example, in 2013–14, women earned only 18 percent of bachelor's degrees in computer and information sciences, as well as only 18 percent of bachelor's in engineering.[7] Clearly something is keeping women from pursuing these fields of study.

The argument that innate gender differences account for the achievement gap in STEM persists despite a growing body of evidence that gender stereotypes and cultural norms, rather than biology, are the primary factors affecting girls' interest and performance in science and math. One study of 34 countries found that higher national levels of implicit gender-science stereotyping (associating "science" with "male") predicted larger gender gaps in science and math achievement among 8th graders.[8] Another study found that among 15-year-olds the gender achievement gap in math was smaller in countries with more gender-equal cultures.[9] The evidence suggests that girls are socialized to believe that they are less competent than boys in science and math, and this socialization process has a significant effect on their success in STEM subjects well before they graduate from high school. It is no surprise, therefore, that so few women enroll in STEM degree programs in college and pursue STEM careers.

Moreover, the impact of gender stereotypes goes beyond education statistics. The same stereotypes that keep many girls from succeeding in math and science to begin with also negatively affect women and girls who have defied the odds and excelled in these subjects. Gender biases create disparities in mentoring, hiring, and salaries for women who enter STEM fields.[10] A *Harvard Business Review* research report on gender in science, engineering, and technology (SET), *The Athena Factor*, notes that "over time, fully 52% of highly qualified females working for SET companies quit their jobs, driven out by hostile work environments and extreme job pressures."[11] Further, *The Athena Factor* cites "hostile macho cultures" as a primary aspect of the negative work environment that women experience, and reports "63% [of women in SET companies] experienced sexual harassment."[12] For many women, the workplace discrimination that they encounter in STEM even further diminishes the appeal of these careers.

Ultimately, the negative stereotypes that keep so many women from succeeding in STEM result in a huge loss of potential talent. According to the U.S. Bureau of Labor Statistics, the occupations that require a bachelor's degree with the highest projected growth rates are almost all related to STEM, and include professions such as personal finance advisors, computer systems analysts, biomedical engineers, and forensic science technicians.[13] ManpowerGroup's 2015 report on global talent shortages found that technicians, accounting and finance staff, and engineers were among the top 10 jobs that U.S. employers struggle the most to fill.[14] As *The Athena Factor* astutely notes, "to fill the skills gap, companies need to turn to female talent in their own backyard."[15] Doing this, however, will require considerable changes in cultural norms and the public's view of women in STEM.

A number of organizations and agencies are attempting to create these cultural changes. Major companies such as Microsoft, Verizon, and 3M have funded initiatives to engage young women in STEM fields.[16] Organizations such as the National Girls Collaborative Project and Girls Who Code are also working to raise interest in STEM among girls through education and mentoring programs.[17] All of these efforts are chipping away at cultural barriers that diminish women's interest and success in science and math fields. However, classroom initiatives, after school programs, and summer camps—programs that are largely focused on girls in kindergarten through high school—do not truly engage the broader American public. To elicit the kind of cultural shift required to make STEM more appealing and more accessible to women and girls on a national level, perceptions must change among the public at large, female and male, young and old. This is where popular media can have a profound impact.

This, of course, brings us to the present work. Television, whether broadcast, cable, or streaming, is one of the most pervasive elements of life in the United States. Nielsen reports that 96 percent of U.S. homes have television access through broadcast, cable, DBS or Telco, or broadband Internet.[18] In the first quarter of 2016, American adults spent an average of 4 hours and 31 minutes watching live television each day, and an additional 33 minutes watching time-shifted TV (DVR).[19] That amounts to an average of 35 hours and 26 minutes per week, which is more than the average American spends at work.[20] Meanwhile, children ages 2–11 watch, on average, more than 20 hours of television (including live and DVR) per week, and teenagers aged 12–17 watch about 15.5 hours per week.[21] Moreover, 50 percent of TV households have subscription video on demand services, such as Netflix or HBO NOW, and the hours spent watching these services are not included in the aforementioned numbers.[22] Needless to say, the cultural impact of television is enormous. This collection of new essays marks the first broad effort to analyze how television portrays women in STEM, and to consider how these portrayals may affect women in the contemporary workplace.

In surveying television series that include women in STEM careers, it quickly becomes evident that these portrayals are complex; they frequently break down certain gender barriers while upholding other problematic gender stereotypes. The essays begin with two that consider how children's television constructs women in STEM. Hope J. Crowell and I analyze three series specifically intended to draw girls to STEM, and discuss the extent to which these series may or may not actually achieve their goal by addressing specific issues that frequently dissuade young women from pursuing STEM studies and careers. Next, Bridget M. Blodgett and Anastasia Salter argue that two animated series featuring women in STEM, *Steven Universe* and *Adventure Time*, both reinforce the idea that women in science and engineering are isolated and lonely, possibly undermining these characters' potentials as positive role models.

The next two essays also provide broad surveys of series with STEM characters; JZ Long focuses on four prime time series, *Arrow*, *Bones*, *Criminal Minds*, and *NCIS*, each with women in science and technology, while I focus specifically on the portrayal of women engineers since the late 1990s on *Star Trek: Voyager*, *Stargate SG-1*, *Scorpion*, and *The 100*. Natalie Krikowa follows up with a more focused analysis of *The 100*, arguing in support of the series' portrayal of Raven Reyes as groundbreaking in terms of both gender and race.

The next two essays, by Lauren Riccelli Zwicky and by Lisa K. Perdigao, provide analyses of the gender politics in two series with overtly feminist themes, *Orphan Black* and *Agent Carter*, respectively, and address the ways in which these series call attention to patriarchal social structures that affect women in general, and women in science more specifically. Erin Nicholes then discusses the role of emotion in *Blindspot*, arguing that the series reinforces gender ideology that suggests that women's emotions affect their proficiency in the STEM workplace. In contrast, Laura Foster and Helen McKenzie discuss the construction of traditionally feminine attributes, including emotionality and nurturing, as beneficial to the female pathologist in *Silent Witness*. Cary M.J. Elza also writes about female pathologists in her analysis of *CSI: Miami* and *Crossing Jordan*, and argues that as sexualized and maternal figures, female medical examiners mediate and translate death and the deceased, but that in order to maintain dominant cultural ideologies, their power is also contained and controlled.

Finally, the last two essays focus on the portrayal of women in science on two BBC series with considerable American fanbases: *Sherlock* and *Doctor Who*. Jennifer Phillips and Kristine Larsen argue, respectively, that *Sherlock*'s Molly and the women of the Moffat Era on *Doctor Who* are strong scientist characters able to hold their own against each series' titular character.

In various ways, the essays in this collection examine how television series reinforce and resist traditional gender ideology in the portrayals of women in STEM. As these essays show, whether in children's programming or on prime time, television producers often seem to struggle to offer portrayals that normalize women's participation in STEM. Nevertheless, the series discussed in this collection generally represent positive steps forward by contributing to a growing body of diverse portrayals of women in STEM that has the potential to shift cultural norms towards a greater acceptance of women in these fields.

If we hope to further encourage women in STEM, both in the United States and globally, it is imperative that we pay close attention to the cultural messages that are broadcast through popular media such as television. This collection, through surveying a broad array of television series, begins that work. However, there is still much work left to do. In the years to come, let us hope that we will see many more female scientists, engineers, and technologists, both on the small screen and in the world.

NOTES

1. The White House Office of the Press Secretary, "Fact Sheet: President Obama Announces Over $240 Million in New STEM Commitments at the 2015 White House Science Fair," *The White House Briefing Room*, March 23, 2015.
2. National Math + Science Initiative, "The STEM Crisis," *National Math + Science Initiative*, 2016.
3. *Ibid.*
4. National Center for Education Statistics, "Table 301.20. Historical Summary of Faculty, Enrollment, Degrees Conferred, and Finances in Degree-Granting Postsecondary Institutions: Selected Years, 1869–70 Through 2013–14," *Digest of Education Statistics*, 2014.
5. *Ibid.* The most recent data available is from 2013–2014.
6. National Center for Education Statistics, "Table 318.45. Number and Percentage Distribution of Science, Technology, Engineering, and Mathematics (STEM) Degrees/Certificates Conferred by Postsecondary Institutions, by Race/Ethnicity, Level of Degree/Certificate, and Sex of Student: 2008–09 Through 2013–14," *Digest of Education Statistics*, 2014.
7. National Center for Education Statistics, "Table 318.30. Bachelor's, Master's, and Doctor's Degrees Conferred by Postsecondary Institutions, by Sex of Student and Discipline Division: 2013–14," *Digest of Education Statistics*, 2014.
8. Brian A. Nosek et al., "National Differences in Gender-Science Stereotypes Predict National Sex Differences in Science and Math Achievement," *PNAS* 106, no. 26 (2009): 10593.
9. Luigi Guiso et al., "Culture, Gender, and Math," *Science* 320, no. 5880 (2008): 1164.
10. Corinne A. Moss-Racusin et al., "Science Faculty's Subtle Gender Biases Favor Male Students," *PNAS* 109, no. 41 (2012): 16477.
11. Sylvia Ann Hewlett et al., *The Athena Factor: Reversing the Brain Drain in Science, Engineering, and Technology* (Cambridge: Harvard Business Review, 2008), i.
12. *Ibid.*
13. Bureau of Labor Statistics, "Occupation Finder," *Occupational Outlook Handbook* (Washington, D.C.: U.S. Department of Labor, 2015). For occupations requiring a minimum of a bachelor's degree, the Occupation Outlook Handbook lists nine professions with expected growth rates of over 20 percent: personal financial advisors, operations research analysts, computer systems analysts, interpreters and translators, substance abuse and behavioral disorder counselors, athletic trainers, biomedical engineers, cartographers and photogrammetrists, and forensic science technicians.
14. ManpowerGroup, *2015 Talent Shortage Survey* (Milwaukee: ManpowerGroup, 2015), 36.
15. Hewlett et al., *The Athena Factor*, i.
16. The White House Office of the Press Secretary, "Fact Sheet: President Obama Announces Over $240 Million."
17. National Girls Collaborative Project, "About NGCP," *National Girls Collaborative Project*, 2016; Girls Who Code, "About Us," *Girls Who Code*, 2017.
18. Nielsen Company, "Nielsen Estimates 118.4 Million TV Homes in the U.S. for the 2016–2017 TV Season," *Nielsen Insights*, August 26, 2016.
19. Nielsen Company, *The Nielsen Total Audience Report: Q1 2016* (New York: The Nielsen Company, 2016), 4.
20. *Ibid.*, 11; OECD, "Hours Worked," *OECD Factbook 2015–2016: Economic, Environmental and Social Statistics* (Paris: OECD Publishing, 2016). According to the OECD Factbook, the average employed American works 34.4 hours per week.
21. Nielsen Company, *The Nielsen Total Audience Report: Q1 2016*, 11.
22. *Ibid.*, 8.

Works Cited

Bureau of Labor Statistics. "Occupation Finder." *Occupational Outlook Handbook*. Washington, D.C.: U.S. Department of Labor, 2015. www.bls.gov/ooh/occupation-finder.htm.

Girls Who Code. "About Us." *Girls Who Code*, 2017. https://girlswhocode.com/about-us/.

Guiso, Luigi, Ferdinando Monte, Paola Sapienza, and Luigi Zingales. "Culture, Gender, and Math." *Science* 320, no. 5880 (2008): 1164–1165.

Hewlett, Sylvia Ann, Carolyn Buck Luce, Lisa J. Servon, Laura Sherbin, Peggy Shiller, Eytan Sosnovich, and Karen Sumberg. *The Athena Factor: Reversing the Brain Drain in Science, Engineering, and Technology*. Cambridge: Harvard Business Review, 2008.

ManpowerGroup. *2015 Talent Shortage Survey*. Milwaukee: ManpowerGroup, 2015. http://www.manpowergroup.com/wps/wcm/connect/db23c560-08b6-485f-9bf6-f5f38a43c76a/2015_Talent_Shortage_Survey_US-lo_res.pdf?MOD=AJPERES.

Moss-Racusin, Corinne A., John Dovidio, Victoria Brescoll, Mark Graham, and Jo Handelsman. "Science Faculty's Subtle Gender Biases Favor Male Students." *PNAS* 109, no. 41 (2012): 16474–16479.

National Center for Education Statistics. "Table 301.20. Historical Summary of Faculty, Enrollment, Degrees Conferred, and Finances in Degree-Granting Postsecondary Institutions: Selected Years, 1869–70 Through 2013–14." *Digest of Education Statistics*, 2014. https://nces.ed.gov/programs/digest/d14/tables/dt14_301.20.asp.

———. "Table 318.30. Bachelor's, Master's, and Doctor's Degrees Conferred by Postsecondary Institutions, by Sex of Student and Discipline Division: 2013–14." *Digest of Education Statistics*, 2014. https://nces.ed.gov/programs/digest/d15/tables/dt15_318.30.asp.

———. "Table 318.45. Number and Percentage Distribution of Science, Technology, Engineering, and Mathematics (STEM) Degrees/Certificates Conferred by Postsecondary Institutions, by Race/Ethnicity, Level of Degree/Certificate, and Sex of Student: 2008–09 Through 2013–14." *Digest of Education Statistics*, 2014. https://nces.ed.gov/programs/digest/d14/tables/dt14_318.45.asp.

National Girls Collaborative Project. "About NGCP." *National Girls Collaborative Project*, 2016. https://ngcproject.org/about-ngcp.

National Math + Science Initiative. "The Stem Crisis." *National Math + Science Initiative*, 2016. https://nms.org/Education/TheSTEMCrisis.aspx.

Nielsen Company. "Nielsen Estimates 118.4 Million TV Homes in the U.S. for the 2016–2017 TV Season." *Nielsen Insights*, August 26, 2016. http://www.nielsen.com/us/en/insights/news/2016/nielsen-estimates-118-4-million-tv-homes-in-the-us—for-the-2016-17-season.html.

Nielsen Company. *The Nielsen Total Audience Report: Q1 2016*. New York: The Nielsen Company, 2016. http://www.nielsen.com/content/dam/corporate/us/en/reports-downloads/2016-reports/total-audience-report-q1-2016.pdf.

Nosek, Brian A., Frederick L. Smyth, N. Sriram, et al. "National Differences in Gender-Science Stereotypes Predict National Sex Differences in Science and Math Achievement." *PNAS* 106, no. 26 (2009): 10593–10597.

OECD. "Hours Worked." *OECD Factbook 2015–2016: Economic, Environmental and Social Statistics*. Paris: OECD Publishing, 2016. http://www.keepeek.com/Digital-Asset-Management/oecd/economics/oecd-factbook-2015-2016/hours-worked_factbook-2015-54-en#.WXUQwYjythE.

The White House Office of the Press Secretary. "Fact Sheet: President Obama Announces Over $240 Million in New STEM Commitments at the 2015 White House Science Fair." *The White House Briefing Room*, March 23, 2015. https://obamawhitehouse.archives.gov/the-press-office/2015/03/23/fact-sheet-president-obama-announces-over-240-million-new-stem-commitmen.

Achievements, Gaps and the "Achievement Gap"

STEM in Children's Programming

ASHLEY LYNN CARLSON
and HOPE J. CROWELL

Researchers in education have long been aware of a persistent achievement gap between girls and boys in science and math. However, as women have made increasing gains in educational attainment across all disciplines, the lack of women in certain STEM fields has become more striking. More bachelor's degrees are awarded to women than men in the United States each year, yet women earn profoundly fewer degrees than men in fields such as physical sciences, technology, computer science, engineering, and mathematics.[1] Looking at assessment data for younger students, it is clear that this achievement gap begins early and grows as students age. The 2015 National Assessment of Educational Progress (NAEP), produced by the U.S. Department of Education, shows that while male and female fourth graders scored similarly in science (with an average score of 154 out of 300 for both groups), by eighth grade males outperformed females by an average of 3 points (155 versus 152), and by twelfth grade the gap had further widened to 5 points (153 versus 148).[2] While girls' slippage in science achievement over time is clear, the decline in girls' interest in and enjoyment of STEM subjects as they grow up is much more extreme, and is likely one of the main causes of the achievement gap. According to one study, in fourth grade, 66 percent of girls and 68 percent of boys enjoy science.[3] But, by eighth grade, boys are twice as likely as girls to be interested in STEM careers.[4] Researchers and educators have increasingly focused on the social factors that contribute to girls' declining interest, as these appear to be the key to increasing STEM participation among young women.

Multiple studies have reported several common issues that affect girls' interest in STEM careers; fear of isolation, stereotypes about women in STEM, and lack of mentorship and role models all appear to be significant contributing factors. Many young women recognize that men dominate certain fields, and concerns about being the only female in a class or workplace may serve to deter them from these pursuits. A study of 852 teen girls produced by Girl Scouts of America found that 47 percent "would feel uncomfortable being the only girl in a group or class."[5] Similarly, many of the girls were concerned that they would be outsiders in STEM careers, with significant variations depending on race.[6] Specifically, 38 percent of African American girls in the study agreed with the statement "Because I am female I would be treated like an outsider if I pursued a career in STEM," while 29 percent of Hispanic girls and 25 percent of Caucasian girls agreed with the statement.[7] These numbers suggest that a large number of young women are concerned that they would not "fit in" in a STEM workplace or in STEM courses. In contrast, girls and young women with positive peer networks in STEM are less likely to struggle with the consequences of gender bias.[8] In other words, when girls feel that they fit in they are more likely to be interested and successful in STEM.

Stereotypes about women in STEM can also affect girls' interests. Stereotype threat occurs when an individual is aware of a negative stereotype and that awareness affects her or his performance. Studies have shown that the suggestion that girls are less competent or capable poses a significant threat to girls' performance in a variety of areas.[9] Moreover, stereotype threat can deter women from pursuing certain careers.[10] Unfortunately, girls may encounter gender stereotypes about women's math and science abilities in a variety of places, including their peers, parents, teachers, and popular media. These stereotypes are not necessarily conveyed intentionally; for example, math anxiety among female elementary school teachers has been shown to adversely affect math achievement among girls and increase the likelihood that girls will believe that boys are better at math.[11] Even in the absence of explicit stereotyping, girls internalize implicit messages about gender difference from their environments.

Exposure to role models has been noted as an effective means of counteracting stereotype threat, but a lack of mentors and role models in STEM has also been recognized as a factor that negatively influences girls' interest in STEM careers.[12] The Girl Scouts of America study found that girls with an interest in STEM were much more likely to know someone in a STEM career—and much more likely to know *a woman* in a STEM career—than girls who were not interested in STEM.[13] In contrast, girls who are unacquainted with any women in STEM professions are less likely to be interested in a related career path. As young women enter college, graduate school, and the workplace, limited mentorship compared to their male peers further diminishes the likelihood that they will stay in STEM fields. Meanwhile, women with effective mentors or sponsors are more likely to see their ideas endorsed in the workplace, and are more likely to be satisfied with their promotions.[14] At all levels, therefore, mentorship and support are key factors in bridging the STEM gender gap.

In recent years, educators, entrepreneurs, non-profit organizations, and major corporations have engaged in numerous projects intended to encourage girls' participation in STEM.[15] There are many STEM-related in-school, after-school, and summer programs for children and young adults, including many that are specifically for girls. There is also a growing body of research on methods for drawing and keeping girls and women in STEM, and various approaches are being implemented in both education and the private sector. Children's television producers have also taken note of the paucity of women in STEM, and have begun to develop new series with a focus on encouraging girls in STEM.

This essay will look at three such series: *Project Mc²*, a Netflix series focused on a group of STEM savvy teen girls who are recruited by a spy agency; *Annedroids*, a Canadian series available in the U.S. on Amazon Video, about an eleven-year-old girl who builds androids; and *SciGirls*, a PBS series billed as "Science Fun for Tween Girls."[16] Although they are not without their flaws, these series provide younger viewers with multiple female role models who can positively affect their perceptions of girls in STEM. Since girls with an interest in STEM are more likely to have done science activities outside of school, this essay will also examine the websites associated with the series, and consider the extent to which online multimedia may further encourage active involvement in STEM.[17]

Project Mc²

In the first season of *Project Mc²*, the series follows the adventures of four girls with STEM interests. McKeyla McAlister (Mika Abdalla) is a teen-age spy who has just started at a new school. She uses broad science skills to complete missions, while also trying to fit in with her peers. Over the course of the season, she recruits three of her classmates to join NOV8, a secret spy organization. Each of the girls has strength in a particular STEM field: Adrienne Attoms (Victoria Vida) is a "culinary chemist," Bryden Bandweth (Genneya Walton) is a computer and social media expert, and Camryn Coyle (Ysa Penarejo) is an engineer. Later seasons add Ember Evergreen (Belle Shouse), whose primary interests are in environmental science and biology, and Devon D'Marco (Alyssa Lynch), an artist, who expands the show's scope to "STEAM" (Science, Technology, Engineering, Art, and Mathematics). In each episode, the girls use their combined strengths and interests to solve mysteries and stop bad guys.

The show has a number of positive attributes. The girls bond over their mutual interest in STEM, thus combatting the concern that girls in STEM are isolated or outcasts. The series also provides young viewers with multiple female role models with interests in a variety of fields; the girls are portrayed as highly intelligent and the show's tagline, "Smart is the new cool," reinforces the idea that girls can be smart and excel in STEM. The cast is also diverse, and includes a Brazilian American (Vida, as Adrienne), a Filipino American (Penarejo, as Camryn), and an African American (Walton, as Bryden). Since STEM participation and achievement are even lower among Hispanic and African American girls, this diversity is especially important.[18] However, what the show offers in terms of racial diversity it lacks in socioeconomic diversity. The girls on the series all appear to be from high-income backgrounds, with seemingly unlimited access to technology, supplies, and extensive wardrobes. As a result, while minority girls may see themselves reflected in these characters, girls from low-income backgrounds may struggle to identify with them.

In perhaps its most overt effort to draw girls to STEM, *Project Mc²* works to resist stereotypes about female scientists as unfeminine. In fact, the series was created in tandem with a line of dolls made by MGA Entertainment, which also produces Little Tikes, Lalaloopsy, and Bratz.[19] In a 2015 interview, the CEO of MGA Entertainment, Isaac Larian, stated that they "didn't just want to make a doll wearing a plastic lab coat."[20] Neither the dolls nor the girls on the show wear attire typically associated with science. Rather than being portrayed in lab coats or coveralls, the girls are almost always dressed in "fashionable" attire: they wear trendy clothes, jewelry, and makeup. Similarly, the line of dolls and toys is very focused on physical appearance and traditional feminine beauty, with branded science kits that let children make their own lip balm, nail polish, and makeup. The show's emphasis on the girls' physical appearance sends viewers the message that STEM is not inherently unfeminine; they can be girly and smart, and scientifically minded.

However, this emphasis is also problematic, as it reinforces other gender stereotypes and is yet another example of televisual media placing undue emphasis on women's physical appearance. The girls' attire often appears more appropriate for a runway show than high school. Adrienne, the "culinary chemist," is particularly fashion-focused, insisting on wearing heels even when it is clearly inconvenient, and always carrying nail polish "for emergencies."[21] The show suggests that girls can look good and do science, but it also tells viewers that looking good is the chief priority for women. Even the dolls and science kits, which are intended to engage girls in science projects at home, are associated with beauty products, and the emphasis in the marketing of these products is beauty, rather than science.

In a similar vein, the show's website is largely focused on marketing for the *Project Mc²* dolls, rather than providing an interactive experience that would be more accessible to girls regardless of income.[22] While the website does include some activities, they are poorly constructed and uninteresting. Rather than providing genuine learning experiences, the online activities are overly simplified. For example, some ask players to drag and drop a few items together to create an experiment or complete a project, with no challenge and little educational value. Quizzes on the website help participants determine "Which Project Mc² Fashion Best Suits You," or "Which Project Mc² Science Accessory Best Fits You," rather asking any STEM related questions. The website provides very little in the way of either knowledge attainment or skill building. Overall, the goal of the website, and indeed the show itself, is largely to sell dolls and related toys, rather than to engage girls in STEM. Thus, while *Project Mc²* directly combats stereotypes about girls in STEM being unfeminine, in many other ways the series and its associated web presence fall short.

Annedroids

While *Project Mc²* has an ensemble cast and connects to a wide variety of STEM fields, *Annedroids* focuses primarily on the main protagonist, Anne (Addison Holley), an adolescent girl with a gift for engineering and programming. In the series, the genius Anne builds androids in her junkyard. Her friends, Nick (Jadiel Dowlin) and Shania (Adrianna Di Liello), are not geniuses, but they do assist her in various projects. Since women make up only 10.1 percent of the electrical and electronics engineering workforce and only 7.9 percent of the mechanical engineering workforce, the series' focus on this field is timely and relevant.[23]

Moreover, robotics and technology, the main topics on the show, are likely to draw in both male and female viewers, and the inclusion of Nick as one of the central figures also increases the odds that it will appeal to both genders. Sexism and sexual harassment directed at women from male colleagues in STEM workplaces poses a significant problem for women's retention in STEM.[24] Further, more than a third of the girls surveyed in the Girl Scout report believed that male colleagues would not treat them equally.[25] Thus, engaging male viewers—and thereby potentially shifting their views about girls—can serve to improve gender equity in STEM workplaces. Many of the efforts to address the gender gap remain focused on changing only girls' attitudes rather than attempting to shift boys' attitudes as well. Through its positive portrayal of girls and boys working together to solve problems and its relatively gender-neutral appeal, *Annedroids* both addresses concerns that girls in STEM are isolated and has the potential to shift both male and female viewers' perceptions about women's participation in engineering.

Annedroids has less racial diversity in its cast than *Project Mc²*, but also portrays characters of more economically modest backgrounds. Anne and Shania are white, while Nick and his mother are Black. Ironically, PAL, the pasty white android who features prominently throughout the series, is voiced by Black actress Millie Davis. The series also portrays diversity in terms of class and family composition. Anne is being raised by a single father whose job apparently provides sufficient income for her to maintain her junkyard and invest in advanced technology. Meanwhile, Nick is being raised by a single mother and Shania is being raised by her grandmother. The characters live in modest houses in what appears to be a lower-income suburban neighborhood (Anne's junkyard is on their block, after all). In the U.S., 44 percent of children live in low-income households, 27 percent live with only one parent, and an additional 3 percent live with a relative other than a parent.[26] Young viewers in these demographics are more likely to relate to the characters on *Annedroids* than on a series like *Project Mc²*, further broadening the potential impact of the show.

In further contrast to the girls on *Project Mc²*, *Annedroid*'s protagonist is not overly feminine or fashion conscious. Instead, Anne is portrayed as a tomboy. For example, in the pilot episode when Nick and Shania first meet Anne, she is wearing a welding helmet and overalls. When she takes off the helmet the other two children are surprised to discover that she is a girl.[27] Anne never shows much interest in stereotypically "girly" activities—in fact, in one episode where Shania attempts to get Anne interested in "girl's day," Anne looks horrified by the amount of pink in Shania's room and is confused by Shania's interest in makeovers and romantic films.[28] Although Anne agrees to participate in a makeover, her expressions throughout the process suggest that she is repulsed. The effect of the makeover is equally horrifying: with bright blue eyeshadow up to her eyebrows and a pink sequined beanie, Anne looks ridiculous rather than glamorous at the end of the episode. While getting dressed up and wearing makeup is constructed as a normal routine for the girls on *Project Mc²*, for Anne it is abnormal and unappealing.

The supermodel image of the teens in *Project Mc²* also stands in stark contrast to Shania, who is decidedly more "girly" than Anne, but still has an appearance that is far from runway ready. Her attire is more traditionally feminine than Anne's—she often wears skirts, pigtails, and lots of pink—but it also reflects typical children's clothing. She's not wearing heels or haute couture, nor does she wear visible makeup. In part, this might be attributed to Shania's age; she is younger than the girls on *Project Mc².* Nevertheless, young viewers are more likely to relate to Shania's "look." The kids' clothing on the show also contributes to the sense that they are typical lower/middle-class children.

On one hand, it may be problematic that the show associates Anne's intelligence and interest in engineering with tomboyish, more masculine behavior and attire. This is particularly evident in the ways that the show contrasts Anne with Shania, who is both more typically feminine and obviously less intellectual. This reinforces the idea that femininity and intelligence are opposing attributes. On the other hand, through both characters the show deemphasizes the importance of young women's appearance in a way that may have a positive effect on viewers' body image.

The difference in emphasis between *Project Mc²* and *Annedroids* is also evident in the shows' websites. While the *Project Mc²* website seems to focus on selling dolls, the *Annedroids* website is full of games designed to introduce children to basic STEM concepts, like programming, spatial reasoning, and physics.[29] Nothing on the *Annedroids* website is overtly gendered, and the focus is clearly educational rather than oriented towards marketing. While the *Annedroids* website does not challenge participants to engage in activities away from the computer, as the *Project Mc²* dolls and toys might, the *Annedroids* web games themselves are much more likely to develop critical thinking, math, and programming skills, and can justifiably be considered engagement with STEM outside of the school setting. In combination, *Annedroids* and its website fill important gaps that *Project Mc²* likely does not.

SciGirls

While *Project Mc²* and *Annedroids* are fictional shows, PBS's *SciGirls* follows real adolescent girls engaging in real STEM projects. In each episode, a different group of junior high school girls tackles a real-world problem with the help of experts in the field. Many of those experts, from biologists to architects to engineers, are also women. The episodes are connected by recurring animated shorts featuring Izzie, a young girl with an interest in science, and her friend Jake. Izzie encounters problems in the animated segments of the show that translate into the projects and experiments carried out by the real "SciGirls."

One of *SciGirls*' greatest attributes is in its portrayal of average kids working through real STEM projects. While *Project Mc²* and *Annedroids* feature outlandish plotlines and technologies that do not actually exist, the SciGirls must solve problems with practical tools and real, existing technology. For example, episodes feature girls developing buoyant robots to improve water quality in the Chesapeake Bay, or designing shoes to walk more safely on slippery ice.[30] Although they are mentored by adults, the girls do most of the work. Since the mentors are usually women, *SciGirls* not only portrays girls doing science, it also provides viewers with many examples of successful women in STEM fields. These mentor figures fill an important need for STEM role models.

Like *Project Mc²* and *Annedroids*, *SciGirls* also successfully portrays racial diversity among the students and mentors alike. Each episode's cast is diverse, with African American, Asian American, and Latina girls and women regularly appearing on the show. Similarly, in the recurring animated portions, Izzie has a darker complexion while Jake is clearly Caucasian. In terms of class, the girls who appear on the series are generally from middle-income backgrounds. The episodes feature brief "profile" segments where each girl has the opportunity to share a little about herself and her interests. These segments generally take place in the girls' homes, and reinforce the idea that they are typical kids with typical interests (that usually are not science-related). For example, Akilah, one of the girls in the episode "Science Cooks!," shares, "I like to play softball [...], I like to read, watch TV, you know what, I'm a regular person."[31] Profiles like these make the girls relatable, and suggest to viewers that many kinds of girls can "fit in" in STEM.

While the projects and experiments in *Project Mc²* and *Annedroids* are often unrealistic, if not technically impossible, it is worth noting that even those on *SciGirls* are usually unachievable for an average child playing at home. The projects often require technology that most children cannot easily access, as well as the mentorship of professionals with extensive knowledge. However, the *SciGirls* website goes much further than either the *Project Mc²* or *Annedroids* sites by providing ideas for accessible activities.[32] The website is significantly more elaborate than the sites for the other two series, with links to games as well as an area where children can create profiles, join an online team, and complete "Questies" to earn points for their team and to level up their skills in a variety of areas, such as "Builder," "Designer," or "Tech Whiz." The "Questies" give players directions to complete tasks either online or offline, after which they can return to the website and record their progress. For example, some of the activities include building and playing a stringed instrument, building a homemade kite and attempting to fly it, drawing a picture of a planet in our solar system, or doing a little research to find out where the participant's favorite fruits and vegetables are grown. Most of the activities will require participants to put in a fair amount of time, but also require limited resources that most people already have around the house, like paper and string. These activities are much more "hands on" than the activities on the *Annedroids* website, but they also require more initiative, since they are not simply online games. Additionally, a second *SciGirls*-related website provides activities and ideas for educators and parents.[33] Overall, the *SciGirls* websites encourage girls to actively participate in science and engineering projects, rather than being passive observers. As such, it is much more likely than the other series' websites to achieve an impact by engaging girls in science projects outside of school.

Conclusions

Project Mc², *Annedroids*, and *SciGirls* all work to promote girls' participation in STEM by addressing some of the key issues that may prevent girls from pursuing their interests in these areas. All three series show girls working with teams and making friends while doing STEM-related activities. Every series has more than one female lead, and the main characters are celebrated for their interests rather than being ostracized. In this way, the shows successfully combat concerns that girls may have about being isolated.

All three series also show young women receiving mentorship from adults. On *Project Mc²*, McKeyla's mother is the head of the spy organization that employs the girls. The character is also played by Danica McKellar, who has a Ph.D. in mathematics and has published several books on math.[34] On *Annedroids*, Anne receives mentorship from her father, Nick's mother, and her teacher. And, on every episode of the *SciGirls*, the team members are mentored by a variety of experts. Thus, each series suggests to young viewers that STEM mentors are available to girls. Of course, the struggle to find mentorship in the real world still exists, but at least these series encourage girls to seek mentoring.

Moreover, all three series and their related websites attempt to engage girls in STEM outside of a school setting. Arguably, the act of watching these shows can be interpreted as a STEM activity itself, but the additional resources associated with the series drive this further. Whether through the *Project Mc²* toys, the *Annedroids* web games, or the *SciGirls* "Questies," it is clear that those involved in producing all three shows hope to provide viewers with opportunities to move from passively watching to actively engaging in STEM at home. That said, perhaps one of the biggest obstacles for these series is in their accessibility. *SciGirls*, which airs on PBS and has free episodes available on its website, is by far the easiest of the three series for U.S. viewers to access regardless of income or other demographics. Ninety-six percent of U.S. homes receive traditional TV signals, meaning that nearly all children in the U.S. can watch the show on television.[35]

The same is not true, however, for *Project Mc²* and *Annedroids*, which are only available online. More than 75 percent of U.S. adults ages 18–49 have home broadband, which means that most children are likely to have Internet access at home.[36] However, only about 53 percent of U.S. adults earning $30,000 or less have home broadband, which suggests that lower income children are much less likely to have access than their higher income peers.

The accessibility divide grows even larger with *Project Mc²* and *Annedroids* because they are only available through online subscription streaming. Forty-five percent of U.S. households subscribe to Netflix, and only 22 percent subscribe to Amazon Prime Video, meaning that *Project Mc²* and *Annedroids*, respectively, have much smaller potential audiences.[37] As a medium for propelling more girls into STEM, television can have a much broader impact if broadcast and cable television follow PBS and streaming services in airing STEM-oriented series that will appeal to young female viewers. Meanwhile, the accessibility of these existing series may impede their impact, particularly among children from low income families.

Still, these three series make important strides towards providing girls with positive STEM role models and combatting problematic assumptions about women in STEM. While *Project Mc²* and *Annedroids* have some issues with stereotypes about women generally as well as women in STEM, in combination the three series demonstrate diversity in terms of interests, backgrounds, and race that can help to defeat assumptions viewers may have. Perhaps most importantly, all three series directly combat the stereotype threat that girls have inherently less aptitude in STEM areas. In addition to inspiring girls' interests, viewing these series may also help diminish the impact of stereotype threat by providing girls with alternative narratives about women in science. Rather than learning that boys are better at science and math, girls watching these shows receive two key messages: girls can do STEM, and STEM fields are exciting and fun. These are important messages that we need to continue to promote in order to successfully close the achievement gap.

Notes

1. National Center for Education Statistics, "Table 318.30. Bachelor's, Master's, and Doctor's Degrees Conferred by Postsecondary Institutions, by Sex of Student and Discipline Division: 2013–14," *Digest of Education Statistics*, 2015.

2. National Center for Education Statistics, "Table 223.10. Average National Assessment of Educational Progress (NAEP) Science Scale Score, Standard Deviation, and Percentage of Students Attaining Science Achievement Levels, by Grade Level, Selected Student and School Characteristics, and Percentile: 2009, 2011, and 2015," *Digest of Education Statistics*, 2015.

3. National Science Foundation, "'Back to School': Five Myths About Girls and Science," *NSF News*, August 27, 2007.

4. Ibid.

5. Kamla Modi, Judy Schoenberg, and Kimberlee Salmond, *Generation STEM: What Girls Say about Science, Technology, Engineering, and Math* (New York: Girl Scouts of America, 2012), 19.

6. Ibid., 23.

7. Ibid.

8. Rachael D. Robnett, "Gender Bias in STEM Fields: Variation in Prevalence and Links to STEM Self-Concept," *Psychology of Women Quarterly* 40, no. 1 (2016): 74–75.

9. Jenessa R. Shapiro and Amy M. Williams, "The Role of Stereotype Threats in Under-

mining Girls' and Women's Performance and Interest in STEM Fields," *Sex Roles* 66 (2012): 176.

10. *Ibid.*, 177.

11. Sian L. Beilock et al., "Female Teachers' Math Anxiety Affects Girls' Math Achievement," *PNAS* 107, no. 5 (2010): 1860.

12. Shapiro and Williams, "The Role of Stereotype Threats," 178.

13. Modi et al., *Generation STEM*, 14.

14. Sylvia Ann Hewlett et al., *Athena Factor 2.0: Accelerating Female Talent in Science, Engineering & Technology* (New York: Center for Talent Innovation, 2014), 3.

15. The National Science Foundation provides grants in support of numerous such projects. Descriptions of programs and past award recipients can be found in NSF publications and on the NSF website.

16. Jordana Arkin (creator), *Project Mc^2* (Netflix: 2015–present); J.J. Johnson and Christin Simms (creators), *Annedroids* (Amazon Video: 2014–present); Richard Hudson (executive producer), *SciGirls* (PBS: 2010–2015).

17. Modi et al., *Generation STEM*, 14.

18. *Ibid.*, 23; National Science Board, *Science & Engineering Indicators, 2016* (Arlington: National Science Foundation, 2016), 15.

19. Heidi Stevens, "Project Mc^2 Dolls Intended to Nudge Girls Toward STEM Careers," *Chicago Tribune*, August 21, 2015.

20. *Ibid.*

21. Jordana Arkin, "Secret Agenting," *Project Mc^2*, season 1, episode 2, directed by Michael Younesi, aired August 7, 2015, on Netflix; Jordana Arkin and Annie Burgstede, "Back to Basics," *Project Mc^2*, season 2, episode 1, directed by Michael Younesi, aired August 12, 2016, on Netflix.

22. See the *Project Mc^2* website, www.projectmc2.com.

23. National Science Board, *Science & Engineering Indicators, 2016*, Appendix Table 3-12.

24. Sylvia Ann Hewlett et al., *The Athena Factor: Reversing the Brain Drain in Science, Engineering, and Technology* (Cambridge: Harvard Business Review, 2008), 7–8.

25. Modi et al., *Generation STEM*, 23.

26. Yang Jiang, Mercedes Ekono, and Curtis Skinner, "Basic Facts About Low-Income Children," *National Center for Children in Poverty*, February 2016; United States Census Bureau, *2016 Current Population Survey Annual Social and Economic Supplement* (Washington, D.C.: U.S. Department of Commerce, 2016).

27. J.J. Johnson and Christin Simms, "Pilot," *Annedroids*, season 1, episode 1, directed by J.J. Johnson, released July 25, 2014, on Amazon Video.

28. J.J. Johnson and Christin Simms, "Parent Swap," *Annedroids*, season 2 episode 4, directed by John May, released July 2, 2015, on Amazon Video.

29. See the *Annedroids* website, www.annedroids.com.

30. Chris Nee, "Aquabots," *SciGirls*, season 2, episode 1, directed by Aya Fukuda, aired October 11, 2012, on PBS; Angie Prindle and Chris Nee, "Mother Nature's Shoes," *SciGirls*, season 2, episode 2, directed by Aya Fukuda, aired October 18, 2012, on PBS.

31. Angie Prindle and Chris Nee, "Science Cooks," *SciGirls*, season 1, episode 8, directed by Aya Fukuda, aired April 2, 2010, on PBS.

32. See the SciGirls website, www.pbskids.org/scigirls.

33. See the SciGirls Connect website, www.scigirlsconnect.org.

34. "Danica McKellar," Biography.com (A&E Television Networks), November 28, 2015.

35. Nielsen Company, "Nielsen Estimates 118.4 Million TV Homes in the U.S. for the 2016–2017 TV Season," *Nielsen Insights*, August 26, 2016.

36. Pew Research Center, "Internet/Broadband Fact Sheet," *Pew Research Center*, January 12, 2017.

37. Christine Wang, "Overwhelming Majority of People Watching Streaming Services Still Choose Netflix," *CNBC*, July 21, 2016.

Works Cited

Arkin, Jordana. *Project MC².* Netflix, 2015–present.
———. "Secret Agenting." *Project Mc²*, season 1, episode 2. Directed by Michael Younesi. Aired August 7, 2015, on Netflix.
Arkin, Jordana, and Annie Burgstede. "Back to Basics." *Project Mc²*, season 2, episode 1. Directed by Michael Younesi. Aired August 12, 2016, on Netflix.
Beilock, Sian L., Elizabeth A. Gunderson, Gerardo Ramirez, Susan C. Levine, and Edward E. Smith. "Female Teachers' Math Anxiety Affects Girls' Math Achievement." *PNAS* 107, no. 5 (2010): 1860–1863.
"Danica McKellar." Biography.com (A&E Television Networks), November 28, 2015. https://www.biography.com/people/danica-mckellar-20970757.
Hewlett, Sylvia Ann, Carolyn Buck Luce, Lisa J. Servon, Laura Sherbin, Peggy Shiller, Eytan Sosnovich, and Karen Sumberg. *The Athena Factor: Reversing the Brain Drain in Science, Engineering, and Technology.* Cambridge: Harvard Business Review, 2008.
Hewlett, Sylvia Ann, Laura Sherbin, Fabiola Dieudonné, Christina Fargnoli, and Catherine Fredman. *Athena Factor 2.0: Accelerating Female Talent in Science, Engineering & Technology.* New York: Center for Talent Innovation, 2014.
Hudson, Richard. *SciGirls.* PBS, 2010–2015.
Jiang, Yang, Mercedes Ekono, and Curtis Skinner. "Basic Facts About Low-Income Children." *National Center for Children in Poverty*, February 2016. http://www.nccp.org/publications/pub_1145.html.
Johnson, J.J., and Christin Simms. *Annedroids.* Amazon Video, 2014–present.
———. "Parent Swap." *Annedroids*, season 2 episode 4. Directed by John May. Released July 2, 2015, on Amazon Video.
———. "Pilot." *Annedroids*, season 1, episode 1. Directed by J.J. Johnson. Released July 25, 2014, on Amazon Video.
Modi, Kamla, Judy Schoenberg, and Kimberlee Salmond. *Generation STEM: What Girls Say About Science, Technology, Engineering, and Math.* New York: Girl Scouts of America, 2012.
National Center for Education Statistics. "Table 223.10. Average National Assessment of Educational Progress (NAEP) Science Scale Score, Standard Deviation, and Percentage of Students Attaining Science Achievement Levels, by Grade Level, Selected Student and School Characteristics, and Percentile: 2009, 2011, and 2015." *Digest of Education Statistics*, 2015. https://nces.ed.gov/programs/digest/d16/tables/dt16_223.10.asp?current=yes.
———. "Table 318.30. Bachelor's, Master's, and Doctor's Degrees Conferred by Postsecondary Institutions, by Sex of Student and Discipline: 2013–14." *Digest of Education Statistics*, 2015. https://nces.ed.gov/programs/digest/d15/tables/dt15_318.30.asp?current=yes.
National Science Board. *Science & Engineering Indicators, 2016.* Arlington: National Science Foundation, 2016. https://nsf.gov/statistics/2016/nsb20161/uploads/1/nsb20161.pdf.
National Science Foundation. "'Back to School': Five Myths About Girls and Science." *NSF News*, August 27, 2007. https://www.nsf.gov/news/news_summ.jsp?cntn_id=109939.
Nee, Chris. "Aquabots." *SciGirls*, season 2, episode 1. Directed by Aya Fukuda. Aired October 11, 2012, on PBS.
Nielsen Company. "Nielsen Estimates 118.4 Million TV Homes in the U.S. for the 2016–2017 TV Season." *Nielsen Insights*, August 26, 2016. http://www.nielsen.com/us/en/insights/news/2016/nielsen-estimates-118-4-million-tv-homes-in-the-us—for-the-2016-17-season.html.
Pew Research Center. "Internet/Broadband Fact Sheet." *Pew Research Center*, January 12, 2017. http://www.pewinternet.org/fact-sheet/internet-broadband/.
Prindle, Angie, and Chris Nee. "Mother Nature's Shoes." *SciGirls*, season 2, episode 2. Directed by Aya Fukuda. Aired October 18, 2012, on PBS.
———. "Science Cooks." *SciGirls*, season 1, episode 8. Directed by Aya Fukuda. Aired April 2, 2010, on PBS.
Robnett, Rachael D. "Gender Bias in STEM Fields: Variation in Prevalence and Links to STEM Self-Concept." *Psychology of Women Quarterly* 40, no. 1 (2016): 65–79.

Shapiro Jenessa R., and Amy M. Williams. "The Role of Stereotype Threats in Undermining Girls' and Women's Performance and Interest in STEM Fields." *Sex Roles* 66 (2012): 175–183.
Stevens, Heidi. "Project Mc^2 Dolls Intended to Nudge Girls Toward STEM Careers." *Chicago Tribune*, August 21, 2015. http://www.chicagotribune.com/lifestyles/ct-sun-0823-balancing-act-20150821-column.html.
United States Census Bureau. *2016 Current Population Survey Annual Social and Economic Supplement.* Washington, D.C.: U.S. Department of Commerce, 2016. https://www.census.gov/hhes/families/.
Wang, Christine. "Overwhelming Majority of People Watching Streaming Services Still Choose Netflix." *CNBC*, July 21, 2016. http://www.cnbc.com/2016/07/21/overwhelming-majority-of-people-watching-streaming-services-still-choose-netflix.html.

The Doctors Who Waited
The Lonely Woman Scientist Trope in Geek TV
Bridget M. Blodgett and Anastasia Salter

The trope of intelligence demanding (and ensuring) isolation recurs with both male and female characters, but is particularly prevalent with the representation of women in STEM. Portrayals of female scientists are scarcer than those of male scientists, thus this representation increases in importance for young women who may base their own identities and expectations upon media depictions. We'll analyze characters from *Adventure Time*[1] and *Steven Universe*[2] who embody this stereotype in different ways through their relationships to the lead characters, the rest of the cast, and their individual careers. These characters are iconic in geek culture, already a space associated with ongoing misogynist discourse, and serve as important keystones for young audiences.

The pervasiveness of the lonely woman in science suggests consequences for women's participation in science, technology, and math fields (hereafter STEM). While such characters can be seen as desirable for the visibility of the representation, they often come with the baggage of desperation and continually unrequited love (as with *Steven Universe*'s Pearl), or they express the dispassionate and distanced viewpoint of someone who has removed themselves from the mundane aspects of normal life (as with *Adventure Time*'s Princess Bubblegum). The relationships of these characters often end disastrously with the woman being either unable or unwilling to actually engage with her passions of both science and the heart. The women of the lonely scientist trope may attempt relationships, but they will always end up alone. For Princess Bubblegum, a relationship is an unnecessary complication to her dedicated focus on scientific research and running a kingdom. In particular, her relationship with Finn is marked explicitly within the text as an unusual departure from her interactions but also intentionally non-romantic and closed in its communication.

Popular culture and the media that creates it are important touchstones for youth looking towards the future about how their lives will develop, especially given the timing of when these shows are consumed with the progression of social development. Young women are more likely to look for greater social acceptance heading into their teen years and more likely to believe media messages than parents' lectures about how STEM works. The tendency of women characters to fall into the lonely scientist trope sends the message to young audiences that the choice of a STEM career is incompatible with social outcomes they might desire, including lasting relationships. Such messages play a role in moving women away from STEM careers.

Portrayals of Women in STEM in the Media

It is a longstanding trend that women participate in STEM related disciplines and careers at disproportionately lower rates than men. From the early 1970s a multitude of initiatives have been developed to help increase the participation of women in these fields but few have found significant long-term success.[3] Many girls begin to lose interest in science at young ages and often struggle to picture themselves as scientists, struggling more with fields like physics than with ones like biology.[4] A major thematic area that arises as a reason for the attrition of girls and young women is that they often feel lonely or isolated in the classroom, being the only or one of a few women present. For many, it is easy to imagine that these feelings will continue into their careers.[5] Drawing from both their experiences in the classroom and from cultural stereotypes like the lone hacker or the individual genius, girls and young women form the impression that STEM-related careers are bound to be solo adventures where one has little interaction with others and few direct connections to the people who are served by their work.[6] Even worse, they often believe that this is how it is meant to be, reinforcing beliefs about simply being an imposter within the field due to natural biological differences.[7]

Recent research has begun to examine the influence that media presentations have upon individuals' expectations and mental models of STEM careers. A series of studies performed by Cheryan, Plaut, Handron, and Hudson found that the cultural depictions of computer scientists could have strong influences upon women's interest in pursuing the field as a career.[8] In particular, those which presented computer scientists as breaking the existing lone hacker stereotypes were actually able to increase women's interest in the field.⁹ The authors argue that media stories are an important tool in shaping and aligning recruitment and retention materials for women who have not yet lost interest in STEM fields.¹⁰ While young women do not inherently feel they don't belong, they do receive strong media messaging that reinforces their existing cultural attitudes and personal experiences with STEM.

Adventure Time and *Steven Universe* both air on Cartoon Network and have found a crossover audience, appealing to children and adult viewers. They share a strong creative pedigree that includes many women directors, creators, artists, and writers, and have often been heralded for progressive depictions of women. However, the status of their depictions as progressive and beneficial is complex, for even as Princess Bubblegum and Pearl offer models of strong women scientists, they are also shown as isolated and alienated from their communities and even from their apparent friends and social groups.

Princess Bonnibel Bubblegum

Princess Bubblegum is introduced in the very first episode of *Adventure Time* and remains one of the most common recurring characters within the show. Throughout much of the early seasons, Princess Bubblegum acts as a love interest for the young protagonist Finn the Human Boy. Her scenes often mix standard damsel in distress tropes with a bit more character development that involves her place as a ruler or interests as a scientist. The first episode has the Princess reanimate dead candy people using a concoction she brewed herself.¹¹ Princess Bubblegum is always shown as being very intelligent and involved in both her royal activities and in the pursuit of scientific research of all varieties. In various episodes she does experiments involving chemistry, biology, genetics, astronomy, physics, psychology, and other strange disciplinary combinations. She is also one of the characters who is regularly shown with a scientific parasite in her pocket. As the *Adventure Time* wiki explains, "Scientific Parasites are a group of creatures in the Land of Ooo who feed on intelligent brain waves. This is why they are commonly found in the pockets of doctors and scientists, such as Princess Bubblegum and Doctor Princess."¹² Overall, Princess Bubblegum is depicted as being more than just a princess; she is a person deeply driven to scientific endeavors.

Beyond being simply interested in science, Princess Bubblegum also defends the sciences as a truth-telling method in a world that involves everyday magic and mysticism. In one notable episode, Princess Bubblegum goes to Wizard Mountain to obtain a cure for the common cold.¹³ Through the course of the entire episode Princess Bubblegum struggles with her assertion that all things magical have a scientific basis at their root and that belief without pursuing understanding is a flaw. In the end, she is unable to acquire the cure but is able to find an alternative that meets the psychological needs of her patient while still making use of the medical knowledge available to her. Overall, Princess Bubblegum represents both the passion for science and the importance of science in her world and ours.

Still, one thing that is presented consistently within the show is Princess Bubblegum's distance from many of the other characters. In general, her closest interactions are with the main characters, Finn and Jake, and with her main helper, Peppermint Butler. However, a major character development arc for Finn revolves around his emotional development and feelings for Princess Bubblegum. The young Finn, just 12 when the show begins, goes through a period of trying to understand his feelings towards the Princess and then determining how he can appropriately act on them. Once Finn gets emotionally close to Princess Bubblegum, she pushes him away and distances her interactions, treating Finn more like a loyal knight than a good friend. When Finn moves on to find a young princess closer to his age, Princess Bubblegum is jealous of their relationship but refuses to admit her motivations.

Princess Bubblegum is also often shown as physically separated from other members of the Candy Kingdom and the world of Ooo. Throughout various episodes, the Princess is shown spending time in her tower with her populous spread out below her. In one scene, she is actually dancing on a small balcony at the top of the tower while everyone else parties below. When she appears on the ground and among her people, they often give her a wide berth, with few characters allowing themselves to come too close. This physical distance is an important marker for the character and represents her difficulty making emotional connections.

To some degree, it is difficult to separate Princess Bubblegum's princessness from her loneliness. Both royalty as well as intelligence could be causes Princess Bubblegum's distance from so many other characters. "The Suitor" in the fifth season focuses on Princess Bubblegum's love life and duty as a royal princess to marry.[14] The guardians of the Candy Kingdom force Peppermint Butler to bring forward one of Princess Bubblegum's royal suitors and make her go on a date. Some humor is presented as Peppermint Butler walks past a line of dusty old men and in one instance a skeleton to find someone suitable to woo the Princess, implying that the Princess has left them waiting for her attention for a long time:

> PEPPERMINT BUTLER: [*sighs then walks down the line of suitors*] All right, you guys. All you guys are gross. How long have you been waiting to court the princess?
> SUITOR #1: 87 years.
> SUITOR #2: 120 years!

SUITOR #3: I'm Gerald.
PEPPERMINT BUTLER: Geez! How long have you been here, Krusty? [*points at Krusty*]
KRUSTY: [*raises fist*] Three hundred years, so what? It's not too late, right, boys?
ALL SUITORS: [*chanting*] It's not too late! Take me on a date! It's my right! Princess all night—[15]

This ends with Peppermint Butler finally finding a suitable candidate, Braco, and bringing him into the Princess's lab to meet her. It does not go well:

BRACO: I want to take you ... on a date.
PRINCESS BUBBLEGUM: [*shocked*] Thank you, Braco. That's very sweet, but no.
PEPPERMINT BUTLER: Princess this lab reeks like brown mist; it's unhealthy. You've got to get outside and do some research on boys [*points at Braco*].
PRINCESS BUBBLEGUM: That is way out of line, Peps, and you guys are donking up my research! [*begins knocking stuff off her table*] Hello! Donk, donk!
BRACO: Princess, I love you! I–I love you so much it hurts. [*Princess Bubblegum stands and goes near him*] The pain it—Huh?
PRINCESS BUBBLEGUM: [*points some kind of laser pointer on Braco's eye*] Hmmm, what you're feeling is called "infatuation." The pain is the product of you overvaluing a projected, imaginary relationship with me.[16]

Bubblegum sees Braco as more of an interesting test subject than a potential suitor and spends much of the episode treating him as such. During several interactions she deliberately studies him, recording his responses and analyzing him using some of her tools. Braco decides to take action and sets out on a quest to help her, taking over for Finn and Jake. In the end we find that the Princess has created a living replica of herself that would be willing to date Braco. She is not able to step away from her royal and scientific duties, even if dating is one of them, but cares deeply enough about Braco's happiness to spend a significant amount of time finding a solution that allows her to both pursue concentrated, individual scientific study and make the connection with Braco.

As the show explains over several seasons, Bubblegum was the creator of her entire kingdom. She used her scientific genius to make a kingdom full of healthy candy people from a toxic waste site. Her royal position arises directly from her scientific nature and interest in improving the world around by her using her intelligence. In season 6 she discusses a potential election with Peppermint Butler:

PRINCESS BUBBLEGUM: I'm studying something that could be real important. Dah! This dumb election. It's not even—[*yawning*] I mean, it's barely even—[*yawns*] barely even legal. [...]
PRINCESS BUBBLEGUM: And even being legal, I mean, I made everyone. I made their homes. The candy people are mercurial, but they're not dillweeds. [...]
PRINCESS BUBBLEGUM: I mean, they know that I love them.[17]

For the Princess it should be obvious that the time she has invested in her people and the scientific work that she has done for them fills in the same roles as being a loving participant in an active relationship with them. Sadly, as she learns in this episode, the candy people do not view her investments the same way and vote to replace her with the King of Ooo, who is more charismatic and willing to talk and interact with them, at least during the campaigning period. This emphasis on extroversion and relatability echoes the rhetorical attacks that frequently haunt women leaders viewed as too intellectual and disconnected, such as Hillary Clinton. Princess Bubblegum's insistence on the pursuit of knowledge as self-evidently of value to the citizens represents similar challenges in communication (which in the context of politics, of course, has historically been gendered as masculine-dominated, with hegemonic traditions of valuing confidence over inquiry).

Within *Adventure Time* Princess Bubblegum represents both a role model for scientifically minded girls and a warning about what their futures could be. She has a significant amount of both royal and intellectual power within the world of Ooo but it doesn't seem to bring her much happiness. In particular, much of her life is shown to be one of distance and work with few attentions paid to the balance of living her life beyond the world of the mind. Her distance from others is presented both emotionally and physically throughout the series. She is a great person but she will only allow admiration from a distance. The Princess is an engaging character with a lot of depth, but not an easy aspirational role model.

Pearl

Like *Adventure Time*, *Steven Universe* centers on a young boy's adventures through a strange and slightly supernatural universe: Steven Universe, the titular character, is a fairly ineffective fighter who tags along with three strong women-identified fighters, Gems from another planet. The three Crystal Gems—Garnet, Amethyst, and Pearl—are the only remnants of a planned Gem colony. They rebelled against the rest of their society when they realized that the planned colonization would destroy Earth and its human inhabitants. While Princess Bubblegum is a mostly accepted but lonely genius, Pearl from *Steven Universe* is a much more tragic figure. She is the team's engineer, serving as a mechanical genius as well as Steven's mentor in Gem technology. Her story is one of lost human connection, and as we follow her journey we learn that she has had to overcome significant stereotypes about what pearls as Gems are supposed to be capable of. Pearl was formerly in love with, and valued as a partner by, Steven's mother, Rose Quartz. She is the most isolated of the three Gems, so desperate for meaningful connection with others that she even resorts to trickery to have an opportunity for fusion—the show's metaphor for love and sexual connection.

Pearl sacrificed a significant amount of personal definition in order to follow Rose Quartz and her rebellion. Although Gem society is very rigid, it does allow for characters to clearly understand their roles and expectations. Pearl completely redefined herself far beyond what most individuals of her Gem type were able to do. She taught herself to fight, learned advanced engineering, and figured out how to survive in the human world. As a result, Pearl is shown as often being personally uncertain. Although her accomplishments are amazing and recognized by the other characters on the show, she seems to feel that she is never good enough. Additionally, Pearl's efforts to change and develop are rewarded by Rose Quartz falling in love with a human man and eventually losing her physical form, leaving Pearl and the other Crystal Gems to raise Steven. While this change demonstrates Rose's emotional progression through a metaphor of change and evolution, Pearl views it differently, seeing herself as the one left behind.

Pearl's primary depiction is as the group's thinker and maker, and she is regularly seen inventing and engineering solutions to problems. However, discussing Pearl as a woman scientist is misleading, as she is perhaps best described as agender:

> While Gems all seem to take on female forms and pronouns (and each of the main three are voiced by female voice actresses), writers and animators from the show have asserted that they are agender, or at least outside the human gender binary (Jones-Quartey). In a recent Reddit AMA, the show's creator Rebecca Sugar specifically stated that "Steven is the first and only male Gem, because he is half human! Technically, there are no female Gems!" (Sugar AMA) The Gems' agender identities are asserted in the actual show as well as in outside comments by creators. Gems have bodies that they are able to change at will, and this magical ability to mutate their bodies makes the standard feminine features that they often display less important in defining their gender.[18]

Still, Pearl uses feminine pronouns and presents and identifies as a woman; thus, the defined body she has chosen to inhabit is that of a woman scientist and fighter. Over the course of several seasons of the show, Pearl's identity has evolved to make her a significant but problematic representation. The episodes discussed here mark pivotal moments in her development.

We see Pearl's loneliness empowering her single-minded approach to science in "Space Race," a first season episode where Steven and his father are building a spaceship for Pearl after Steven is moved by her desire to return home.[19] The effort is humorous and doomed until they seek out Pearl's advice, and she brings an unexpected seriousness to the venture. As she thinks over the idea: "I hear what you're saying, and I agree—it would be incredibly dangerous; a fool's errand.... But aren't the true fools the ones who don't seize an opportunity, despite all the inherent risks? And I'd be able to show Steven the wonders of the cosmos! And maybe, just for a second, from a distance, I could see what's been going on without me."[20]

"Space Race" establishes Pearl's scientific mind and determination: even as Steven and his father grow increasingly wary of the task at hand, Pearl engages in everything from making rocket fuel (while showing Steven her methodology, of course) to engineering. We see Pearl both relying on existing knowledge and using ingenuity with the limited human tools and equipment available. Her alienation and distance (physical and emotional) are so powerful that she throws them into the task, and even builds a prototype and launches away from the Earth with Steven. This dialogue ensues when Pearl and Steven are beginning to launch:

> PEARL: This will be perfectly fine, just a pop over to the nearest star system. I'll give him back in 50 years.
> MR. UNIVERSE: 50 years? What?! I'll be dead in 50 years! Pearl, you bring him back right now, or I'll Hello? Hello?!
> STEVEN: Pearl, I'm not supposed to go. Pearl!
> PEARL: Oh, this is so exciting! Steven, you're gonna love it.[21]

Pearl's usual reason and grounded personality disappear at the prospect of the journey. There is also the suggestion that Pearl's personal desires and strong-minded pursuit of the goal of the rocket ship actually make her a danger to Steven. The episode ends with Pearl returning Steven to the ground safely, full of regret for letting her project get out of control; the moment demonstrates her growing arc of self-awareness with regards to her own scientific tendencies.

Later in the first season, in the episode "Rose's Scabbard," the Gems find the scabbard to Rose's sword at the site of a battleground. For Pearl, it holds exultant memories: "Your mother led us to glorious victory! The odds were against us, and our hearts were uncertain. But we chose to fight alongside Rose, and here we made our stand against our Homeworld!"[22] She gives the scabbard to Steven, but notes that it is empty without the sword: "That's just the scabbard, Steven. It held your mother's sword. Nothing else could fit so perfectly inside. For all this time it's been … incomplete."[23] The words echo, clearly meaning more to Pearl, reflecting her own emptiness—an emptiness that has been a constant state since Rose's transference of her Gem and essence to Steven. Pearl is haunted by the resemblance, as she notes when Steven asks her what Rose was like: "She was courageous, and brilliant … and beautiful…. Sometimes, you look so much like her."[24]

As the episode progresses, Pearl is faced with evidence that her relationship with Rose wasn't as close or reliable as she thought: Steven is already in possession of Rose's sword, hidden inside the magical Lion who is also apparently connected to Rose and who has taken Steven to spaces Pearl thought were private to herself and Rose. This adds doubt to Pearl's Rose-centric view of herself: "Everything I ever did, I did for her. Now she's gone, but I'm still here. Sometimes, I wonder if she can see me through your eyes. What would she think of me now?"[25] This episode is the first to strongly establish Pearl's loneliness and isolation: we see her as longing for Rose, who apparently did not feel the same, at least based on the physical artifacts that have all been left to Steven's care. This unequal relationship is at the core of Pearl's character, and several episodes explore Pearl's dependency and longing for her past connection with Rose.

One of the most telling episodes for Pearl's character is her mentorship of Connie in "Sworn to the Sword."[26] Pearl is initially wary of the idea of teaching Connie to fight, but she is moved by Connie's desire when Connie invokes Steven: "I wanna be there for Steven, to fight by his side! The Earth is my home too, can't I help protect it?"[27] Pearl sees herself in Connie, and the parallels are strong: Connie is a geeky character, physically inferior to the Gems by simple virtue of her humanity. As the physically weakest of the Gems, Pearl connects to Connie's struggle. However, the training quickly becomes about Pearl shaping Connie into the type of devoted defender that she herself was to Rose, as she expresses in the lyrics of the song "Do It for Her."[28]

Pearl's physicality is unusual among depictions of women scientists (who are rarely allowed to be both analytical and powerful), but her warrior-like instincts are also suggested to be something other than inherent later in the lyrics of "Dot It for Her."[29] Those lyrics are apparently as true for Pearl as they are for Connie. Pearl's level of devotion is even a subject of concern for Garnet, who herself is a fusion of a lesbian couple of Gems: "Back during the war, Pearl took pride in risking her destruction for your mother. She put Rose Quartz over everything; over logic, over consequence, over her own life."[30] Garnet warns Steven that Pearl is trying to inspire Connie to fill a similar role for him. Fan reviews of the episode noted that this is one of the first confirmations of Pearl's love for Rose:

> When Pearl outlines her notion of respect, status, and authority—embodied in the concept of a knight, "completely dedicated to a person and a cause"—we understand even more how adrift Pearl is. She muses to herself that she was only a few thousand years old when she began fighting with Rose, a woman we increasingly gather she loved. What's 10 years in the wake of a relationship that powerful, for a person that old? Rebuilding those bonds takes time.[31]

Thus, Pearl was once defined by her love for Rose, and now she is defined by the lack of that love—by the ultimate loneliness, stranded far away from her home planet.

Throughout the first and second season, Pearl's isolation is further evident as we only occasionally see her engage in fusion, the show's metaphor for a binding together of two characters. When Pearl engages in fusion, she is participating in a sexually encoded act:

> There can be no doubt that Fusion is a semi-sexual or at least desire-coded occurrence. Apart from the fact that Pearl deems the dance inappropriate for young Steven to see, there is the body language of the dance itself. When Pearl and Garnet attempt to teach Steven the process of Fusion, there is obviously a coded desire between them in the closeness and movement of their dance which includes flushed cheeks, heavy breathing, and daringly deep dips.[32]

Thus, it is unsurprising that the one episode that serves as the greatest testament to Pearl's isolation is "Cry for Help," which centers on Pearl's fusion with Garnet as Sardonyx. Fusion is a complex Gem interaction: it is more than a relationship; it is a subsuming of two (or more) selves into a collective with its own thoughts, tensions, and battles for control. Garnet's character is already a fusion of two Gems, Ruby and Sapphire, who are in a permanent relationship so close that they prefer to never spend time apart or un-fused.

Pearl's dependence is self-destructive; her feelings of loneliness, and lack of completion, are a threat to her health and friendship. Pearl's intense desire to be like Garnet—to be fused, and in a stable relationship—leads to her tricking Garnet into a fusion, causing a rift between them. She is caught by the others after sabotaging a tower in order to create an artificial need for Garnet to fuse with her, and in the confrontation Garnet is confused even as Pearl tries to explain: "I'm sorry.... I—It's just ... so much fun being Sardonyx with you."[33] Pearl acknowledges the rift with Garnet that follows as a reflection of her own weakness: "But it's true! No matter how hard I try to be strong like you.... I'm just a Pearl. I'm useless on my own. I need someone to tell me what to do.... When we fuse, I can feel what it's like to be you. Confident and secure, and complete. You're perfect. You're the perfect relationship, you're always together, I just.... I wanted to be a part of that."[34] Her emotional loneliness and feeling of inferiority drive much of Pearl's development across the show's two seasons. Her story is very much defined as that of someone who deliberately went against her natural inclinations and is suffering as a consequence. Even though Pearl has had strong relationships in the past she is still not happy, and it appears that all the things she has changed about herself are those that cause her the most dissatisfaction.

Pearl's departure from the normal nature of her Gem-type is brought to the forefront when she is confronted with Peridot's natural talents as an engineer and technician. This means that Pearl must deal with the similarities and differences between herself and Peridot in a relationship that highlights just how far from her "natural state" she has come:

> [Peridot claps her hands in command. Pearl continues to stand there, looking incredulously at Peridot.]
> PERIDOT: [whispering to Steven] How do you get her to leave?

> PEARL: Excuse me, I am not leaving.
> STEVEN: Yeah! She's gotta stay here to help us build the drill thing, right?
> PERIDOT: [*laughing slightly*] No, no. You're confused. A pearl can't build a thing like this.
> STEVEN: Why not?
> PERIDOT: Because pearls aren't for this! They're for standing around, and looking nice, and holding your stuff for you … right?[35]

The encounter between Pearl and Peridot has shadows of the fake geek girl debate.[36] Pearl's traditional femininity and association with an object emblematic of impractical beauty lead Peridot to question her ability to be useful, much less to be an engineer. Peridot's dismissive treatment of Pearl will resonate with any feminine-presenting technical woman:

> PERIDOT: This is pointless! There's no way you're gonna beat me! You're an accessory! Somebody's shiny toy! Where do you get off acting like your own Gem?! [*Peridot's robot rips one of the arms off of Pearl's robot.*] You're just a PEARL!
> PEARL: [*grimaces, but her expression becomes determined.*] That's right! I am a pearl! [*punches Peridot in the face*][37]

The rhetoric of Peridot's insults is particularly suggestive of gendered microaggressions, and seems poised to put Pearl into her place. Pearl's insecurities and Peridot's heckling culminate in a giant robot fight between the two Gems, after which Peridot acknowledges Pearl's potential worth:

> PERIDOT: I have to admit, it's … remarkable that a Pearl such as yourself could become such a … knowledgeable technician. Mmm… [*holds up the power drill*] Why don't we get started?
> PEARL: [*takes the power drill*] You're holding it upside down. [*hands the drill back*][38]

At the end Pearl is surrounded by her fellow Gems despite losing the fight, while Peridot is left alone with a hollow victory, seeking the attention and affection Pearl receives. This episode shows a surprising amount of character development as Pearl initially feels the sting of Peridot's assumptions about her very deeply but fights to overcome those perceptions and eventually finds a strong belief in her own efficacy and the strength of her bonds with the other Crystal Gems.

Since she wasn't made naturally for technology and fighting, Pearl doubts the technical skills she taught herself while serving Rose Quartz and feels like she'll be forever an imposter. The changes she made turned her into an anomaly in a culture that doesn't allow for any differences to exist from the enforced social order. But, the support she receives from the Gems helps her find that she is both talented and not alone in the world. Pearl learns to accept her own uniqueness as a strength and turns that talent into genuine confidence. Although they may not be the romantic companions she had originally planned to have, they do help her feel whole and connected. Pearl's arc offers potential hope to the young viewer, while simultaneously reinforcing the promise of romantic isolation that comes from following in her footsteps.

Conclusion

Adventure Time and *Steven Universe* are dominant cultural markers for many American children. As these children go forward they will use the messages encoded in these works to help shape and guide their decisions about their own lives. While the characters Princess Bubblegum and Pearl represent interesting women in STEM-related professions, their depictions come with some potential negative associations as well. Both characters are shown as being good role models for children and overall express more positive dispositions to STEM pursuits than negative, but their physical and emotional separation from others, feelings of inadequacy, and social coding as "different from normal" reinforce negative traits. These particular messages can further support beliefs that young girls have about STEM as something that suits them and their interests. As these shows are marketed towards an audience that includes young and pre-adolescent viewers, who are engaged in processes of self-reflection and realization regarding both sexuality and their future interests and careers, the arcs of these characters might discourage young people from seeing similar choices positively.

This is a very different message than similar media aimed at the same age group but featuring boys in STEM-associated roles. *Phineas and Ferb*, a show airing on the Disney Channel and focused upon the exploits of two half-brothers, presents technical and scientific skills as being both a good thing and socially welcomed.[39] The woman scientist is shown as a loner, whose actions are rarely praised or accepted by the community, while Phineas and Ferb are shown as collaborative and social. They are accepted by the community as boy geniuses, and their inventiveness is a continual source of wonder and diversion for their friends. While their actions sometimes have unexpected or apparently destructive consequences, they are only viewed in a negative light by their sister, who acts as an enforcer of social norms. In sharp contrast, Princess Bubblegum and Pearl are othered by their intellectual interests. Their engagements in STEM activities are viewed with suspicion and even cast as a threat to others, as with Pearl's rocket ship and Princess Bubblegum's formulas.

All three of these shows are framed around young men as the central character. There is a strong bias towards showing men as the default viewpoint across media, and all three shows keep this in common by using a young teen boy as the dominant interpreter of the actions that happen each episode. While this simply reinforces a media trend in *Phineas and Ferb*, it helps to cast the actions of the women in *Adventure Time* and *Steven Universe* into a more critical light. Women's actions are often more socially judged for breaking with traditional norms and more universalized as representing a whole group. Audiences may not interpret *Phineas and Ferb* as representing all potential futures for men in STEM, but Princess Bubblegum and Pearl are more likely to be interpreted as demonstrative of women's roles in STEM because they are among a relatively few number of representations. Girls will attempt to see themselves in these women and judge what the future is likely to be for them if they enter a STEM career.

The lack of diverse representation within STEM majors and careers is a complex issue that needs to be dealt with in more nuanced fashions. Research on older interventionist models of change has begun being analyzed and many within the scientific community are finding flaws with previous methodologies.[40] In order to achieve any significant impact, interventions must target not only increasing women's participation but also changing the culture that surrounds STEM and helps shape girls' connections to the fields. Women are often not considered as active participants in their own decision-making process when it comes to discussions about the STEM pipeline, but they do read the cultural context, see their own experiences with STEM topics, and interpret from there what their futures will likely hold. When presented with negative experiences and stereotyped representations of female scientists and engineers, it is to be expected that young women choose to go down a different path.

NOTES

1. Pendleton Ward (creator), *Adventure Time* (Cartoon Network: 2010–present).
2. Rebecca Sugar (creator), *Steven Universe* (Cartoon Network: 2013–present).
3. Jacob Clark Blickenstaff, "Women and Science Careers: Leaky Pipeline or Gender Filter?" *Gender and Education* 17, no. 4 (2005): 369–386; Terrell L. Strayhorn, James M. DeVita, and Amanda M. Blakewood, "Broadening Participation Among Women and Racial/Ethnic Minorities in Sciences, Technology, Engineering and Maths," in *Social Inclusion and Higher Education*, eds. Tehmina N. Basit and Sally Tomlinson (Cambridge: Polity Press, 2012), 65–81.
4. Dale Baker and Rosemary Leary, "Letting Girls Speak Out About Science," *Journal of Research in Science Teaching* 4, no. 1 (2003): S200; Phillip M. Sadler et al., "Stability and Volatility of STEM Career Interest in High School: A Gender Study," *Science Education* 96, no. 3 (2012): 411–427; Rob Semmens, Chris Piech, and Michelle Friend, "Who Are You? We Really Wanna Know ... Especially If You Think You're Like a Computer Scientist," *GenderIT '15 Proceedings of the Third Conference on GenderIT* (2015): 40–43.
5. Suzanne Brainard and Linda Carlin, "A Six-Year Longitudinal Study of Undergraduate Women in Engineering and Science," *Journal of Engineering Education* 87, no. 4 (1998): 369–375.
6. Anita Borg, "What Draws Women to and Keeps Women in Computing?" *Annals of the New York Academy of Sciences* 869 (1999): 102–105; Valerie A. Clarke and G. Joy Teague, "Characterizations of Computing Careers: Students and Professionals Disagree," *Computers and Education* 26, no. 4 (1996): 241–246.
7. Nikki A. Falk et al., "Expanding Women's Participation in STEM: Insights from Parallel Measures of Self-Efficacy and Interests," *Journal of Career Assessment*, September 11,

2016; Nancy N. Heilbronner, "The STEM Pathway for Women: What Has Changed?" *Gifted Child Quarterly* 57 (2013): 39–55.
    8. Sapna Cheryan et al., "The Stereotypical Computer Scientist: Gendered Media Representations as a Barrier to Inclusion for Women," *Sex Roles* 69, no. 1–2 (2013): 58–71.
    9. *Ibid.*
    10. *Ibid.*
    11. Pendleton Ward, "Slumber Party Panic," *Adventure Time*, season 1, episode 1, directed by Larry Leichliter, aired April 5, 2010, on Cartoon Network.
    12. "Scientific Parasite," *Adventure Time Wiki*, accessed September 5, 2016.
    13. Jesse Moynihan, "Wizards Only, Fools," *Adventure Time*, season 5, episode 26, directed by Nate Cash, aired July 1, 2013, on Cartoon Network.
    14. Pendleton Ward, "The Suitor," *Adventure Time*, season 5, episode 21, directed by Nate Cash, aired May 20, 2013, on Cartoon Network.
    15. *Ibid.*
    16. *Ibid.*
    17. Kent Osborne and Jack Pendarvis, "Hot Diggity Doom," *Adventure Time*, season 6, episode 42, directed by Andres Salaff, aired June 5, 2015, on Cartoon Network.
    18. Eli Dunn, "Steven Universe, Fusion Magic, and the Queer Cartoon Carnivalesque," *Gender Forum: An Internet Journal for Gender Studies* 56 (2016).
    19. Rebecca Sugar and Joseph D. Johnston, "Space Race," *Steven Universe*, season 1, episode 28, directed by Ian Jones-Quartey, aired October 9, 2014, on Cartoon Network.
    20. *Ibid.*
    21. *Ibid.*
    22. Rebecca Sugar and Raven Molisee, "Rose's Scabbard," *Steven Universe*, season 1, episode 45, directed by Ian Jones-Quartey, aired March 9, 2015, on Cartoon Network.
    23. *Ibid.*
    24. *Ibid.*
    25. *Ibid.*
    26. Joseph D. Johnston and Jeff Liu, "Sworn to the Sword," *Steven Universe*, season 2, episode 9, directed by Ian Jones-Quartey, aired June 15, 2015, on Cartoon Network.
    27. *Ibid.*
    28. *Ibid.*
    29. *Ibid.*
    30. *Ibid.*
    31. Eric Thurm, "*Steven Universe*: 'Sworn to the Sword,'" *A.V. Club*, June 15, 2015.
    32. Dunn, "Steven Universe, Fusion Magic, and the Queer Cartoon Carnivalesque." A flashback to Pearl and Rose's fusion dance was edited out of the UK airings of the show. See Charles Pullman-Moore, "Cartoon Network UK Is Editing Out the Queer Magic of 'Steven Universe,'" *Fusion*, January 6, 2016.
    33. Rebecca Sugar and Joseph D. Johnston, "Friend Ship," *Steven Universe*, season 2, episode 18, directed by Ian Jones-Quartey, aired July 17, 2015, on Cartoon Network.
    34. *Ibid.*
    35. Rebecca Sugar and Joseph D. Johnston, "Back to the Barn," *Steven Universe*, season 2, episode 23, directed by Joseph D. Johnston, aired October 8, 2015, on Cartoon Network.
    36. Joseph Reagle, "Geek Policing: Fake Geek Girls and Contested Attention," *International Journal of Communication* 9 (2015): 19.
    37. *Ibid.*
    38. *Ibid.*
    39. Dan Povenmire and Jeff Marsh (creators), *Phineas and Ferb* (Disney Channel: 2007–2015).
    40. Bridget Blodgett and Anastasia Salter, "#1ReasonWhy: Game Communities and the Invisible Woman," in *Proceedings of the 9th International Conference on the Foundations of Digital Games*, eds. Michael Mateas, Tiffany Barnes, and Ian Bogost (Liberty of the Seas, Caribbean: Society for the Advancement of the Science of Digital Games, 2014); Anna Vitores and Adriana Gil-Juárez, "The Trouble with 'Women in Computing': A Critical Examination

of the Deployment of Research on the Gender Gap in Computer Science," *Journal of Gender Studies* 25, no. 6 (2015): 666–680.

WORKS CITED

Baker, Dale, and Rosemary Leary. "Letting Girls Speak Out About Science." *Journal of Research in Science Teaching* 40, no. 1 (2003): S200.
Blickenstaff, Jacob Clark. "Women and Science Careers: Leaky Pipeline or Gender Filter?" *Gender and Education* 17, no. 4 (2005): 369–386.
Blodgett, Bridget, and Anastasia Salter. "#1ReasonWhy: Game Communities and the Invisible Woman." In *Proceedings of the 9th International Conference on the Foundations of Digital Games*, edited by Michael Mateas, Tiffany Barnes, and Ian Bogost. Liberty of the Seas, Caribbean: Society for the Advancement of the Science of Digital Games, 2014. http://www.fdg2014.org/proceedings.html.
Borg, Anita. "What Draws Women to and Keeps Women in Computing?" *Annals of the New York Academy of Sciences* 869 (1999): 102–105.
Brainard, Suzanne G., and Linda Carlin. "A Six-Year Longitudinal Study of Undergraduate Women in Engineering and Science." *Journal of Engineering Education* 87, no. 4 (1998): 369–375. doi:10.1109/FIE.1997.644826.
Cheryan, Sapna, Victoria C. Plaut, Caitlin Handron, and Lauren Hudson. "The Stereotypical Computer Scientist: Gendered Media Representations as a Barrier to Inclusion for Women." *Sex Roles* 69, no. 1–2 (2013): 58–71.
Clarke, Valerie A., and G. Joy Teague. "Characterizations of Computing Careers: Students and Professionals Disagree." *Computers and Education* 26, no. 4 (1996): 241–246. doi:10.1016/0360-1315(96)00004-8.
Dunn, Eli. "Steven Universe, Fusion Magic, and the Queer Cartoon Carnivalesque." *Gender Forum: An Internet Journal for Gender Studies* 56 (2016). http://www.genderforum.org/issues/transgender-and-the-media/steven-universe-fusion-magic-and-the-queer-cartoon-carnivalesque/.
Falk, Nikki A., Patrick J. Rottinghaus, Tracy N. Casanova, Fred H. Borgen, and Nancy E. Betz. "Expanding Women's Participation in STEM: Insights from Parallel Measures of Self-Efficacy and Interests." *Journal of Career Assessment*, September 11, 2016.
Heilbronner, Nancy N. "The STEM Pathway for Women: What Has Changed?" *Gifted Child Quarterly* 57 (2013): 39–55.
Johnston, Joseph D., and Jeff Liu. "Sworn to the Sword." *Steven Universe*, season 2, episode 9. Directed by Ian Jones-Quartey. Aired June 15, 2015, on Cartoon Network.
Moynihan, Jesse. "Wizards Only, Fools." *Adventure Time*, season 5, episode 26. Directed by Nate Cash. Aired July 1, 2013, on Cartoon Network.
Osborne, Kent, and Jack Pendarvis. "Hot Diggity Doom." *Adventure Time*, season 6, episode 42. Directed by Andres Salaff. Aired June 5, 2015, on Cartoon Network.
Povenmire, Dan, and Jeff Marsh. *Phineas and Ferb*. Disney Channel, 2007–2015.
Pullman-Moore, Charles. "Cartoon Network UK Is Editing Out the Queer Magic of 'Steven Universe.'" *Fusion*, January 6, 2016. http://fusion.net/story/252111/cartoon-network-steven-universe-queer/.
Reagle, Joeseph. "Geek Policing: Fake Geek Girls and Contested Attention." *International Journal of Communication* 9 (2015): 1–19.
Sadler, Philip M., Gerhard Sonnert, Zahra Hazari, and Robert Tai. "Stability and Volatility of STEM Career Interest in High School: A Gender Study." *Science Education* 96, no. 3 (2012): 411–427.
"Scientific Parasite." *Adventure Time Wiki*. Accessed September 5, 2016. http://adventuretime.wikia.com/wiki/Scientific_Parasite.
Semmens, Rob, Chris Piech, and Michelle Friend. "Who Are You? We Really Wanna Know ... Especially If You Think You're Like a Computer Scientist." *Gender IT '15 Proceedings of the Third Conference on GenderIT* (2015): 40–43.
Strayhorn, Terrell L., James M. DeVita, and Amanda M. Blakewood, "Broadening Participation Among Women and Racial/Ethnic Minorities in Sciences, Technology, Engineering

and Maths." In *Social Inclusion and Higher Education*, edited by Tehmina N. Basit and Sally Tomlinson, 65–81. Cambridge: Polity Press, 2012.
Sugar, Rebecca. *Steven Universe*. Cartoon Network, 2013–present.
Sugar, Rebecca, and Joseph D. Johnston. "Back to the Barn." *Steven Universe*, season 2, episode 23. Directed by Joseph D. Johnston. Aired October 8, 2015, on Cartoon Network.
_____. "Cry for Help." *Steven Universe*, season 2, episode 14. Directed by Ian Jones-Quartey. Aired July 13, 2015, on Cartoon Network.
_____. "Friend Ship." *Steven Universe*, season 2, episode 18. Directed by Ian Jones-Quartey. Aired July 17, 2015, on Cartoon Network.
_____. "Space Race." *Steven Universe*, season 1, episode 28. Directed by Ian Jones-Quartey. Aired October 9, 2014, on Cartoon Network.
Sugar, Rebecca, and Raven Molisee. "Rose's Scabbard." *Steven Universe*, season 1, episode 45. Directed by Ian Jones-Quartey. Aired March 9, 2015, on Cartoon Network.
Thurm, Eric. "*Steven Universe*: 'Sworn to the Sword.'" *A.V. Club*, June 15, 2015. http://www.avclub.com/tvclub/steven-universe-sworn-sword-220161.
Vitores, Anna, and Adriana Gil-Juárez. "The Trouble with 'Women in Computing': A Critical Examination of the Deployment of Research on the Gender Gap in Computer Science." *Journal of Gender Studies* 25, no. 6 (2015): 666–680.
Ward, Pendleton. *Adventure Time*. Cartoon Network, 2010–present.
_____. "Slumber Party Panic." *Adventure Time*, season 1, episode 1. Directed by Larry Leichliter. Aired April 5, 2010, on Cartoon Network.
_____. "The Suitor." *Adventure Time*, season 5, episode 21. Directed by Nate Cash. Aired May 20, 2013, on Cartoon Network.

Girl Geniuses

Anti-Intellectual Stereotypes of Women in STEM Careers in Contemporary Televisual Culture

JZ LONG

"The world of everyday life is not only taken for granted as reality by the ordinary members of society.... It is [also] a world that originates in their thoughts and actions, and is maintained as real by these."
—Peter Berger and Thomas Luckmann[1]

"This is exactly why you squints should stay in the lab. You guys don't know anything about the real world."
—FBI Special Agent Seeley Booth, *Bones*[2]

That women are underrepresented in STEM careers has already been well established. According to statistics from the U.S. National Science Foundation, while women in the United States earn 57 percent of all bachelor's degrees and almost half of all undergraduate degrees, they continue to see declines in such traditional STEM-related fields as computer science, mathematics, and engineering (and astonishingly, and respectively, by 10, 5, and 1 percent).[3] While recent scholarship has demonstrated how outright discrimination contributes to this state of affairs,[4] other researchers have used such critical lenses as gender,[5] ethnicity,[6] education,[7] and nationality[8] in order to interrogate how and why women continue to remain underrepresented in these careers. Scholars have even focused their research on how specific forms media (including cinema, television, and video games) contribute to the reception of STEM-related issues amongst viewers.[9] Adding to the growing literature on the effects of these mediated representations of science, this essay constructs a close reading of several contemporary television dramas in order to better understand how they perpetuate negative stereotypes about women in STEM-related careers.

Building on previous research illustrating how contemporary televisual representations of geniuses in such series as *Bones*, *House*, and *Star Trek* proved problematic in their use of character quirks and flaws as a means for allowing viewers to uncritically distance themselves from engagement with the protagonists' intellectuality,[10] this essay examines the narrative trajectories of forensic scientist Abby Sciuto (Pauley Perrette, *NCIS*), cybersecurity whiz Felicity Smoak (Emily Bett Rickards, *Arrow*), Daisy Wick (Carla Gallo), one of Dr. Temperance Brennan's (Emily Deschanel) revolving cast of "squinterns" (*Bones*), and FBI analyst Penelope Garcia (Kirsten Vangsness, *Criminal Minds*) in order to further illustrate how these representations contribute to the contemporary anti-intellectual and anti-feminist climate.[11]

In each of these instances, female characters find themselves in a profound double bind: whereas male characters are often disregarded for their intellect but respected for their work, female characters who exhibit intellectual brilliance are not only marginalized for their vast knowledge (anti-intellectualism) but also because of their sex and sexuality (anti-feminism). This bind plays itself out in contemporary broadcast television programming insofar as these female scientists are not just given various quirks and attributes which allow viewers to distance themselves from their scientific intellectuality but are also found in supporting roles focused on their romantic relationships. As a result, this analysis can help us to think more critically about the utility of such texts in order to fight both the anti-intellectual and anti-feminist tides in our everyday lives.

One of the ways in which contemporary scholars study such media stereotypes is by using constructivist theories like cognitive schema theory. Constructivist theories posit that, since humans "organize and interpret experience by applying cognitive structures called cognitive schemata," the careful analysis of individuals' cognitive schema—as the "networks of strongly connected cognitive elements that represent the generic concepts stored in memory"—reveals how the specific schemes in our heads help to construct our everyday reality.[12] These schema are activated in individuals' minds when they encounter objects (both actual and virtual) within their perceptual environment. As a result, scholars have developed cognitive schema theory, which states that there are four distinct types of cognitive schema—prototypes, constructs, stereotypes, and scripts—that operate to make sense of the world around us (or, more particularly given the case here, the world in front of us).[13] Given the immense power of contemporary mass media to affect viewer's attitudes and beliefs, it behooves us to examine how these schemata operate within specific media texts, such as those involving women in STEM-based careers, to construct representations that become internalized in the minds of viewers.

If prototypes can be viewed as "the most representative example of a category" (that is, an ideal type that exists only in our minds), then constructs are "bipolar, mental yardstick[s] we use to measure people and situations" against our existing prototypes.[14] For example, what do you think of as the "best," or most representative, example of a female scientist? This prototype (say, Marie Curie) then serves as a mental construct for subsequent comparisons to other individuals. Who else is like Curie? Famous doctors on TV (Dr. Oz, Dr. Phil)? Fictional doctors like Dr. House, Dr. McCoy, or Dr. Watson? Your family doctor? In making such assessments, our minds fold specific individuals into our cognitive schema and evaluates in relation to our prototypes. As "cognitive schemes or mental templates that apply to the thoughts, behaviors, characteristics, and qualities of people,"[15] then, these interpersonal constructs are not only "the primary cognitive structures through which we interpret events"[16] but also "the basic cognitive structures through which we perceive and understand the social world."[17] Some of these structures, often reduced to binaries, include experienced/not experienced, fair/not fair, intelligent/not intelligent, knowledgeable/not knowledgeable, and trustworthy/not trustworthy.[18] Though our prototypes and constructs are often in conflict, they are both repetitive enough that they lead, over time, into generalizations that we apply as a type of cultural shorthand when we meet specific individuals who exhibit specific constructs. These generalizations are called stereotypes.

As noted by cognitive psychologists, stereotypes can be defined as "beliefs about the characteristics, attributes, and behaviors of members of certain groups."[19] Thus, stereotypes exist, on one level, as "intrapersonal, mental structures" that operate inside of our heads to help us create (a) sense of the world around us by making assumptions about how the world works. On another, and generally lesser realized, level, however, stereotypes operate as "extrapersonal, world structures," or external constructions or representations impinging on the mind from the outside world.[20] Levels, perhaps, is not the right word for what we are working with here, for it is important to note that these two modes of stereotyping are co-constitutive. That is, neither one can exist without the other and, in fact, are both continually implicated in the creation of both interpersonal and intercultural meaning. As Strauss and Quinn put it, "meanings are the product of current events in the public world interacting with mental structures [such as stereotypes], which are in turn the product of previous interactions with the public world."[21]

Given enough experiences in the social world, individuals begin to write cultural scripts—"a type of automatic pilot providing guidelines on how to act when one encounters new situations"[22]—to help them navigate the world even more easily. As scholars note, these scripts can also be conceptualized as "the social environment in which a youngster is raised [which] has an important influence on the development of social skills across childhood, adolescence, and into adulthood."[23] When faced with decisions in everyday life, our minds seek to integrate the various facets of the situation, not just by stereotyping the environment but also by responding to such stereotypes as if they were actually reflective of individuals' realities.

In the following case studies, then, a close reading of the narrative arcs of several female television characters involved in STEM careers is conducted in order to illustrate the types of cultural meanings such representations affirm. While I have primarily focused on such police procedurals as *Arrow*, *Bones*, *Criminal Minds*, and *NCIS*, examination of other programs, like the ones included in this volume, will undoubtedly provide further support for the current state of female stereotypes in televisual science.

Case Study 1: Forensics Specialist Abigail Sciuto

If first impressions are any indication, Abby Sciuto's was not an especially flattering one. In the pilot episode of *NCIS* (patriotically entitled "Yankee White"), Abby's character, denoted as a "forensics specialist," is first introduced. The introduction, however, is one in which she is not present. Waiting for Abby's arrival, the following conversation takes place between the morgue assistant Gerald Jackson (Pancho Demmings) and head NCIS Special Agent Leroy Gibbs (Mark Harmon):

JACKSON: I found Abby. She's on the way in.
GIBBS: Yeah, did you wake her up?
JACKSON: No. Called her on her cell. That must have been one phat party.

While the intern then leaves the room with a smile on his face, Gibbs' expression is much different: a short stare, a quizzical raising of the eyebrows, and the following half-hearted question to head medical examiner Donald "Ducky" Mallard (David McCallum): "Why would Abby go to a fat party?"[24] Before we even meet Abby, then, viewers have already been primed to think of her character as both unconscionable (why was she not already at work?) and deviant (why was she at a party on a work night?).

The following scene greets us with the introduction of Abby, a smiling young white woman with black hair, bright lipstick, and a silver necklace with a large eagle on it. Her first conversation is with a colleague, where Abby not only points out that she has "a futon by the cabinet over there" (in case of emergencies or late nights?) but also irreverently asks if her colleague was "her priest" after he said "Bless you" in response to her willingness to help out (rather than, perhaps, a less sarcastic note of simple thanks).[25] Then it is off to work, and off the screen, as the next scene moves us forward some inordinate (and incalculable) amount of time only to find Dr. Mallard contextualizing Abby's long, hard, and, again, off-screen work before she responds directly to several questions from the other primary members of the show: "Well, I did a fibrinogen test. The procoagulant numbers were high, but they weren't off the charts [...] I only iso'd epinephrine that was injected when he got 'jouled and juiced' on the plane [...] the [victim] was an organic freak. I mean, he probably whizzed green. But none of that'll cottage-cheese your blood."[26] At this point, even her boss, in the midst of all of the primary characters of the episode, briefly tilts his head down in apparent shame. If shame is, here, the correct affect, then we are left to wonder what we, as viewers, are supposed to feel shamed about: shame, no doubt, about a protégé who uses colorful language about "jouled and juiced" victims and "cottage-cheese[d]" blood. Both a supervisory and generational critique is at work here, as the genius of Abby's background in forensic science is overshadowed by her gothic look and inappropriate discourse. After digressing for a moment about the victim's last meal and his poor diet, Abby ends the scene by asking the group's special guests if "You dudes in the Secret Service ever think about throwing yourselves in front of the President's diet?"[27] After the head investigator smiles, everyone else smiles, and the tension is diffused and the situation returns to normal (even if, unsurprisingly, we never do get an honest answer to her now rhetorical question).

The number of negative stereotypes presented in this inaugural episode alone are startling. We are greeted with two males talking about Abby's absence, but the conversation quickly moves to an engagement with her non-work life. This immediately primes viewers to perceive Abby's character anti-intellectually, as in the above scenes where she is portrayed as simultaneously unreliable, inappropriate, and deviant (as in not of the norm). She is further hyper-sexualized by her unique "goth" style, consisting of bright red lipstick, Pippi Longstocking bangs, and silver barbs on her black dog-collar choker. In the popular Halloween episode "Witch Hunt," for example, Abby's unexpectedly slow-motion twirl in Marilyn Monroe's iconic costume leaves her male colleagues DiNozzo (Michael Weatherly) and McGee (Sean Murray) starry-eyed. After McGee surreptitiously takes a high-resolution picture of her backside (in which, we, too, see for the first time the large black-and-white cross tattoo), Abby turns back and, seeing both men watching her, engages in the following exchange:

> SCIUTO: Why are you looking at me like that? Do I have food in my teeth or something?

DINOZZO: [*chuckles*] I'll just stick with the "or something." Need to run our dead guy's photo against mug shots.
SCIUTO: Give me.
DINOZZO: [*slaps McGee*] The camera, McGee.
MCGEE: The camera, sorry.[28]

In the next scene, Abby is found twirling around the lab in her iconic dress while the three of them talking about zombie movies and wait for the results from a lab report. In what would clearly be a case study of sexual harassment in the workplace, Abby turns to McGee and says, "McGee, can you invert the image? As soon as you're done undressing me with your eyes."[29] As usual, her co-workers' behaviors are not only familiar cultural scripts but they also serve to emphasize Abby's body rather than her mind.

Such attitudes undoubtedly serve as reasons for her continued status as a forensics specialist, especially after fourteen seasons of demanding and fast-paced work. Given the combination of her high intelligence and idiosyncrasies, however, her character remains largely behind the scenes, literally, as she is almost always working from her laboratory at NCIS headquarters. Even the few scenes in which she leaves headquarters, though, exhibit further anti-feminist stereotypes by placing Abby using common cultural scripts of the damsel in distress. Her narrative slowly develops over the years until her inevitable kidnapping and torture, which occurs during Abby's special appearance on fellow drama *NCIS: Los Angeles*. In "Random on Purpose," she is sent to L.A. to help their team find a throat-slashing serial killer Abby has dubbed "The Phantom."[30] Between announcing "Oops, I think I took a wrong turn" and "Wow, I think this place is pretty cool," Abby's initial black gothic outfit leads even the head of the L.A. division to point out that Abby is "the first NCIS employee [she's] ever met with a sense of style."[31] Finding time to go out for a drink (at a club called Steampunk, no less) after being asked out by one of her new colleagues, Abby is kidnapped by The Phantom. While the team searches her web log for clues, Abby is cuffed to a chair while the killer streams the encounter over the Internet. Using her adept dactylogical skills, Abby leads the detectives to The Phantom just before she is beheaded with an axe. Or, as the Internet Movie Database's entry for the episode puts it, "Abby [...] lends a hand, gets into a mess, and solves 15 murders."[32] All, apparently, in a day's work.

While Abby exhibits great knowledge of computing and forensic science, such knowledge is overshadowed by her unusual quirks and lack of social etiquette. Once again, a character's intellectuality is elided, but this time with added critique that her gender and sexuality are as problematic as her brilliant mind. This is a common theme and one that parallels those of other female characters on television.

Case Study 2: IT Expert Felicity Smoak

Racing out of the elevator in a short black shirt and low-cut white blouse, Felicity Smoak barges into the office of Walter Steele (Colin Salmon), the CEO of Queen Consolidated, and proceeds to engage him in the following conversation:

> SMOAK: I've got one question: Why am I being fired?
> STEELE: Ms. Smoak, isn't it?
> SMOAK: Yes, and I am without a doubt the single most valuable member of your technical division. That's including my so-called "supervisor" [*makes air quotes*]. Letting me go would be a major error for this company.
> STEELE: I agree, which is why you're not being fired.
> SMOAK: Uh, I assumed when you brought me up here, it was because ... [*imitates slicing her own throat*].
> STEELE: It's because I wanted you to look into something for me [...] I was hoping you could find out some of the details of the transaction for me.
> SMOAK: Find out...
> STEELE: Dig up discreetly.
> SMOAK: I'm your girl. [*Starts to walk away.*] I mean, I'm not your girl. I wasn't making a pass at you. [*Starts walking away again.*] Thank you for not firing me. [*Walks out the door.*][33]

An awkward beginning, to be sure. Initially designed as a secondary cast member, Felicity's undercover work eventually leads her to Oliver Queen (Stephen Amell), son of the owner of Queen Consolidated as well as The Arrow, a local vigilante and archer. Shot by his own mother while disguised as The Arrow, Oliver enlists Felicity's help to get him back to his hideout.[34] Now an integral member of "Team Arrow," Felicity slowly develops romantic feelings for Oliver, even as Oliver pursues his former lover, Laurel Lance. After being repeatedly rebuffed by Oliver, Felicity's character does look for other love interests (with, one should note, a simultaneously increasing attention to her own bodily appearance, as evidenced by the decreasing hem lines). Felicity's other attempts at romantic relationships are also highlighted, including her cross-series pursuit of Barry Allen (aka The Flash, played by Grant Gustin) and her tortured relationship with Ray Palmer (aka The Atom, played by Brandon Routh).[35]

By the beginning of season three, however, her narrative takes a turn for the worse. Having dispatched Deathstroke (Manu Bennett), the major villain from the first two seasons, the show's new writers decided to focus on the relationship between Felicity and Oliver, much to the dismay of many fans. Renaming the couple "Olicity," viewers quickly grew weary of their overly emotional and clichéd romantic rhetoric at the expense of new villains and character development. As one fan argued online, "More screen time has seen her become arrogant, hypocritical, whiny, and act as if her opinion holds more weight than anyone else on the team, including Oliver's. If she doesn't get her way, she just throws a little temper tantrum until everyone agrees with her."[36] If the first episode of the third season saw Oliver and Felicity on their first official date, the twentieth episode would see the two having passionate sex amidst the wispy candles and red sheets of Ra's Al Ghul's exotic castle.[37] And just three episodes later, in the third season finale, Oliver decides to retire from being The Arrow to live happily ever after with Felicity.[38] In the season four premiere, Oliver attempts to propose to Felicity but is interrupted by the new mega-villain Damien Darhk (Neal P. McDonough).[39] In the mid-season finale, Oliver's second attempt to propose to Felicity is cut short when she is shot and paralyzed by Darhk.[40] In the following episode, however, Oliver once again proposes and this time with more success.[41]

All of this sounds like a television soap opera, focused more on the cultural script of romantic love rather than on the technical expertise needed to supervise a super-powered crime fighting team. As indicated by Andrew Kreisberg, one of *Arrow*'s executive producers, at this point in the series Oliver and Felicity are "very openly a couple and living together. It has a very different feel to see whatever struggles they face; at the end of the day, they're two people who love each other. There will be lighter, nice, heartwarming end-of-episode, curled-up-on-the-couch moments for our two lovers who are no longer star-crossed."[42] In portraying Felicity's character less as a highly-regarded scientist and CEO and more like a revolving lover, the program reinforces negative stereotypes about the roles even STEM-educated women should follow.

The hypersexualization of Felicity as both lover and fiancée effectively elides her importance as an information technology expert for viewers. Having slept with Oliver a mere five episodes after sleeping with Ray Palmer,[43] we are left to wonder, among other things, what such dalliances have to do with her status as a highly intelligent and competent technologist. Such stereotypical depictions are nothing new, however, and occur with all-too-common frequency. Coupled with anti-social behavior, however, as in the case of *Bones*' Daisy Wick, the results are even more concerning.

Case Study 3: "Squintern" Daisy Wick

The very first scene of *Bones* suggests more of the same type of hypersexualization of its female scientists. Awaiting Dr. Temperance "Bones" Brennan's flight from Guatemala, one of her assistants, Angela Montenegro (Michaela Conlin), is frantically searching the airport for information about her arrival. With the electronic terminals on the fritz and the clerk at the information desk preoccupied, Angela immediately resorts to her sexuality: she suggestively lifts up her skirt in order to get both the clerk's and, of course, the viewer's attention. Several scenes later, we are witness to two shots where Dr. Brennan's bust is prominently displayed: the first, a scene in the lab (while putting bones together as electronic music plays in the background) and, more provocatively, a scene at her home (where she is seen in her negligee, holding a bat, as she prepares to confront a suspicious sound from another room).[44] Before seeing even a hint of their intellectual capacities, we are privy to their breasts and thighs.

Later in the episode, as they arrive at the crime scene, FBI Special Agent Seeley Booth (David Boreanaz) famously (and derogatorily) refers to Dr. Brennan's assistants as "squints":

> BOOTH: Typical squint.
> BRENNAN: I don't know what that means.
> BOOTH When cops get stuck they bring in people like you. Squints; you know, who squint at things.
> BRENNAN Oh, you mean people with very high IQs and basic reasoning skills?[45]

Such jabs reach their dénouement at the end of season three, when it is revealed that Bones' primary intern, Zack Addy (Eric Millegan), has become the assistant to a serial killer called Gormogon. As a result of Addy's arrest, season four begins with the show utilizing a revolving door of new "squinterns," all of whom, like Bones' other assistants, are saddled with unique idiosyncrasies and quirks.

Not surprisingly, all but one of the seven new squinterns are men, and the female squintern, Daisy Wick, is given a number of particularly unnerving characteristics. For example, in her very first episode on the show, Daisy is fired after constantly referring to Dr. Brennan as her "hero," failing to inform a supervisor before testing an important specimen, and speaking up before Bones even asked for her name.[46] Though rehired, even Wick's later development as a love interest for a colleague is not enough to garner her much sympathy. Rather, as one fan site notes, Wick "quickly became one of the show's least-liked characters because of her constant chattering and lack of self-awareness."[47] Echoing these sentiments, one viewer refers to Wick as a "chatterbox, straitlaced, obnoxious, wimp,"[48] while another viewer writes that "I wish Daisy would never show up in the rotation again, because she may be the most irritating character I've ever seen. She's annoyingly perky, completely self-centered, has no filter, and no sense of how to deal with people. Everyone in the lab seems to hate her, which was funny to watch the first few times, but is just irritating now."[49] And still another fan notes, "I hate her voice, her annoying behavior and her general stupid inability to shut her mouth when other characters are fed up of her yapping."[50] The general consensus is that Wick is not simply one of those "characters that you just want to throttle because they are so irritating"[51] but also one "you just utterly loathe so much that they actually make you want to fast forward their scenes."[52] As one fan notes, these quirks are designed "to reinforce the scientific nerd stereotype and they always appear like caricatures next to characters with actual developed personalities."[53]

As a "squintern," Daisy's character does not appear in every episode. Her continued presence on the show, however, eventually leads to a romantic relationship with FBI psychologist Lance Sweets (her "Sweet Lancelot"). From season four to season six, Daisy and Lance are a couple, and this is more often the focus of the show rather than her stellar scientific work. Two failed wedding proposals later, the relationship finally ends. By this point in the series, other female scientists are also being primarily characterized by their relationship status, most notably Brennan with Booth and Angela with Jack Hodgins (who both become married with children). In the season 10 premiere, however, it is arbitrarily revealed that Daisy is pregnant with Lance's child (Seeley Lance Wick-Sweets, or "Little Lance," as she calls him). As Daisy puts it to Booth, "Lance and I bumped into each other a few times this past year, and one of those bumps turned into a bump."[54] Later in the same episode, however, Sweets is abruptly killed by a government assassin and Daisy is left alone with her child. After showing up later in the season to give birth to her son, Daisy's character has receded into the background. Like many of the women on *Bones*, Daisy's narrative overemphasizes cultural scripts of romantic love and marriage at the expense of those of knowledge and intelligence.

Case Study 4: Technical Analyst Penelope Garcia

In the premiere of *Criminal Minds*, the introduction of the show's four primary male leads—FBI Behavioral Analysis Unit (BAU) Chief Aaron Hotchner (Thomas Gibson), Senior Supervisory Special Agent Jason Gideon (Mandy Patinkin), and Supervisory Special Agents Derek Morgan (Shemar Moore) and Dr. Spencer Reid (Matthew Gray Gubler)—is juxtaposed with the abduction of one young, white woman and the screams of another white woman, blindfolded, as her nails are being trimmed by an unknown male serial killer. Twenty-five minutes later, we meet former hacker and current BAU Technical Analyst Penelope Garcia, who is introduced to us through the following exchange with Agent Morgan:

> GARCIA: You've reached Penelope Garcia. In the FBI's Office of Supreme Genius.
> MORGAN: Hey it's Morgan. I need you to work some magic here. I've got a program called Deadbolt Defense and a girl with only a couple hours to live so what do you know?

GARCIA: You've got a problem. Deadbolt's the number one password crack-resistant software out there. You're gonna have to get inside this guy's head to get the password.
MORGAN: I thought I was calling the Office of Supreme Genius.
GARCIA: Well, gorgeous, you've been rerouted to the Office of Too Friggin' Bad.[55]

This exchange, lasting less than a minute, is the only scene featuring Garcia's character throughout the entire pilot episode. Though viewers will soon learn her prowess as a technical analyst and computer programmer, the audience's first impression here is displaced onto her unique sense of humor and sexual innuendo. In fact, this unusual way of answering her official FBI phone becomes a common quirk of the character's all-too-colorful personality. When not answering from the "Office of Supreme Genius" or "Office of Unfettered Omniscience,"[56] Garcia has also variously referred to herself as the "Oracle of Quantico"[57] and the "Queen of All Knowledge."[58]

Though designed as a means of establishing a connection between Garcia and Morgan, not only does this kind of innuendo grow stale but it also leads to embarrassment in front of her colleagues and supervisors. In "From Childhood's Hour," for example, after Agent Morgan says "Talk to me, momma," Garcia replies that her "high performance engine may purr like a puma on the prowl, but this time, Derek, you have seriously overheated my engines and I will seriously require some cool down laps upon your return if you know what I mean by that." Unsurprisingly, Agent Morgan responds with "Baby girl, you're on speaker."[59] In "In Name and Blood," Garcia answers the phone with "Talk dirty to me," only to hear that it is senior Section Chief Erin Strauss on the line. Garcia responds that "it goes without saying that I was expecting it to be someone else, ma'am."[60] Later in the episode, Morgan and Garcia are on the phone when the following exchange takes place:

MORGAN: Garcia, baby girl, please tell me something I want to hear.
GARCIA: You're a statuesque god of sculpted chocolate thunder.
MORGAN: Something I don't already know.
GARCIA: I have a sweet tooth?[61]

While "baby girl" and "baby doll" can certainly be read as terms of affection, they can just as easily be seen as an infantilization of this female analyst and her (again, largely off-screen) work.

In "Compulsion," the second episode of the series, viewers are also treated to the reality of Garcia's job: in a room barely lit with a couple of adjustable desk lamps, Garcia sits at a table surrounded by eleven computer monitors, a plethora of computer accessories (multiple keyboards, mice, and speakers), and a random collection of trinkets (including a stress ball, Lego figures, and ragged copies of *Forbes* and *USA Today*).⁶² Her hair up in pigtails (are FBI analysts allowed to wear pigtails, or is Garcia an exception due to the fact that she does not frequently go out and interact with the public?), Garcia is later asked to run a voice analysis of an "unsub" (unknown subject) and proceeds to have the following exchange, again with Agent Morgan:

> GARCIA: Okay, you know how on *Star Trek* when Captain Kirk asked McCoy to do something totally impossible, and McCoy says, "Dammit, Jim, I'm a doctor not a miracle worker?"
> MORGAN: Hey, what are you telling me? Not to expect a miracle?
> GARCIA: No, I'm saying I'm not a doctor.
> MORGAN: That's my girl.⁶³

While the writers' invocation of the *Star Trek* series is stereotypical of the cultural appreciation by nerdy, asocial scientists, the unusual sexual tension between these two characters suggests new narrative possibilities. The show, however, will never resolve this tension, preferring to utilize it, whenever needed, to lighten the narrative load amidst the disturbing flow of arsonists, serial killers, and rapists. In fact, just as Agent Gideon uncovers the motive for the episode's killer (a college student who likes to set people on fire), we are again witness to a conversation between Garcia and Morgan:

> GARCIA: Hey, gorgeous, I've put this thing through every audio filter I've got. There's only one thing I can tell you for sure. This guy isn't saying "Karen." It's more like "Ka-Rone."
> MORGAN: Garcia, what the hell is "Ka-Rone"?
> GARCIA: If I figure it out, does it earn me a night of passionate lovemaking?
> MORGAN: Most definitely, sweetness ... with Reid.
> GARCIA: Uh...
> MORGAN: Bye.⁶⁴

Morgan then turns around to inform a puzzled Agent Reid of the information passed along by Garcia.

This type of violent narrative inevitably reaches into the personal life of Garcia, as she is not only stalked and shot by a crooked law enforcement officer in season three but is also placed in witness protection during season eleven after uncovering evidence of an online group of hitmen seeking something called "the dirty dozen."⁶⁵ After learning that this sublime object is none either than Garcia herself, she is confined to BAU headquarters until further notice.⁶⁶ While holed up for her own protection, Garcia's character can be seen in various states of emotionality, including anxiety and panic (complete with hand-wringing, stuttering, and rapid speech).⁶⁷ Once the BAU finds not just the hitmen but their NSA-led drug cartel employers (a truly long story), Garcia returns to work and the show returns to its traditional procedural format.

Seeing Garcia's strong skills as an FBI analyst overshadowed by the "damsel-in-distress" cliché is certainly a major concern. Even more problematic, however, is that most of the time her character "[b]asically solves all of the cases but never gets credit."[68] As one online critic (and fan) puts it, each episode always seems to involve asking

> Garcia (who mostly stays in Quantico surrounded by a bank of computers) to "Find someone matching these Extremely Specific Characteristics, Penelope! Time is running out!" And, of course, as fast as she can type, Penelope ("hacking" databases that would be patently illegal IRL) finds the UNSUB's name, age, address, psych history, tattoos, meds, high school class rank, favourite Rolling Stones tune, the names and manufacturers of all his stuffed animals—oh, and she'll triangulate his cell phone and find him, too.[69]

As with our other female scientists, the economy of television prevents young fans of the show not only from seeing the hard work required to make such forensics look "easy" but also, and more problematically, from seeing a strong female scientist publicly lauded for her efforts.

Girl Geniuses

As I teach to all of my students, there are two fundamental dangers of all stereotypes: on the one hand, negative stereotypes lead to negative actions (Hitler is perhaps the most obvious example, or prototype, here); on the other, individuals tend to live up to their stereotypes. This second danger is more insidious than the first insofar as the act of living up to one's stereotype is largely unconscious. Understanding how stereotypes fit into our natural perceptual processes (for example, understanding that entirely eliminating generalizations of others is an impossible task given the structure of our cognitive capacities) allows us to start a critical conversation with ourselves regarding the origin of such generalizations.

As illustrated throughout this essay, popular television programs like *Arrow*, *Bones*, *Criminal Minds*, and *NCIS* utilize a number of negative stereotypes that prevent viewers of these shows from understanding the hard work required by today's women entering careers in science, technology, engineering, and mathematics. One major stereotype is that female television scientists are almost always subordinated to male counterparts, and, if they are not, they are characterized by idiosyncrasies (especially those, as in the cases of Abby and Penelope, involving appearance) designed to infer that such quirks render them ineligible for leadership. Here the double bind is that while intelligence is necessary for strong leadership, such displays by female characters are met with anti-intellectualism, disdain, and dismissal.

Another key stereotype promoted in these shows is that the intense training and knowledge needed to succeed in STEM-based careers is virtually non-existent; rather, these female scientists are seen completing forensic tasks faster than a speeding bullet (pardon the double pun). As demonstrated elsewhere, this "CSI Effect" has already had negative repercussions in both courtrooms and universities.[70] In all of these shows characters are expected to have answers immediately, and are often dismissed by other characters when their discourse becomes too scientific. In this regard, the double bind is between always already having the right answer or being criticized for not having it fast enough. In popular television programs featuring women in STEM-based careers, then, female scientists like the ones discussed here are stereotyped in a number of problematic ways, including hypersexualization, trivialization, and even infantilization.[71]

It is important to remind ourselves here that researchers have repeatedly illustrated how we all—students, parents, and teachers alike—have internalized negative stereotypes and continue to underestimate our own students' abilities for future success in these scientific disciplines. As several scholars have noted, stereotypes start to function "as educational gatekeepers, constraining who enters these fields,"[72] by establishing generalizable qualities to which real individuals are unfairly measured against. These stereotypes, moreover, are most often transmitted via individual persons, cultural environments, and media communications.[73]

Given the broad reach of media communications like television, it is important, therefore, to analyze these media representations in order to better understand how they affect our own cognitive schema. As evidenced by the above examples, popular American television programming remains a prevalent site for negative representations of women in STEM careers. Given the pervasive reach of contemporary media, correcting these stereotypes will not be easy. This is especially true if we have unconsciously absorbed these stereotypes over years of media consumption. Developing a critical media literacy, like the examination set out it this essay, can at least mitigate the impact of such stereotypes by bringing to light the ways in which they are presented in our popular culture.

NOTES

1. Peter L. Berger and Thomas Luckmann, *The Social Construction of Reality* (New York: Penguin, 1966), 33.

2. Hart Hanson, "Pilot," *Bones*, season 1, episode 1, directed by Greg Yaitanes, aired September 13, 2005, on Fox.

3. National Science Board, *Science and Engineering Indicators 2016* (Arlington: National Science Foundation, 2016).

4. Sylvia C. Nassar-McMillan et al., "New Tools for Examining Undergraduate Students' STEM Stereotypes: Implications for Women and Other Underrepresented Groups," *New Directions for Institutional Research*, no. 152 (2011): 87–98.

5. Edna Tan et al., "Desiring a Career in STEM-Related Fields: How Middle School Girls Articulate and Negotiate Identities-in-Practice in Science," *Journal of Research in Science Teaching* 50, no. 10 (2013): 1143–1179; Josimeire M. Julio and Arnaldo M. Vaz, "Latent

Masculinity in School Physics Investigation Activities: Microanalysis of Small Groups and Whole Class Interactions," in *Contemporary Science Education Research: Scientific Literacy and Social Aspects of Science*, eds. Gultekin Cakmakci and Mehmet Fatih Tasar (Ankara, Turkey: Pegem Akademi, 2010), 333–337.

    6. Kareen Ror Malone and Gilda Barabino, "Narrations of Race in STEM Research Settings: Identity Formation and Its Discontents," *Science Education* 93, no. 3 (2009): 485–510; Maria Teresa V. Taningco, *Latinos in STEM Professions: Understanding Challenges and Opportunities for Next Steps: A Qualitative Study Using Stakeholder Interviews* (Los Angeles: University of Southern California, 2008).

    7. Vanessa L. Wyss, Diane Heulskamp, and Cathy J. Siebert, "Increasing Middle School Student Interest in STEM Careers with Videos of Scientists," *International Journal of Environmental and Science Education* 7, no. 4 (2012): 501–522; Henriette Tolstrup Holmegaard, Lene Moller Madsen, and Lars Ulriksen, "A Journey of Negotiation and Belonging: Understanding Students' Transition to Science and Engineering in Higher Education," *Cultural Studies of Science Education* 9, no. 3 (2014): 755–786.

    8. Gregor Cerinsek et al., "Which Are My Future Career Priorities and What Influenced My Choice of Studying Science, Technology, Engineering or Mathematics? Some Insights on Educational Choice," *International Journal of Science Education* 35, no. 17 (2013): 2999–3025; David Miller, Alice H. Eagly, and Marcia C. Linn, "Women's Representation in Science Predicts National Gender-Science Stereotypes: Evidence from 66 Nations," *Journal of Educational Psychology* 107, no. 3 (2015): 631–644.

    9. Elizabeth Whitelegg, R. Holliman, and J. Carr, "Exploring Gendered Stereotypes on Science Television with Children and Young People: Towards a Classroom Application," *Contemporary Science Education Research: Scientific Literacy and Social Aspects of Science*, eds. Gultekin Cakmakci and Mehmet Fatih Tasar (Ankara, Turkey: Pegem Akademi, 2010), 277–280; Jon D. Miller et al., "Adult Science Learning from Local Television Newscasts," *Science Communication* 28, no. 2 (2006): 216–242.

    10. JZ Long, "Mediated Genius, Anti-Intellectualism, and the Detachment(s) of Everyday Life," in *Genius on Television: Essays on Small Screen Depictions of Big Minds*, ed. Ashley Lynn Carlson (Jefferson, NC: McFarland, 2015), 32–48.

    11. Donald P. Bellisario and Don McGill (creators), *NCIS* (CBS: 2003–present); Greg Berlanti, Marc Guggenheim, and Andrew Kreisberg (creators), *Arrow* (The CW: 2012–present); Hart Hanson (creator), *Bones* (Fox: 2005–2017); Jeff Davis (creator), *Criminal Minds* (CBS: 2005–present).

    12. Julia T. Wood, *Communication Mosaics: An Introduction to the Field of Communication*, 7th edition (Boston: Wadsworth, 2014), 45; Claudia Strauss and Naomi Quinn, *A Cognitive Theory of Cultural Meaning* (New York: Cambridge University Press, 1997), 6.

    13. Wood, *Communication Mosaics*, 45.

    14. Ibid.

    15. Brant Burleson, "Constructivism: A General Theory of Communication Skill," in *Explaining Communication: Contemporary Theories and Exemplars*, eds. Bryan B. Whaley and Wendy Samter (Mahwah, NJ: Lawrence Erlbaum Associates, 2007), 119.

    16. Brant R. Burleson and Jessica J. Rack, "Constructivism Theory: Explaining Individual Differences in Communication Skill," in *Engaging Theories in Interpersonal Communication: Multiple Perspectives*, eds. Leslie A. Baxter and Dawn O. Braithwaite (Thousand Oaks, CA: SAGE Publications, 2008), 53.

    17. Burleson, "Constructivism," 120.

    18. Wood, *Communication Mosaics*, 46.

    19. James L. Hilton and William von Hippel, "Stereotypes," *Annual Review of Psychology* 47 (1995): 240.

    20. Strauss and Quinn, *A Cognitive Theory*, 6.

    21. Ibid.

    22. James M. Honeycutt, "Imagined Interaction Theory: Mental Representations of Interpersonal Communication," in *Engaging Theories in Interpersonal Communication: Multiple Perspectives*, eds. Leslie A. Baxter and Dawn O. Braithwaite (Thousand Oaks, CA: SAGE Publications, 2008), 78.

23. Burleson, "Constructivism," 132.
24. Donald Bellisario, "Yankee White," *NCIS*, season 1, episode 1, directed by Donald Bellisario, aired September 23, 2003, on CBS.
25. *Ibid.*
26. *Ibid.*
27. *Ibid.*
28. Steven Kriozere, "Witch Hunt," *NCIS*, season 4, episode 6, directed by James Whitmore, Jr., aired October 31, 2006, on CBS.
29. *Ibid.*
30. Speed Weed, "Random on Purpose," *NCIS: Los Angeles*, season 1, episode 9, directed by Steven DePaul, aired November 24, 2009, on CBS.
31. *Ibid.*
32. IMDb, "Random on Purpose," *IMDB (Internet Movie Database)*, 2016.
33. Moira Kirkland and Lana Cho, "An Innocent Man," *Arrow*, season 1, episode 4, directed by Vince Misiano, aired October 31, 2012, on The CW.
34. Andrew Kreisberg and Marc Guggenheim, "The Odyssey," *Arrow*, season 1, episode 14, directed by John Behring, aired February 6, 2013, on The CW.
35. Compare, for example, Felicity's flirtatious behavior with Barry (The Flash) in "The Scientist" (*Arrow*, season 2, episode 8), her vigil by his hospital bed in "Blast Radius" (*Arrow*, season 2, episode 10), and an awkward double-date with Barry Allen's old crush in "Going Rogue" (*The Flash*, season 1, episode 4), with the following season's melodrama with Palmer Technologies CEO Ray Palmer (The Atom), from her initial introduction as a prospective employee in "The Calm" (*Arrow*, season 3, episode 1) to her breaking out in tears in front of him in "Sara" (*Arrow*, season 3, episode 2) to her mother's attempts at running interference in "Corto Maltese" (*Arrow*, season 3, episode 3).
36. Shazam37, "Why 'Olicity' Is Killing Arrow," *Comic Book Movie*, April 23, 2015.
37. Marc Guggenheim and Jake Coburn, "The Calm," *Arrow*, season 3, episode 1, directed by Glen Winter, aired October 4, 2014, on The CW; Wendy Mericle and Oscar Balderrama, "The Fallen," *Arrow*, season 3, episode 20, directed by Antonio Negret, aired April 22, 2015, on The CW.
38. Marc Guggenheim and Jake Coburn, "My Name Is Oliver Queen," *Arrow*, season 3, episode 23, aired May 13, 2015, on The CW.
39. Marc Guggenheim and Wendy Mericle, "Green Arrow," *Arrow*, season 4, episode 1, directed by Thor Freudenthal, aired on October 7, 2015, on The CW.
40. Wendy Mericle and Ben Sokolowski, "Dark Waters," *Arrow*, season 4, episodes 9, directed by John Behring, aired on December 9, 2015, on The CW. Far from an arbitrary decision, this storyline echoes the Joker's paralysis of Commissioner Gordon's daughter, Barbara Gordon, in Alan Moore's *Batman: The Killing Joke*, and her subsequent reappearance in the DC Universe as Oracle, a paraplegic computer whiz who works behind the scenes to help Batman and other superheroes.
41. Oscar Balderrama and Sarah Tarkoff, "Blood Debts," *Arrow*, season 4, episode 14, directed by Jesse Warn, aired on January 20, 2016, on The CW.
42. Sydney Bucksbaum, "'Arrow' Bosses Tease Game-Changing Season 4 Villain, Challenges for Olicity," *Hollywood Reporter*, October 7, 2015.
43. Erik Oleson and Ben Sokolowski, "Nanda Parbat," *Arrow*, season 3, episode 15, directed by Gregory Smith, aired on February 25, 2015, on The CW; Wendy Mericle and Oscar Balderrama, "The Fallen," Arrow, season 3, episode 20, directed by Antonio Negret, aired on April 22, 2015, on The CW.
44. Hanson, "Pilot."
45. *Ibid.*
46. Carla Kettner and Mark Lisson, "The Man in the Outhouse," *Bones*, season 4, episode 3, directed by Steven DePaul, aired September 10, 2008, on Fox.
47. "Daisy Wick," *Buddy TV*, accessed June 25, 2017.
48. "Daisy Wick," *F*** Yeah, Controversial Characters* (blog), December 23, 2012.
49. Sarah Braun, "Top 5 Most Disliked TV Characters," *Big Damn TV Geek* (blog), July 25, 2012.

50. anabananadog, "The Characters and Relationships of Bones," *Previously TV* (blog), January 30, 2015.
51. VanMitch, "Top Twenty Annoying TV/Movie Characters," *Van's Wisdom* (blog), May 3, 2012.
52. "I Don't Like You: Daisy Wick," *Shep Herds TV* (blog), March 22, 2012.
53. crippledscholar, "I Wish Bones Had Killed Off Dr. Jack Hodgins," *crippledscholar* (blog), April 22, 2016.
54. Stephen Nathan and Jonathan Collier, "The Conspiracy in the Corpse," *Bones*, season 10, episode 1, directed by Ian Toynton, aired September 25, 2014, on Fox.
55. Jeff Davis, "Extreme Aggressor," *Criminal Minds*, season 1, episode 1, directed by Richard Shepard, aired September 22, 2005, on CBS.
56. Edward Allen Bernero, "Plain Sight," *Criminal Minds*, season 1, episode 4, directed by Matt Earl Beesley, aired October 12, 2005, on CBS.
57. Ed Napier, "Somebody's Watching," *Criminal Minds*, season 1, episode 18, directed by Paul Shapiro, aired March 29, 2006, on CBS.
58. Andrew Wilder, "North Mammon," *Criminal Minds*, season 2, episode 7, directed by Matt Earl Beesley, aired November 1, 2006, on CBS.
59. Bruce Zimmerman, "From Childhood's Hour," *Criminal Minds*, season 7, episode 5, directed by Anna J. Foerster, aired October 19, 2011, on CBS.
60. Chris Mundy, "In Name and Blood." *Criminal Minds*, season 3, episode 2, directed by Edward Allen Bernero, aired October 3, 2007, on CBS.
61. Mundy, "In Name and Blood."
62. Jeff Davis, "Compulsion," *Criminal Minds*, season 1, episode 2, directed by Charles Haid, aired September 28, 2005, on CBS.
63. *Ibid.*
64. *Ibid.*
65. Breen Frazier, "The Job," *Criminal Minds*, season 11, episode 1, directed by Glenn Kershaw, aired September 30, 2015, on CBS.
66. Jim Clemente, "Target Rich," Criminal Minds, season 11, episode 7, directed by Glenn Kershaw, aired November 11, 2015, on CBS.
67. *Ibid.*
68. Melissa Fraser, "Criminal Minds Review," *Ruthless Reviews*, February 4, 2015.
69. *Ibid.*
70. Corey Call et al., "Seeing Is Believing: The CSI Effect Among Jurors in Malicious Wounding Cases," *Journal of Social, Behavioral, and Health Sciences* 7, no. 1 (2013): 53–66; Graeme Paton, "*CSI* Fuels Forensic Science Degree Rise," *The Telegraph*, October 16, 2009.
71. Elizabeth A. Gunderson et al., "The Role of Parents and Teachers in the Development of Gender-Related Math Attitudes," *Sex Roles* 66, no. 3 (2012): 153–166.
72. Sapna Cheryan, Allison Master, and Andrew N. Meltzoff, "Cultural Stereotypes as Gatekeepers: Increasing Girls' Interest in Computer Science and Engineering by Diversifying Stereotypes," *Frontiers in Psychology* 6, article 49 (2015): 1–2.
73. *Ibid.*, 5.

Works Cited

anabananadog. "The Characters and Relationships of Bones." *Previously TV* (blog), January 30, 2015. http://forums.previously.tv/topic/16830-the-characters-and-relationships-of-bones/.
Balderrama, Oscar, and Sarah Tarkoff. "Blood Debts." *Arrow*, season 4, episode 14. Directed by Jesse Warn. Aired on January 20, 2016, on The CW.
Bellisario, Donald P. "Yankee White." *NCIS*, season 1, episode 1. Directed by Donald Bellisario. Aired September 23, 2003, on CBS.
Bellisario, Donald P., and Don McGill. *NCIS*. CBS: 2003–present.
Berger, Peter L., and Thomas Luckmann. *The Social Construction of Reality*. New York: Penguin, 1966.
Berlanti, Greg, Marc Guggenheim, and Andrew Kreisberg, *Arrow*. The CW: 2012–present.

Bernero, Edward Allen. "Plain Sight." *Criminal Minds*, season 1, episode 4. Directed by Matt Earl Beesley. Aired October 12, 2005, on CBS.
Braun, Sarah. "Top 5 Most Disliked TV Characters." *Big Damn TV Geek* (blog), July 25, 2012. http://www.bigdamntvgeek.com/2012/07/top-5-most-disliked-tv-characters/.
Bucksbaum, Sydney. "'Arrow' Bosses Tease Game-Changing Season 4 Villain, Challenges for Olicity." *Hollywood Reporter*, October 7, 2015. http://www.hollywoodreporter.com/live-feed/arrow-season-4-olicity-829087.
Bureau of Labor Statistics. "American Time Use Survey." *Bureau of Labor Statistics*. Washington, D.C.: U.S. Department of Labor, 2016. http://www.bls.gov/news.release/atus.nr0.htm.
Burleson, Brant R. "Constructivism: A General Theory of Communication Skill." In *Explaining Communication: Contemporary Theories and Exemplars*, 113–139. Edited by Bryan B. Whaley and Wendy Samter. Mahwah, NJ: Lawrence Erlbaum Associates, 2007.
Burleson, Brant R., and Jessica J. Rack. "Constructivism Theory." In *Engaging Theories in Interpersonal Communication: Multiple Perspectives*, 51–63. Edited by Leslie A. Baxter and Dawn O. Braithwhite. Thousand Oaks, CA: SAGE Publications, 2008.
Call, Corey, Amy K. Cook, John D. Reitzel, and Robyn D. McDougle. "Seeing Is Believing: The CSI Effect Among Jurors in Malicious Wounding Cases." *Journal of Social, Behavioral, and Health Sciences* 7, no. 1 (2013): 53–66.
Cerinsek, Gregor, Tina Hribar, Natasa Glodez, and Slavko Dolinsek. "Which Are My Future Career Priorities and What Influenced my Choice of Studying Science, Technology, Engineering or Mathematics? Some Insights on Educational Choice." *International Journal of Science Education* 35, no. 17 (2013): 2999–3025.
Cheryan, Sapna, Allison Master, and Andrew N. Meltzoff. "Cultural Stereotypes as Gatekeepers: Increasing Girls' Interest in Computer Science and Engineering by Diversifying Stereotypes." *Frontiers in Psychology* 6, article 49 (2015).
Clemente, Jim. "Target Rich." *Criminal Minds*, season 11, episode 7. Directed by Glenn Kershaw. Aired November 11, 2015, on CBS.
crippledscholar. "I Wish Bones Had Killed Off Dr. Jack Hodgins." *crippledscholar* (blog), April 22, 2016. http://crippledscholar.wordpress.com/2016/04/22/i-wish-bones-had-killed-off-dr-jack-hodgins/.
"Daisy Wick." *Buddy TV*. Accessed June 25, 2017. http://www.buddytv.com/bones/characters/daisy-wick.aspx.
"Daisy Wick." *F*** Yeah, Controversial Characters* (blog), December 23, 2012. http://fyeahcontroversialcharacters.tumblr.com/post/38669542450/character-daisy-wick-fandom-bones-reason-for.
Davis, Jeff. "Compulsion." *Criminal Minds*, season 1, episode 2. Directed by Charles Haid. Aired September 28, 2005, on CBS.
———. *Criminal Minds*. CBS: 2005–present.
———. "Extreme Aggressor." *Criminal Minds*, season 1, episode 1. Directed by Richard Shepard. Aired Sep 22, 2005, on CBS.
Frazier, Breen. "The Job." *Criminal Minds*, season 11, episode 1. Directed by Glenn Kershaw. Aired September 30, 2015, on CBS.
Guggenheim, Marc, and Jake Coburn. "The Calm." *Arrow*, season 3, episode 1. Directed by Glen Winter. Aired October 4, 2014, on The CW.
———. "My Name Is Oliver Queen." *Arrow*, season 3, episode 23. Aired May 13, 2015, on The CW.
Guggenheim, Marc, and Wendy Mericle. "Green Arrow." *Arrow*, season 4, episode 1. Directed by Thor Freudenthal. Aired on October 7, 2015, on The CW.
Gunderson, Elizabeth A., Gerardo Ramirez, Susan C. Levine, and Sian L. Beilock. "The Role of Parents and Teachers in the Development of Gender-Related Math Attitudes." *Sex Roles* 66, no. 3–4 (2012): 153–166.
Hanson, Hart. *Bones*. Fox: 2005–present.
———. "Pilot." *Bones*, season 1, episode 1. Directed by Greg Yaitanes. Aired September 13, 2005, on Fox.
Hilton, James L., and William von Hippel. "Stereotypes." *Annual Review of Psychology* 47 (1995): 237–271.

Holmegaard, Henriette Tolstrup, Lene Moller Madsen, and Lars Ulriksen. "A Journey of Negotiation and Belonging: Understanding Students' Transition to Science and Engineering in Higher Education." *Cultural Studies of Science Education* 9, no. 3 (2014): 755–786.

Honeycutt, James M. "Imagined Interaction Theory: Mental Representations of Interpersonal Communication." In *Engaging Theories in Interpersonal Communication: Multiple Perspectives*, 77–87. Edited by Dawn O. Braithwaite and Paul Schrodt. Thousand Oaks, CA: SAGE Publications, 2008.

"I Don't Like You: Daisy Wick." *Shep Herds TV* (blog), March 22, 2012. http://shepherdstv.wordpress.com/2012/03/22/i-dont-like-you-daisy-wick/.

Julio, Josimeire M., and Arnaldo M. Vaz. "Latent Masculinity in School Physics Investigation Activities: Microanalysis of Small Groups and Whole Class Interactions." In *Contemporary Science Education Research: Scientific Literacy and Social Aspects of Science*, 333–337. Edited by Gultekin Cakmakci and Mehmet Fatih Tasar. Ankara, Turkey: Pegem Akademi, 2010.

Kettner, Carla, and Mark Lisson. "The Man in the Outhouse." *Bones*, season 4, episode 3. Directed by Steven DePaul. Aired September 10, 2008, on Fox.

Kirkland, Moira, and Lana Cho. "An Innocent Man." *Arrow*, season 1, episode 4. Directed by Vince Misiano. Aired October 31, 2012, on The CW.

Kreisberg, Andrew, and Marc Guggenheim. "The Odyssey." *Arrow*, season 1, episode 14. Directed by John Behring. Aired February 6, 2013, on The CW.

Kriozere, Steven. "Witch Hunt." *NCIS*, season 4, episode 6. Directed by James Whitmore, Jr. Aired October 31, 2006, on CBS.

Long, JZ. "Mediated Genius, Anti-Intellectualism, and the Detachment(s) of Everyday Life." *Genius on Television: Essays on Small Screen Depictions of Big Minds*, 32–48. Edited by Ashley Lynn Carlson. Jefferson, NC: McFarland, 2015.

Malone, Kareen Ror, and Gilda Barabino. "Narrations of Race in STEM Research Settings: Identity Formation and Its Discontents." *Science Education* 93, no. 3 (2009): 485–510.

Mericle, Wendy, and Ben Sokolowski. "Dark Waters." *Arrow*, season 4, episodes 9. Directed by John Behring. Aired on December 9, 2015, on The CW.

Mericle, Wendy, and Oscar Balderrama. "The Fallen." *Arrow*, season 3, episode 20. Directed by Antonio Negret. Aired April 22, 2015, on The CW.

Miller, David L., Alice H. Eagly, and Marcia C. Linn. "Women's Representation in Science Predicts National Gender-Science Stereotypes: Evidence from 66 Nations." *Journal of Educational Psychology* 107, no. 3 (2015): 631–644.

Miller, Jon D., Eliene Augenbraun, Julia Schulhof, and Linda G. Kimmel. "Adult Science Learning from Local Television Newscasts." *Science Communication* 28, no. 2 (2006): 216–242.

Mundy, Chris. "In Name and Blood." *Criminal Minds*, season 3, episode 2. Directed by Edward Allen Bernero. Aired October 3, 2007, on CBS.

Napier, Ed. "Somebody's Watching." *Criminal Minds*, season 1, episode 18. Directed by Paul Shapiro. Aired March 29, 2006, on CBS.

Nassar-McMillan, Sylvia C., Mary Wyer, Maria Oliver-Hoyo, and Jennifer Schneider. "New Tools for Examining Undergraduate Students' STEM Stereotypes: Implications for Women and Other Underrepresented Groups." *New Directions for Institutional Research*, no. 152 (2011): 87–98.

Nathan, Stephen, and Jonathan Collier. "The Conspiracy in the Corpse." *Bones*, season 10, episode 1. Directed by Ian Toynton. Aired September 25, 2014, on Fox.

National Science Board. *Science and Engineering Indicators 2016*. Arlington: National Science Foundation, 2016. http://www.nsf.gov/statistics/2016/nsb20161/uploads/1/nsb20161.pdf.

Oleson, Erik and Ben Sokolowski. "Nanda Parbat." *Arrow*, season 3, episode 15. Directed by Gregory Smith. Aired February 25, 2015, on The CW.

Paton, Graeme. "CSI Fuels Forensic Science Degree Rise." *The Telegraph*, October 16, 2009. http://www.telegraph.co.uk/education/6348107/CSI-fuels-forensic-science-degree-rise.html.

Shazam37. "Why 'Olicity' Is Killing Arrow." *Comic Book Movie*, April 23, 2015. https://www.comicbookmovie.com/dc_tv/arrow/why-olicity-is-killing-arrow-a119361.
Speed Weed. "Random on Purpose." *NCIS: Los Angeles*, season 1, episode 9. Directed by Steven DePaul. Aired November 24, 2009, on CBS.
Strauss, Claudia, and Naomi Quinn. *A Cognitive Theory of Cultural Meaning*. New York: Cambridge University Press, 1997.
Tan, Edna, Angela Calabrese Barton, Hosun Kang, and Tara O'Neill. "Desiring a Career in STEM-Related Fields: How Middle School Girls Articulate and Negotiate Identities-in-Practice in Science." *Journal of Research in Science Teaching* 50, no. 10 (2013): 1143–1179.
Taningco, Maria Teresa V. *Latinos in STEM Professions: Understanding Challenges and Opportunities for Next Steps: A Qualitative Study Using Stakeholder Interviews*. Los Angeles: University of Southern California, 2008.
VanMitch. "Top Twenty Annoying TV/Movie Characters." *Van's Wisdom* (blog), May 3, 2012. https://vanswisdom.wordpress.com/2012/05/03/top-twenty-annoying-tvmovie-characters/.
Whitelegg, Elizabeth, Richard Holliman, and Jennifer Carr. "Exploring Gendered Stereotypes on Science Television with Children and Young People: Towards a Classroom Application," *Contemporary Science Education Research: Scientific Literacy and Social Aspects of Science*, 277–280. Edited by Gultekin Cakmakci and Mehmet Fatih Tasar. Ankara, Turkey: Pegem Akademi, 2010.
Wilder, Andrew. "North Mammon." *Criminal Minds*, season 2, episode 7. Directed by Matt Earl Beesley. Aired November 1, 2006, on CBS.
Wood, Julia T. *Communication Mosaics: An Introduction to the Field of Communication* (7th edition). Boston: Wadsworth, 2014.
Wyss, Vanessa L., Diane Heulskamp, and Cathy J. Siebert. "Increasing Middle School Student Interest in STEM Careers with Videos of Scientists." *International Journal of Environmental and Science Education* 7, no. 4 (2012): 501–522.
Zimmerman, Bruce. "From Childhood's Hour." *Criminal Minds*, season 7, episode 5. Directed by Anna J. Foerster. Aired October 19, 2011, on CBS.

"One of the Guys"
Female Engineers on Television
Ashley Lynn Carlson

In 2015, an article in *Scientific American* declared, "the complete absence of female engineers in popular culture has huge implications for public perceptions of the STEM fields."[1] The author, Jayde Lovell, was one of the winners of that year's "The Next MacGyver" competition, which aimed to crowdsource ideas for television series featuring female engineers as the main protagonists. Whether intentionally or not, Lovell was a bit hyperbolic. While it's true that popular culture has a significant impact on public perception, women engineers are not entirely absent from the scene. In fact, some of the most memorable television engineers from the past twenty years have been women.[2] In the late 1990s and early 2000s, women with extraordinary engineering abilities were central characters in two of the most popular science fiction series of the time: *Star Trek: Voyager* (1995–2001) and *Stargate SG-1* (1997–2007).[3] More recently, female engineers play central roles in *Scorpion* (2014–present) and *The 100* (2014–present).[4]

The female engineers on *Voyager*, *SG-1*, *Scorpion*, and *The 100* have, and have had, the potential to serve as role models for young women considering careers in a field that is heavily male dominated. As of 2013, the most recent data available, only 15 percent of the engineering workforce is made up of women.[5] The numbers are even grimmer in certain specialties, particularly mechanical engineering, where women make up only 8 percent of the workforce.[6] It is therefore particularly important to consider the implications of popular portrayals of women in engineering fields, as these portrayals can have a significant impact on both how women in engineering are perceived and women's interests in related careers. In each series discussed here, the characters demonstrate time and again that women can be exceptional engineers, which is an important step towards fighting gender bias.

However, each of the engineers discussed in this essay is also an outsider or Othered in her respected universe, and thus reinforces the notion that women who design and build things, and particularly women who work with machines, are unusual and "different." Further, this difference is often at least partially constructed through an emphasis on the female characters' physical strength, aggressiveness, and other traits commonly (albeit problematically) associated with masculinity. Studies have shown that women in engineering often adopt behaviors associated with masculinity as a means of fitting in.[7] Powell, Bagilhole, and Dainty, for example, build on Judith Butler's work on gender performativity and argue that women in engineering "actively perform masculinity."[8] They note a number of tactics that women use to cope with the male-dominated environment in engineering, including "acting like one of the boys," "achieving a reputation," and "adopting an 'anti-woman' approach."[9] These tactics are reflected in the on-screen construction and performance of gender across the four series discussed in this essay. While gender can be understood as a construct, the repetition of the portrayal of female engineers as masculine in popular culture contributes to the conception that masculine traits are necessary, or even natural, for those who excel in the profession. Thus, while it is promising to see women engineers on television, these portrayals risk supporting hegemonic masculinity, and may ultimately deter many young women from pursuing the profession.

B'Elanna Torres, Star Trek: Voyager

The *Star Trek* franchise has a history of breaking new ground. The diverse cast of *The Original Series* (1966–1969) challenged contemporary notions of gender, race, and nationality.[10] Notably, Lieutenant Uhura (Nichelle Nichols) made television history as a Black female communications officer and member of the Enterprise's bridge crew. Later spin-offs of *Star Trek* continued the franchise's legacy of portraying diversity within the egalitarian society of the United Federation of Planets.

When *Star Trek: Voyager*, the fourth series in the franchise, premiered in 1995, most of the media buzz was about Captain Kathryn Janeway (Kate Mulgrew), the first female captain in a leading role on a *Star Trek* series. Yet the series featured another lead female who also broke ground by filling a traditionally male role: B'Elanna Torres (Roxann Dawson), the half-Klingon, half-human who became *Voyager*'s chief engineer.[11] Interestingly, the series pilot opens not with a scene featuring Captain Janeway, but with one in which B'Elanna saves the crew of a Maquis ship by getting "creative" with her engineering skills, thus making B'Elanna, rather than Janeway, the first strong female character to appear on the show.[12] Throughout all seven seasons,

B'Elanna served as an important representation of a female engineer while also reflecting and resisting various cultural ideologies relating to both gender and race.

In the series premiere of *Star Trek: Voyager*, the crews of two ships, one Starfleet (the *Voyager*), one Maquis (a resistance organization that has resorted to terrorist tactics, and that Starfleet is attempting to quell), are pulled by an alien force over 70,000 light-years away from Earth, to the Delta Quadrant. Finding themselves in an uncharted sector of space where they are completely isolated from communication with the Alpha Quadrant (the region of space that is home to Earth) the two crews must work together. After the destruction of the Maquis ship, they ultimately merge into one crew aboard the *Voyager*. B'Elanna Torres is a central focus of the second episode of the series, "Parallax," in which Captain Janeway and her new first officer, Commander Chakotay (the former captain of the now destroyed Maquis ship, played by Robert Beltran), work to assimilate the rebellious former Maquis into the Starfleet crew.[13] The episode is central in establishing B'Elanna's character and the personal and professional struggles she faces throughout the series.

"Parallax" opens with acting chief engineer Lieutenant Carey (Josh Clark), an angry, white, human male, yelling "She's not just out of control; she's out of her mind."[14] "She," it turns out, is B'Elanna, who has broken Lt. Carey's nose in three places over "a disagreement about the power grid."[15] Thus, the very first line of the episode intersects with problematic gender stereotypes: B'Elanna is the madwoman, emotionally out of control, and therefore fundamentally unfit (at least in Lt. Carey's view) to work in engineering. Yet B'Elanna's emotional struggles, as well as her physical aggressiveness, simultaneously serve to masculinize her: rather than the typical "hysterical" woman, B'Elanna expresses anger through physical violence, a trait more commonly associated with men. B'Elanna is characterized as "out of her mind" above all because she is behaving outside of her prescribed gender role.

B'Elanna's struggle to behave professionally is also linked to her Klingon heritage, and since species difference in the *Star Trek* universe can be likened to racial difference, her character can also be linked to racial stereotypes (Roxann Dawson is Hispanic, and Klingons are depicted as dark-complected). As Robin Roberts writes, "B'Elanna's tendency toward violence and aggression and her warlike orientation are depicted as stemming from her Klingon heritage; they are presented as racialized masculine cultural characteristics that are valuable but that must be kept under tight control."[16] Moreover, as the only Klingon on the *Voyager*, B'Elanna's species difference specifically serves to cast her as Other, and further separates her from the rest of the crew. As such, B'Elanna's introduction on the series is troubling in terms of both gender and race.

In spite of her rocky start aboard the *Voyager*, B'Elanna is promoted to chief engineer above Lt. Cary because, as Chakotay says, she's "a better engineer than he is."[17] Indeed, he tells Captain Janeway that B'Elanna is "the best engineer I've ever known."[18] Janeway gets sufficient proof of this later in "Parallax" when B'Elanna's ingenuity helps save the *Voyager*, ultimately leading to B'Elanna's promotion. On one hand, the promotion suggests not only that women can be engineers, but that they can outperform men, in opposition to the longstanding stereotype that women have naturally less aptitude in science and math. On the other hand, the details here are problematic, as B'Elanna's gender and species (racial) difference threaten to undermine the evaluation of her performance, thereby suggesting that women must be exceptional (in this case, exceptionally gifted in engineering) in order to achieve the same success that is open to (often less exceptional) men. This reflects women's perception that they can overcome gender discrimination by achieving a reputation in the field; unfortunately, this perception is often false, as women in engineering continue to face discrimination regardless of their abilities and achievements.[19] Similarly, B'Elanna struggles in her career despite her abilities.

Over the seven seasons of *Star Trek: Voyager*, B'Elanna's character develops more fully, and in ways that define her as an invaluable member of the crew. Yet, her temper continues to be one of the most prominent aspects of her personality throughout the series, even if that temper is increasingly in check. For example, in the season four episode "Random Thoughts" B'Elanna's violent thoughts cause her to be accused of a crime on an alien world. As Lieutenant Tuvok (Tim Russ) says in the episode, "this isn't the first time that Lieutenant Torres' violent proclivities have created problems."[20] In season five, B'Elanna suffers from emotional problems following the death of some of her previous crewmates, and as a result she nearly kills herself by running dangerous combat simulations on the holodeck with the safety protocols turned off.[21] The episode highlights both her impressive physical strength and her violent tendencies. Later in season five, when Captain Janeway chooses B'Elanna to lead an away mission, her emotional stability is again called into question, as Tuvok argues "B'Elanna is unpredictable, Captain, under these circumstances her volatile nature could compromise the mission."[22] These are only a few of the many instances in which the series draws attention to B'Elanna's physicality and aggression, and each one serves to reinforce her construction as Other.

Interestingly, one noteworthy and potentially positive aspect of B'Elanna's development is that she is the only woman on the show who manages to forge and maintain a healthy relationship over the course of the series, eventually marrying her love interest, Tom Paris (Robert Duncan McNeill), and, in the series finale, giving birth to their child.[23] Other characters' story arcs repeatedly reflect discord between one's professional and personal life; Janeway has left her husband behind in the Alpha Quadrant, Kes (Jennifer Lien) and Neelix (Ethan Phillips) break up as Kes matures and becomes more independent, and in the final episode the budding romance between Chakotay and Seven (Jeri Ryan) is nearly derailed by the mere possibility that in the future Seven's death in the line of duty will take an emotional toll on Chakotay. In contrast, B'Elanna and Tom date for several years before finally marrying and starting a family. Through their relationship, the series provides an important portrayal of a woman who successfully pursues both a professional life and a personal life.

Although B'Elanna's personal and professional development throughout *Star Trek: Voyager* can be read as largely positive, it nevertheless problematically supports certain detrimental stereotypes. B'Elanna repeatedly saves the crew and ship through her ingenuity and skills, and by the series finale there is no doubt that she is a competent and trustworthy officer, in addition to being a talented engineer. Still, her Klingon characteristics of physical strength and aggression serve to masculinize her, while her emotional volatility reinforces the perception that women's emotions interfere with rationality and can directly conflict with job performance in engineering. While B'Elanna is undoubtedly a strong female character and an excellent engineer, these issues make it difficult to definitively categorize her as a positive role model for women interested in engineering.

Samantha Carter, Stargate SG-1

Building on the success of the film *Stargate* (1994) and following in the footsteps of successful science fiction series like *Star Trek*, *Stargate SG-1* first aired on Showtime in 1997. The show quickly became a hit. In 1998 Jerry Offsay, then president of programming at Showtime, stated that *Stargate SG-1* was "the most widely watched thing on our network[...]; it outperforms every theatrical movie on our air."[24] The show followed a structure that was very similar to *Star Trek*: in each episode the SG-1 team visited new worlds and encountered alien landscapes and civilizations. However, rather than flying around in a ship, the SG-1 team began their voyages on Earth, travelling through the Stargate, a portal that allowed them to instantly reach distant worlds. In the early seasons, SG-1 had four members: Colonel Jack O'Neill (Richard Dean Anderson), the team leader, Daniel Jackson (Michael Shanks), an archeologist and language expert, T'ealc (Christopher Judge), an extraterrestrial with knowledge of other planets, and Samantha Carter (Amanda Tapping), a theoretical astrophysicist and Air Force Captain whose practical contributions to the team include a broad range of technological and engineering skills. Although Carter is not labeled as an engineer, she nevertheless fulfills this role in many episodes. She frequently works with both terrestrial and alien technologies, building and repairing machines and systems in order to support the team. For this reason, I have included her as an example of a female engineer.

Because *Stargate SG-1* is set in the present day (the late 90s when it first aired), contemporary views about women as scientists and military officers are reflected more overtly in this series than in *Voyager*. In Carter's first scene in the pilot episode, she joins a group of other officers, all men, to discuss a mission through the Stargate. In the first few moments, Carter's gender identity is questioned because she prefers to go by "Sam." She comments, "you don't have to worry, Major, I played with dolls when I was a kid," seemingly to clarify her sexual orientation, to which the Major responds, "G.I. Joe?"[25] Carter's remark that the Major does not need "to worry" seems to allude to the "Don't Ask, Don't Tell" policy that was instituted in 1993, just a few years before the first episode of *SG-1*.[26] The Major's response indicates that he will continue to assume that Carter is masculine, even as she resists situating herself in that way. As the scene continues, the men at the table question Carter's ability to handle the physical demands of travelling through the Stargate. When Carter informs Colonel O'Neill that "just because my reproductive organs are on the inside instead of the outside, doesn't mean I can't handle whatever you can handle," her comment is met with literal eye-rolls from the men seated across the table.[27] Thus, in Carter's first two minutes on screen, the series calls attention to the rarity of women in military and scientific roles and suggests that, in the mainstream consciousness at least, gender informs women's professional opportunities and choices. The scene reflects an important reality for women in male-dominated fields: that they are viewed as either "'honorary men' or 'flawed women.'"[28] While the Major suggests that Carter is a flawed woman, she attempts to assert herself as an honorary man, capable of the same feats as her male colleagues.

Carter's gender is at the forefront throughout the first season, and frequently serves to set her as apart from the rest of the all-male SG-1 team. In the show's third episode, "Emancipation," the SG-1 team visits a planet inhabited by descendants of the Mongols.[29] The women in the community are seen as property and cannot show their faces in public. In order to conform with the law of the land, Carter is forced to wear a dress. When the men on the team first see her in her new attire, their mouths gape, and O'Neill tells her "it kinda works for me," pointedly calling her "Samantha" rather than Sam or Carter.[30] In a dress she is also recognized for the first time as "beautiful" by one of the Mongols, and as a result of her physical appearance she is kidnapped, sold, and threatened with rape. Seemingly by virtue of a simple change in attire, a dress rather than military fatigues, Carter is transformed into both a beautiful object and a victim. The implication here is that traditional femininity, symbolized by a dress rather than military garb, is associated with a loss of agency.

Apparently unable to help herself, Carter is "rescued" when her team purchases her back from her warlord captor. Yet, at the end of the episode when she is back in her military fatigues, she defeats the same warlord in physical combat. This scene serves to emphasize that Carter's physical strength is on par with men; she gains respect through her physicality, despite the fact that her primary contribution to her team is scientific. This moment links Carter's capacity as a SG-1 member to traditionally masculine characteristics, reinforcing the link between masculinity and success in science and engineering, much like the presentation of B'Elanna on *Voyager*. Moreover, as long as she is dressed like the men, she is able to position herself as an "honorary man."

Carter's victory in combat with the warlord ultimately leads all of the women in the community to be "free" (they remove their veils in public).[31] The episode is brimming with problematic material, from the blatant Orientalism in the portrayal of the planet's "Mongolian" inhabitants to the obvious white-savior trope. Despite serious issues in the construction of race, however, it is worth noting that the episode attempts to portray Carter in a positive light, as a "liberated" woman. Unfortunately, Carter's liberation is also constructed as eschewing traditional femininity in the form of a dress, suggesting that women can either be strong or feminine, but not both.

While several of the early episodes of the first season pointedly show that Carter is as strong and competent as the men, later episodes in the season continue to suggest that Carter is treated differently because of her gender. In the episode "Hathor," she tells a female colleague "Maybe it's just me, but I can't figure out how to feel like one of the guys with these guys, you know what I mean? I always feel like I'm the girl."[32] This comment directly addresses one of the most common obstacles for women in STEM fields: feeling isolated in a male-dominated workplace. It also reflects the tendency among women in engineering to actively pursue behaviors that will help them "blend in and become 'one of the boys.'"[33] Ironically, being "the girl" proves an asset in the episode, as Carter leads the women at Stargate Command to save the day after a female Goa'uld (an alien race that is a recurring enemy on the series) puts the men under her spell and takes control of the base. Yet even this basic plot reinforces the idea of innate gender difference: Carter is one of the "girls" at Stargate Command, but also the only girl on the SG-1 team. In certain situations this might provide an advantage, but overall it is also an important dividing line between her and the rest of the team.

Similarly, in the following episode Carter is singled out from the team to care for an orphaned girl.[34] Despite her expertise in astrophysics, she is reassigned from her duties to observe a black hole and essentially ordered to babysit instead. Whereas the dress in "Emancipation" clearly makes Carter uncomfortable, in this episode Carter almost immediately takes on a nurturing role, reinforcing gendered expectations through her maternalistic instincts and emotional attachment to the girl. Once again, this episode draws specific attention to Carter's gender as a key feature that sets her apart from the rest of her team. Later in the episode, the team discovers that the girl has a kind of bomb inside her body that will wipe out Stargate Command. Without a means to remove or disable the bomb, the team moves the child to a deep underground bunker where the explosion will be contained. Carter defies a direct order and insists on staying with her, even though doing so will only mean Carter's death (the child's death, at this point, is a foregone conclusion). In the end, the device fails to detonate, and both Carter and the girl are saved. Nevertheless, the episode makes it clear that Carter's roles as a scientist and military officer are secondary to her role as a woman, which is constructed as innately nurturing and driven by emotion rather than reason. Her gender can be read as alternately a strength or a weakness, but above all it is a clear difference that affects her professional performance and necessarily makes her Other.

Over the ten years that *SG-1* aired, Carter's gender became less and less of an emphasis on the show; like B'Elanna, she became increasingly accepted as both an integral member of the team and a foremost expert in multiple fields. Notably, in the eighth season she was promoted to Lieutenant-Colonel and replaced O'Neill as the leader of *SG-1*.[35] One moment from the final season that highlights the changes in Carter's character can be found at the very beginning of the of the third-to-last episode, "Family Ties."[36] The episode opens with a shot of two pairs of high-heeled boots, and the camera quickly pans up to reveal Carter and Vala Mal Doran (an additional female member of SG-1 who joined the team in season 10, played by Claudia Black) wearing dresses and carrying multiple shopping bags each. The women are walking through the halls of Stargate Command, and in the background several men appear distracted by their attire. The camera angle and the men in the background are clearly intended to construct the women as objects of sexual desire. However, when they run into Lt. Commander Cameron Mitchell (another addition to the *SG-1* team, played by Ben Browder), he is surprised by their unusual attire but does not gape or make inappropriate comments, as Carter's teammates do in the season one episode "Emancipation." Carter's behavior is also markedly different; here she appears as self-confident and comfortable in a dress as in her usual gear.

Although the moment is brief, it reveals the extent to which Carter's character transformed over the series' ten-year run. In this scene, and in the next, when Carter is called to the Stargate before she has time to change into her uniform, it is evident that her femininity is no longer, or at least less, at odds with her physical strength, engineering capabilities, or scientific interests. It's also worth noting that this scene is one of a very few moments in the final season that emphasize Carter's gender at all, in comparison to the repeated full-episode narratives that focused on gender in season one. The addition of Vala to *SG-1* also diminishes the construction of Carter as a gendered Other, as she is no longer the sole female and thus default outsider on the team.

While gender issues prevail in the early episodes of both *Voyager* and *Stargate SG-1*, they become increasingly irrelevant to each woman's performance as the series continue. Presumably, as both the audience and the series' writers became accustomed to seeing women in engineering roles, gender ceased to be a focal point or potential source of conflict in the professional settings on each series. In essence, for viewers the two series normalize the presence of women in engineering and technical fields. Nevertheless, both B'Elanna and Carter are largely constructed as "tomboys," and thereby reinforce cultural expectations that those with mechanical interests and abilities are more masculine.

Happy Quinn, Scorpion, *and Raven Reyes,* The 100

Since 2014, two new shows featuring women engineers have aired on primetime television: *Scorpion* and *The 100*. *Scorpion* is about a team of geniuses who solve a variety of major problems for governments and other clients. The sole female genius on the team is Asian-American Happy Quinn (Jadyn Wong), a mechanical engineer. Happy's first scene in the series is immediately reminiscent of the portrayal of B'Elanna Torres in early episodes of *Voyager*; after rigging the wiring in the team's warehouse to steal electricity, she climbs down from the ladder and explains that the reason she hasn't picked up payment for her last gig is that the client called her "Sugar," so she "hit him in the mouth."[37] Her "tough guy" attitude is one of her character's trademarks. At one point, Happy explains that to "deal with stress [...] I smash things,"[38] and she is regularly shown threatening to hit people, throwing things, or hammering away her frustrations in the garage. Like B'Elanna, she's brilliant and strong-willed, but also like B'Elanna, she is characterized as angry, physically aggressive, and prone to violence.

The psychiatrist on the team, Toby (Eddie Kaye Thomas), describes her as suffering from "hostility and anger dissonance syndrome."[39] This is not a real diagnosis; "anger dissonance syndrome" is a fictional syndrome apparently invented by the series' writers, but the implication is that there is something wrong with Happy.[40] Admittedly, all of the geniuses on *Scorpion* have psychological issues. Nevertheless, Happy's issues are problematically linked directly to her mechanical prodigy and simultaneously constructed in opposition to traditional gender roles. Toby persistently attempts to convince Happy to date him throughout the first season, but whenever he acts on "instincts" (Toby's word) to protect her, she reacts with anger and frustration. In doing so, the series suggests that Happy is unable to fit into her role as a woman, which in the context of the series, and Toby's psychobabble, appears to be biologically prescribed. Thus, the show constructs Happy as a "flawed woman" and reinforces both traditional gender ideology—man as protector and woman as needing protection—and that mechanical aptitude runs counter to femininity.

It is promising to see that the female team member on *Scorpion* is the mechanical engineer and not, for example, the psychiatrist (a field that has more women than men).[41] It is also exciting to see a team of crime fighters where the woman is described as "the toughest on the team."[42] Yet this, too, echoes the problematic performance of gender that Powell et al. describe; Happy can be understood as "adopting an 'anti-woman' approach," which is sometimes associated with "appearing more 'macho' than some men."[43] In Happy's case, she is more macho than any of the men on the team. Additionally, she demonstrates a lack of interest and sometimes even disdain for the one other female character on the show, the non-genius Paige (Katherine McPhee), who exudes traditional gender ideology in her emotionality and unwavering focus on her role as a mother. Powell et al. note that "adopting an 'anti-woman' approach is another way to distance oneself from one's own gender identity [but] any career success among such women is unlikely to promote the interests of women in the sector generally."[44] Given the limited portrayals of engineers, particularly female engineers, on television, it is difficult not to read every portrayal of a woman engineer as a sign of progress. Nevertheless, the portrayal of an extremely macho and masculinized female engineer such as Happy does little to disrupt problematic stereotypes that may discourage women and girls from pursuing careers in engineering.

In this way, *The 100* has perhaps been more successful in making engineering appear less gendered as a career choice. *The 100* is set in the future following a nuclear disaster on Earth. The survivors of the disaster have lived aboard a space station known as "The Arc" for nearly a century, but with the Arc's systems failing, those in charge send 100 teenaged delinquents back to Earth's surface to determine whether it is safe for everyone else. On the series, Raven Reyes (Lindsey Morgan), is the "youngest Zero-G mechanic" in over fifty years, making her, like all of the women discussed here, particularly gifted in engineering.[45]

Essentially all of the main characters on *The 100* are gritty non-conformists, and gender divisions are less clearly defined in the dystopian future than in contemporary American society, making it more difficult to describe Raven as masculinized in comparison to other characters on the series. Still, her physical strength is emphasized throughout the series, even as she struggles with serious injuries that lead to a permanent physical disability that requires her to use a brace to walk. As with all of the other women discussed here, Raven's strength and endurance are notable. She insists on pushing herself physically despite chronic pain, even to the point of potentially worsening her condition.[46] Also like all of the women discussed in this essay, Raven is clearly constructed as fighter, both physically and mentally. In season three, as Raven fights to regain self-control after an artificial intelligence (AI) takes over her mind, the AI remarks that Raven is "so much stronger than the rest of you."[47] Indeed, Raven is the only person who seems able to resist the AI at all. Similarly, at the beginning of season four, one of her peers remarks that Raven has "been through more than anyone," to which she responds, "There's nothing like a little pain to remind you you're alive."[48] This coincides with female engineers' performance of masculinity by avoiding and criticizing "feminine tactics (such as crying)," another aspect of the "anti-woman" approach.[49] The one saving grace on *The 100* may be that many of the female characters show similar behaviors; they push through pain and attempt to put their emotions on hold because their survival in the post-apocalyptic environment of the series often depends upon it.

While Raven may not be so obviously masculine when compared to other characters on *The 100*, both she and Happy share some other noticeable qualities aside from their engineering skills that serve to set them apart as different. Both characters are marked as criminal in their first moments on the series; Raven breaks into areas of the Arc that are off-limits and Happy is busy stealing electric service. Both characters are defiant of authority, acting impulsively and even potentially violently at times. Both characters are also racial minorities, which is particularly problematic as their characteristics may be at least partially tied to racial stereotypes rather than assumptions related to their professions. Regardless, both characters reinforce the perception that engineering is a profession for those with masculine qualities.

Conclusion

It is promising to see women engineers on television, and if this trend continues it may well propel more young women to seek career paths in engineering. A similar trend has occurred in forensic science over the past 30 years, with numerous series portraying female forensic scientists while an increasing number of women have actually entered the field (women now make up close to 74 percent of graduates in forensic science).[50] However, television needs to continue to portray more diversity among women in engineering—not just racial diversity, but diversity in personality types. Persistently portraying female engineers as physically strong, aggressive, combative, and masculine reinforces problematic stereotypes that tie math and science to masculinity. This translates to the same "double bind effect" that Powell et al. describe: "women engineers who perform in highly feminine ways are likely to be considered incompetent and competent women engineers are seen as unfeminine; thereby instilling a norm whereby only male masculinity is likely to be accepted in the current situation."[51] As the engineers across these four series are all competent, they are also seen as unfeminine, and in this respect, therefore, little progress has been made since the 1990s.

Women's share in the engineering workforce has slowly increased, from 9 percent in 1995 when *Voyager* first aired to approximately 15 percent in 2013, but there is still much progress that needs to be made.[52] Shows like *Scorpion* and *The 100* have the potential to draw a new generation of young women into engineering, but if popular portrayals are to have a larger impact, it is imperative that TV producers cease to link masculine traits to engineers. The recurrent performance of masculinity among female engineers on television does little challenge the perception that engineering itself is masculine; indeed, quite the opposite. Perhaps this is most obvious in the case of the new *MacGyver*, which premiered in September of 2016 on CBS.[53] Despite the 2015 competition to create a female "Next MacGyver," this MacGyver is, alas, still a man.

Notes

1. Jayde Lovell, "MacGyvering a Female Engineer onto Television," *Scientific American*, August 26, 2015.
2. I use the term "engineer" broadly to examine four female characters with obvious strengths in mechanics and engineering, although not all of them have the specific title of "engineer." All of these characters are charged with designing, building, and maintaining machines and technology. As such, this essay is largely concerned with mechanical engineers.
3. Rick Berman, Michael Piller, and Jeri Taylor (creators), *Star Trek: Voyager* (UPN: 1995–2001); Jonathan Glassner and Brad Wright (creators), *Stargate SG-1* (Showtime: 1997–2002, Sci-Fi Channel 2002–2007).
4. Nick Santora (creator), *Scorpion* (CBS: 2014–present); Jason Rothenberg (creator), *The 100* (The CW: 2014–present).
5. National Science Board, *Science & Engineering Indicators 2016* (Arlington: National Science Foundation, 2016), 85.
6. *Ibid.*, 84.
7. Laura A. Rhoton, "Distancing as a Gendered Barrier: Understanding Women Scientists' Gender Practices," *Gender and Society* 25, no. 6 (2011): 698; Abigail Powell, Barbara Bagilhole, and Andrew Dainty, "How Women Engineers Do and Undo Gender: Consequences for Gender Equality," *Gender, Work, and Organization* 16, no. 4 (2009): 412.
8. Powell et al., "How Women Engineers Do and Undo Gender," 418.
9. *Ibid.*, 418–420.

10. Gene Roddenberry (creator), *Star Trek* (NBC: 1966–1969).
11. Another female engineer, Dr. Leah Brahms (Susan Gibney), appeared in several episodes of *Star Trek: The Next Generation*, but was not a main character.
12. Michael Piller and Jeri Taylor, "Caretaker," *Star Trek: Voyager*, season 1, episode 1, directed by Winrich Kolbe, aired January 16, 1995, on UPN.
13. Brannon Braga, "Parallax," *Star Trek: Voyager*, season 1, episode 2, directed by Kim Friedman, aired January 23, 1995, on UPN.
14. *Ibid.*
15. *Ibid.*
16. Robin A. Roberts, "Science, Race, and Gender in Star Trek: Voyager," in *Fantasy Girls: Gender in the New Universe of Science Fiction and Fantasy Television*, ed. Elyce Rae Helford (Lanham, MD: Rowman & Littlefield 2000), 211.
17. Braga, "Parallax."
18. *Ibid.*
19. Powell et al., "How Women Engineers Do and Undo Gender," 419–420.
20. Kenneth Biller, "Random Thoughts," *Star Trek: Voyager*, season 4, episode 10, directed by Alexander Singer, aired November 19, 1997, on UPN.
21. Kenneth Biller, "Extreme Risk," *Star Trek: Voyager*, season 5, episode 3, directed by Cliff Bole, aired October 28, 1998, on UPN.
22. Bryan Fuller, Nick Sagan, and Kenneth Biller, "Juggernaut," *Star Trek: Voyager*, season 5, episode 21, directed by Allan Kroeker, aired April 26, 1999, on UPN.
23. Kenneth Biller and Robert Doherty, "Endgame," *Star Trek: Voyager*, episode 7, season 24, directed by Allan Kroeker, aired May 23, 2001, on UPN.
24. Andy Meisler, "Not Even Trying to Appeal to the Masses," *New York Times*, October 4, 1998.
25. Jonathan Glassner and Brad Wright, "Children of the Gods," *Stargate SG-1*, season 1, episode 1, directed by Mario Azzopardi, aired July 27, 1997, on Showtime.
26. Policy Concerning Homosexuality in the Armed Forces, 10 U.S.C. §654 (1993).
27. *Ibid.*
28. Powell et al., "How Women Engineers Do and Undo Gender," 412.
29. Kathryn Powers, "Emancipation," *Stargate SG-1*, season 1, episode 3, directed by Jeff Woolnough, aired August 8, 1997, on Showtime.
30. *Ibid.*
31. *Ibid.*
32. David Bennet Carren, J. Larry Carroll, and Jonathan Glassner, "Hathor," *Stargate SG-1*, season 1, episode 13, directed by Brad Turner, aired October 24, 1997, on Showtime.
33. Powell et al., "How Women Engineers Do and Undo Gender," 418.
34. Robert Cooper, "Singularity," *Stargate SG-1*, season 1, episode 14, directed by Mario Azzopardi, aired October 31, 1997, on Showtime.
35. Robert Cooper, "New Order: Part 2," *Stargate SG-1*, season 8, episode 2, directed by Andy Mikita, aired July 9, 2004, on SciFi.
36. Joseph Mallozzi and Paul Mullie, "Family Ties," *Stargate SG-1*, season 10, episode 18, directed by Peter DeLuise, aired June 8, 2007, on SciFi.
37. Nick Santora, "Pilot," *Scorpion*, season 1, episode 1, directed by Justin Lin, aired September 22, 2014, on CBS.
38. Elizabeth Beall and David Foster, "Revenge," *Scorpion*, season 1, episode 11, directed by Mel Damski, aired December 8, 2014, on CBS.
39. Nick Santora and Nicholas Wootton, "A Cyclone," *Scorpion*, season 1, episode 3, directed by Gary Felder, aired October 6, 2014, on CBS.
40. A Google search for the term only brings up references to the series.
41. In 2015, women accounted for 57 percent of medical residents in psychiatry. Lyndra Vassar, "How Medical Specialties Vary by Gender," *AMA Wire*, February 18, 2015.
42. Nick Santora and Alex Katsnelson, "Forget Me Nots," *Scorpion*, season 1, episode 15, directed by Jann Turner, aired January 19, 2015, on CBS.
43. Powell et al., "How Women Engineers Do and Undo Gender," 420.
44. *Ibid.*, 421.

45. Jason Rothenberg, "Earth Skills," *The 100*, season 1, episode 2, directed by Dean White, aired March 26, 2014, on The CW. In Season 2, Raven's role as a "mechanic" rather than an "engineer" is referenced as she develops a relationship with Wick (Steve Talley), who has the job title of engineer. Despite the job titles, it is clear as they work together than Raven is an equally competent engineer.

46. Charlie Craig, "Hakeldama," *The 100*, season 3, episode 5, directed by Tim Scanlan, aired February 18, 2016, on The CW.

47. Charmaine DeGraté and Javier Grillo-Marxauch, "Fallen," *The 100*, season 3, episode 10, directed by Matt Barber, aired April 7, 2016, on The CW.

48. Jason Rothenberg, "Echoes," *The 100*, season 4, episode 1, directed by Dean White, aired February 1, 2017, on The CW.

49. Powell et al., "How Women Engineers Do and Undo Gender," 421.

50. National Center for Education Statistics, "Table 318.30. Bachelor's, Master's, and Doctor's Degrees Conferred by Postsecondary Institutions, by Sex of Student and Discipline Division: 2013–14," *Digest of Education Statistics*, 2015.

51. Powell et al., "How Women Engineers Do and Undo Gender," 425.

52. National Science Board, *Science & Engineering Indicators 2016*, 85.

53. Peter M. Lenkov and Lee David Zlotoff (creators), *MacGyver* (CBS: 2016–present).

Works Cited

Beall, Elizabeth, and David Foster. "Revenge." *Scorpion*, season 1, episode 11. Directed by Mel Damski. Aired December 8, 2014, on CBS.

Berman, Rick, Michael Piller, and Jeri Taylor. *Star Trek: Voyager*. UPN, 1995–2001.

Biller, Kenneth. "Extreme Risk." *Star Trek: Voyager*, season 5, episode 3. Directed by Cliff Bole. Aired October 28, 1998, on UPN.

_____. "Random Thoughts." *Star Trek: Voyager*, season 4, episode 10. Directed by Alexander Singer. Aired November 19, 1997, on UPN.

Biller, Kenneth, and Robert Doherty. "Endgame." *Star Trek: Voyager*, episode 7, season 24. Directed by Allan Kroeker. Aired May 23, 2001, on UPN.

Braga, Brannon. "Parallax." *Star Trek: Voyager*, season 1, episode 2. Directed by Kim Friedman. Aired January 23, 1995, on UPN.

Carren, David Bennet, J. Larry Carroll, and Jonathan Glassner. "Hathor." *Stargate SG-1*, season 1, episode 13. Directed by Brad Turner. Aired October 24, 1997, on Showtime.

Cooper, Robert. "New Order: Part 2." *Stargate SG-1*, season 8, episode 2. Directed by Andy Mikita. Aired July 9, 2004, on SciFi.

_____. "Singularity." *Stargate SG-1*, season 1, episode 14. Directed by Mario Azzopardi. Aired October 31, 1997, on Showtime.

Craig, Charlie. "Hakeldama." *The 100*, season 3, episode 5. Directed by Tim Scanlan. Aired February 18, 2016, on The CW.

DeGraté, Charmaine, and Javier Grillo-Marxauch. "Fallen." *The 100*, season 3, episode 10. Directed by Matt Barber. Aired April 7, 2016, on The CW.

Fuller, Bryan, Nick Sagan, and Kenneth Biller. "Juggernaut." *Star Trek: Voyager*, season 5, episode 21. Directed by Allan Kroeker. Aired April 26, 1999, on UPN.

Glassner, Jonathan, and Brad Wright. "Children of the Gods." *Stargate SG-1*, season 1, episode 1. Directed by Mario Azzopardi. Aired July 27, 1997, on Showtime.

_____. *Stargate SG-1*. Showtime, 1997–2002, Sci-Fi Channel, 2002–2007.

Lenkov, Peter M., and Lee David Zlotoff. *MacGyver*. CBS, 2016–present.

Lovell, Jayde. "MacGyvering a Female Engineer onto Television." *Scientific American*, August 26, 2015. https://blogs.scientificamerican.com/voices/macgyvering-a-female-engineer-onto-television/

Mallozzi, Joseph, and Paul Mullie. "Family Ties." *Stargate SG-1*, season 10, episode 18. Directed by Peter DeLuise. Aired June 8, 2007, on SciFi.

Meisler, Andy. "Not Even Trying to Appeal to the Masses." *New York Times*, October 4, 1998. http://www.nytimes.com/1998/10/04/arts/television-radio-not-even-trying-to-appeal-to-the-masses.html

National Center for Education Statistics. "Table 318.30. Bachelor's, Master's, and Doctor's Degrees Conferred by Postsecondary Institutions, by Sex of Student and Discipline Division: 2013–14." *Digest of Education Statistics*, 2015. https://nces.ed.gov/programs/digest/d15/tables/dt15_318.30.asp?current=yes.

National Science Board. *Science & Engineering Indicators, 2016*. Arlington: National Science Foundation, 2016. https://nsf.gov/statistics/2016/nsb20161/uploads/1/nsb20161.pdf.

Piller, Michael, and Jeri Taylor. "Caretaker." *Star Trek: Voyager*, season 1, episode 1. Directed by Winrich Kolbe. Aired January 16, 1995, on UPN.

Policy Concerning Homosexuality in the Armed Forces. 10 U.S.C. §654, 1993.

Powell, Abigail, Barbara Bagilhole, and Andrew Dainty. "How Women Engineers Do and Undo Gender: Consequences for Gender Equality." *Gender, Work, and Organization* 16, no. 4 (2009): 411–427.

Powers, Kathryn. "Emancipation." *Stargate SG-1*, season 1, episode 3. Directed by Jeff Woolnough. Aired August 8, 1997, on Showtime.

Rhoton, Laura A. "Distance as a Gendered Barrier: Understanding Women Scientists' Gender Practices." *Gender and Society* 25, no. 6 (2011): 696–716.

Roberts, Robin A. "Science, Race, and Gender in Star Trek: Voyager." In *Fantasy Girls: Gender in the New Universe of Science Fiction and Fantasy Television*, edited by Elyce Rae Helford, 203–221. Lanham, MD: Rowman & Littlefield 2000.

Roddenberry, Gene. *Star Trek*. NBC, 1966–1969.

Rothenberg, Jason. *The 100*. The CW, 2014–present.

_____. "Earth Skills." *The 100*, season 1, episode 2. Directed by Dean White. Aired March 26, 2014, on The CW.

_____. "Echoes." *The 100*, season 4, episode 1. Directed by Dean White. Aired February 1, 2017, on The CW.

Santora, Nick. "Pilot." *Scorpion*, season 1, episode 1. Directed by Justin Lin. Aired September 22, 2014, on CBS.

_____. *Scorpion*. CBS, 2014–present.

Santora, Nick, and Alex Katsnelson. "Forget Me Nots." *Scorpion*, season 1, episode 15. Directed by Jann Turner. Aired January 19, 2015, on CBS.

Santora, Nick, and Nicholas Wootton. "A Cyclone." *Scorpion*, season 1, episode 3. Directed by Gary Felder. Aired October 6, 2014, on CBS.

Vassar, Lyndra. "How Medical Specialties Vary by Gender." *AMA Wire*, February 18, 2015. https://wire.ama-assn.org/education/how-medical-specialties-vary-gender.

STEM and Diversity on Primetime Television
The Representation of Gender and Race in The 100

Natalie Krikowa

Television depicts "a very specific and consistent set of occupational images" and occupational roles are central to most television stories.[1] Television reaches a wide audience in Western culture, and as a cultural artifact, has become the U.S.'s primary storyteller.[2] The mass media, and television in particular, are powerful sites of cultural (re)production where dominant (Anglo, male) ideological beliefs about race, ethnicity, sex, and gender are reinforced and re-circulated through the use of stereotypes.[3] Historically, women were portrayed on television only in traditional gender roles, predominantly as housewives involved in domestic chores, and these portrayals perpetuated stereotypes about women and work.[4] While these portrayals have changed over time, with women on television now increasingly portrayed as lawyers, doctors, and politicians, there remains a slow movement towards television featuring women, especially women from diverse backgrounds, working as STEM professionals. Given the continued influence television has for general audiences across international borders, this essay argues for the importance of a continued focus on the need for women to be featured in these roles. This serves audiences who are diverse in their interests, backgrounds, and experiences, and particularly the next generation of young women who may be influenced by the way they see working women framed on television.

It is also a social and theoretical imperative to continue to discuss how minorities are depicted on television, as well as how those portrayals have or have not changed over time.⁵ Latinas have been underrepresented in terms of both their gender and their ethnicity, and have historically been confined to a narrow set of stereotypical, often negative, characterizations.⁶ According to Debra Merskin, beliefs about race, ethnicity, sex, and gender are reinforced through television. She suggests that stereotypes become naturalized through their repetition; they support cultural beliefs and values about certain groups of people based on distorted presentations of qualities.⁷ Monk-Turner et al. argue that the images viewers see on network television continue to have the potential to impact how different ethnic and racial groups perceive one another.⁸ Although Latinos are currently the largest ethnic minority in the United States, comprising approximately 17.5 percent of the population, content analytic research shows that they only constitute approximately 5 percent of characters featured on primetime television.⁹ Diverse and complex (counter-stereotypical) television portrayals of racial minorities, particularly in STEM occupations, can have a significant impact on viewers in both the depicted minority group and the wider population. As such, this essay examines Raven Reyes, a STEM-oriented Latina character from The CW's Sci-Fi drama, *The 100*.¹⁰

As a woman of non–Latina heritage, I acknowledge the inherent challenges of speaking to these issues in place of women of color. Despite the unease it brings, I also recognize the importance in speaking up at the inequality that still exists in television representation. I defer to Charles Ramírez Berg's preference of the term "Latino/a" over the more imprecise and bureaucratic designation "Hispanic."¹¹ I also acknowledge the term "Latinx"¹² as a gender-neutral term being preferred by some academics, activists, and journalists in recent times in an attempt to move beyond gender binaries and gendered language, to language that is inclusive of the intersecting identities of Latin American descendants, as well as for individuals who identify as trans, queer, agender, non-binary, gender non-conforming, or gender fluid. As this essay focuses primarily on a female character, I have opted to employ "Latina" to avoid confusion with previous studies in this field.

To undertake this examination this essay uses content analysis and Cultivation Theory,¹³ to demonstrate how nuanced and complex television portrayals of young women of color can shift ideologies in young adult Western audiences. These approaches are uniquely suited because their frameworks focus specifically on the processes of stereotype formation, application, and reception within a Western English-speaking mass-media context. In analyzing the portrayal of Raven Reyes within the Cultivation Theory framework, it is clear that this character counters the dominant Latina stereotypes. Yet, her potential to positively impact current and future audiences by inspiring more young women of color to pursue STEM occupations remains to be seen.

Raven Reyes: Stereotype or Trailblazer?

In 2014, The CW released a young adult series *The 100*, featuring a female protagonist and cast of diverse female characters. *The 100* is an American post-apocalyptic sci-fi drama based on the young adult book series of the same name by Kass Morgan. Set in the future after a catastrophic nuclear event, the series follows a group of one hundred young delinquents who are sent down to Earth from a collective of space stations known as "The Ark" to see if Earth is survivable. The series also follows those characters left behind on the Ark, including 19-year-old Raven Reyes (played by Lindsey Morgan), the Ark's youngest Zero-G mechanic in over fifty years. With the survival of the human race resting on the shoulders of the delinquents, Raven becomes integral to their survival throughout the series. During the first season, Raven rebuilds a hundred-year-old escape pod and pilots it to Earth, uses spare parts from her escape pod to build rockets and launch them into the atmosphere, makes two-way radios out of toy cars and spare parts, and rigs a video communication system to talk to The Ark.[14] She assembles bullets and bombs, and while bleeding out from a gunshot wound to her back, talks someone (with no technical experience) through literal rocket science.[15]

In season two we are reunited with Raven, as she lies dying from the bullet wound to her back.[16] She undergoes traumatic spinal surgery (without any anesthesia) and lives, but with a permanently paralyzed leg.[17] The second season follows her physical and emotional struggle as she comes to terms with her permanent disability. Using a leg brace to allow her to walk more freely, she continues to serve as a mechanic for her people, even building a radio beacon.[18] In the episode entitled "Spacewalker" we learn more about Raven's past, her pain from being neglected by her mother, and her desire to achieve her goals despite her health setbacks.[19] Raven experiences significant grief and suffering but never gives up. Her intellect and problem-solving skills help in bringing down the enemy, disabling weapons, and planning and executing missions.

The third season depicts Raven suffering from chronic pain associated with her injuries from the previous season. Initially she pushes through the pain, rebuilding and driving a rover and riding on horseback.[20] But in a mission to save her people from a missile attack, for the first time we see Raven lose faith in herself, admitting she feels broken.[21] Eventually the physical and emotional pain becomes overwhelming. She allows an artificial intelligence (AI) to take over her brain in order to alleviate the pain, but she soon realizes that she can no longer remember anything that brought her pain, including those she has loved and lost.[22] After successfully battling the AI with the help of her friends, she is equipped with enhanced knowledge of computer technology.[23] She remarks: "I can barely walk and my shoulder's killing me but my brain is all kinds of awesome."[24] As the only former AI-enslaved human with enhanced computational ability, Raven uses the AI's code against it, creating a backdoor that allows her access to the virtual kill switch.[25]

Raven Reyes is just one of a few Latina characters on television who counter the dominant stereotype surrounding Latina women. In earlier studies, Gary D. Keller and Charles Ramírez Berg found that Latinas were portrayed in Hollywood film in limited stereotypes, each with negative characteristics or connotations. Keller organized the Latina stereotypes into three categories:

> 1. *Cantina Girl.* "Great sexual allure, teasing, dancing, and behaving in an alluring fashion," are hallmark characteristics of this stereotype. She is most often represented as a sexual object, a "naughty lady of easy virtue" ([Keller] 40).
> 2. *Faithful, self-sacrificing senorita.* This woman usually starts out good, but goes bad by the middle of the film or television program. This character realizes she has gone wrong and is willing to protect her Anglo love interest by placing herself between the bullet/sword/posse/violence intended for him.
> 3. *Vamp.* Whereas Cantina Girl is most often presented physically as an available sexual object, the Vamp uses her intellectual and devious sexual wiles to get what she wants. She often brings men to violence and enjoys doing so. She is a psychological menace to males who are ill equipped to handle her.[26]

Keller notes that the three main Latina stereotypes function mainly in relationship to an Anglo male love interest. Similarly, Ramírez Berg noted three female stereotypes, closely linked to their male counterparts:

> *The Halfbreed Harlot* [...] is lusty and hot-tempered [...] a slave to her passions; her character is based on the premise that she is a nymphomaniac. In true stereotypical fashion, motivation for her actions is not given—she is a prostitute because she likes the work, not because social or economic forces have shaped her life. [...]
> *The Female Clown* [...] represents a way to neutralize the overt sexual threat posed by the Halfbreed Harlot. The strategy is to negate the Latin female's eroticism by making her an object of comic derision. [...]
> *The Dark Lady* [...] is mysterious, virginal, inscrutable, aristocratic—and alluring precisely because of these characteristics. Her cool distance is what makes her so fascinating to Anglo males. She is circumspect and aloof, whereas her Anglo sister is direct and forthright; she is reserved, whereas the Anglo is boisterous; she is opaque, whereas the Anglo woman is transparent.[27]

Although Raven Reyes has both sexual and platonic relationships with men, her role in the series is not defined by these relationships. She does not use her sexuality or intellect for self-gain or to further the plot of the male protagonist, thus breaking away from the Latina stereotypes theorized above by Keller and Ramírez Berg. She is not there purely as titillation for the male gaze or as the comic relief for the white male audience. There are moments in the series, however, where Raven uses sex to distract her from emotional and physical pain. Although these acts do not place her into one of the above negative stereotypes, she is shamed for her choices by the men she has just slept with. In her sexual encounters with Bellamy (season one) and Wick (season two) Raven initiates the sex and afterwards is met with hostility. These sexual encounters were never about the men she was sleeping with, but rather her own personal feelings. Raven exits each encounter the way she entered, with intent and agency. It is precisely this agency that places Raven outside of the existing stereotypes. She becomes far more interesting when analyzed not simply as a body for the male gaze, but as a complex and contradictory character.

Mastro and Behm-Morawitz's framework, which focuses on the portrayal of a character's status (socioeconomic status, social authority, and job authority), physical attributes (race, age, attire, attractiveness, accent, and body type), and character traits (motivation, intelligence, respect, work ethic, articulation, temperament, physical aggression, verbal aggression, and sexual aggression) highlights how Raven Reyes is a rarity among representations of Latina women.[28] Raven is a major character in *The 100*. Her occupation as a Zero-G mechanic indicates her intellectual and physical capacity for specific skilled labor. The occupation has medium authority as she still reports to superiors, but she is later called upon as an invaluable source of knowledge and skill. Mastro and Behm-Morawitz's study found that Latinos had lower job authority, but the tendency to depict them as subordinate was decreasing.[29] Raven Reyes certainly furthers this trend. She is portrayed as being from a low socioeconomic class, although not dissimilar from many of the other characters. Among the juvenile delinquents, she maintains high social authority; her opinions and ideas are respected and often sought out. Though she is not one of the two main leaders of the delinquents, she is part of the leadership group, thus giving her higher social and job authority than typical representations.[30] She has no family left (after her mother passed away), which diverts from the typical portrayal of Latinas as being most often identified as family members.[31] Moreover, the social status she holds is closely tied to her knowledge and skill in the STEM fields, as her scientific and mechanical knowledge often saves lives.

Raven Reyes' race is never directly referred to in the canon of the show, however actress Lindsey Morgan has self-identified as having Mexican, Spanish, and Irish heritage.[32] Her physical attributes, including age, attire, attractiveness, accent, and body type are on par with those of her on-screen counterparts but still reflect the dominant trend to portray young adults as attractive and sexually appealing. Mastro and Behm-Morawitz found that the Latinas were generally portrayed as thin and attractive, depicting them as "addictively romantic, sensual, sexual, and even exotically dangerous."[33] Raven embodies these characteristics, being in her late teens, with a slim yet athletic build, as well as being sexually forward. She adopts a standard American accent, free from a stereotypically Latin accent. Her portrayal shows counter-stereotyping to that seen in previous studies where Latinas were significantly more likely to be depicted with an accent.[34] While the removal of her accent may be deemed as problematic, it is discussed in the canon of the series that many races and nationalities formed The Ark, and as such all people aboard adopted the standard American accent.

Raven is portrayed as highly motivated, intelligent, and articulate. She is greatly respected among her peers and superiors, and she has a strong work ethic. These character traits diverge from the stereotypical representations, which present Latinas as often lazier, less intelligent, and less articulate than their on-screen counterparts.[35] Notably Latinas are most often portrayed as having the lowest work ethic, which Raven fully contradicts. She is seen throughout the series as being studious and determined. Raven is, however, hot-tempered, with high levels of physical, verbal, and sexual aggression (but no higher than many of her on-screen counterparts). She is often quick to react, sassy, sexually forward, and willing to question authority. In these ways she is in line with previous on-screen portrayals of Latinas as more verbally aggressive than their counterparts.

When analyzed within this framework it is clear that Raven Reyes does not embody the majority of negative characteristics seen in the Latina stereotypes that are perpetuated in mass media. Although she adopts the sexually forward and self-confident characteristics of her on-screen predecessors, she is not shown to be typical vamp or harlot. Mastro and Greenberg note that "ethnic minorities historically were seen in more disparaging roles than ethnic majorities," and this is particularly true for Latinos.[36] The role of Raven is far from disparaging, and contrarily depicts the Latina minority as having higher social status than many of her ethnic majority counterparts. But can Raven be a catalyst for change, the trailblazer needed to break down the negative stereotypes that pervade our screens?

Cultivation Theory assumes that stereotypical portrayals are so frequent as to be unavoidable, and in their frequency, one will find comparatively invariant presentations of attributes.[37] Raven Reyes is one variant from the typical, and on her own cannot possibly change the dominant perception of Latinas (as established by the mass media), but she does present a counter-stereotype. Mastro and Tukachinsky, focusing on the positive stereotypes of Latinos in media, suggest that increasing favorable media depictions of minority ethnic groups and including audience's pre-existing cognitions, such as positive stereotypes, will improve representation and therefore social values and ideologies.[38] Mastro and Greenberg argue that given few opportunities for viewing Latino characters, persistent exposure to a single series with one or more counter-stereotypical Latino characters (such as *The 100*) may provide the strongest opportunity to create, reinforce, and/or alter social perceptions.[39]

Diversifying the Portrayal of Women in STEM Fields

A 2012 study by the Geena Davis Institute on Gender in Media found that although women make up between 60–65 percent of the U.S. television viewership, they only account for 39 percent of characters in primetime programs.[40] The report revealed that the portrayal of work on television is still largely gendered and that although women appeared in a range of careers and positions of authority across the various occupational sectors, they occupied only 21 percent of jobs in STEM fields on primetime television, with not one female engineer or mathematician shown. The majority of STEM occupations for women were as forensic pathologists, medical examiners, computer scientists, and technologists.[41]

It is not only on television where we see this disparity. The U.S. government, industry, and academic leaders suggest increasing the overall STEM workforce as a top economic priority. One area of focus has been to reduce disparities in STEM employment by gender and race. According to the U.S. Census Bureau, although women's involvement in STEM occupations has increased since the 1970s, they remain significantly underrepresented in engineering and computer occupations, which make up more than 80 percent of all STEM employment.[42] Although women make up nearly half of the working population, they made up only 26 percent of STEM workers in 2011.[43] Women's underrepresentation in STEM is a result of their significant underrepresentation in engineering and computer occupations. While women's representation has continued to grow in math and science occupations since the 1970s, growth has declined in engineering.[44] And, while the Latino/a share of the workforce has increased significantly from 3 percent in 1970 to 15 percent in 2011, they made up only 7 percent of the STEM workforce in 2011.[45] Unfortunately, the Census Bureau report did not note how many Latinas were working in STEM fields or how race and gender intersect. Similarly, the Geena Davis Institute on Gender in Media study did not explore the relationship between race and gender in the portrayals of STEM professions on television. It is therefore hard to situate the portrayal of Raven Reyes within the broader media landscape when the studies of women are not interrogated further.

Still, there's reason to believe that Raven is a positive role model. In an interview with Latin Post, actress Lindsey Morgan described her character as "helping girls become interested in science, engineering, and mechanics.

She makes it look cool."⁴⁶ In portraying Raven, Morgan is providing a new generation of young women (among others) with a powerful role model to look up to. It is important to note that during its third season run in 2016, *The 100* was criticized for its portrayal of people of color and LGBT people, with deaths of beloved characters falling into long-established, disturbing tropes. The show's creator and writers have also been criticized by fans and critics alike for how Raven's storyline has focused on her constant physical, emotional, and mental suffering. Whilst these views are valid, Raven continues to be portrayed as a complex and nuanced woman of color who defies most of the Latino stereotypes that still pervade our culture.

Why Is Raven Reyes So Important for Young Viewers?

By the end of the 1990s, the "girl power" movement was in full swing, ushering in a new "tough woman" aesthetic showing that women could physically compete with men.⁴⁷ The aggressive attitude and muscular physique popularized by Sigourney Weaver in the *Alien* franchise, Linda Hamilton in *Terminator 2: Judgment Day* (1991), and Lara Croft in the *Tomb Raider* computer games, spawned a new kind of protagonist, the action chick, that quickly infiltrated the television medium. Characters including Xena: Warrior Princess, Buffy the Vampire Slayer, Nikita on *La Femme Nikita*, and Max on *Dark Angel*, continued the reframing of notions of womanhood and femininity taking place in films, music, and games.⁴⁸ These women challenged traditional notions of women's physicality and what it meant to be a strong woman.⁴⁹

While female action heroes excelled, there were other women protagonists using brains over brawn to save the day, most notably, Samantha Carter (Amanda Tapping) on *Stargate SG-1* (1997–2006) and Dana Scully (Gillian Anderson) on *The X-Files* (1993–2002, 2016–present).⁵⁰ These two shows, among others, portrayed women working in historically male-dominated occupations, including STEM fields. Samantha Carter is a United States Air Force Captain (later promoted) with a Ph.D. in theoretical astrophysics and Dana Scully is an FBI Agent who holds an MD and an undergraduate degree in physics. When these two characters first appeared, the social and cultural interest in STEM that exists in many of today's television dramas had yet to dominate; before Olivia Dunham (*Fringe*), Temperance Brennan (*Bones*), Jane Rizzoli and Maura Isles (*Rizzoli and Isles*), or Abby Sciuto (*NCIS*),⁵¹ it was Dana Scully's superior brain power that made her the hero. Dana Scully was rational, courageous, and often, unapologetically, the smartest person in the room. She carried herself as a highly competent and reliable woman: people trusted in her ability, and the cool authority with which she ruled her career—and her life—inspired countless young women to forge careers in STEM fields.

The influx of young women pursuing STEM careers due to growing up watching Dana Scully is known as the "Scully Effect." This unintended consequence of the show's popularity among young women demonstrated that this "girl power," seen in action series like *Buffy* and *Xena*, extended to the STEM fields. Dana Scully continues to be an inspiring role model for today's generation of young women, with *The X-Files* now syndicated and available on Netflix and Hulu. At the 2013 San Diego Comic-Con International, Gillian Anderson noted that she has long been aware of the "Scully Effect," stating: "We got a lot of letters all the time, and I was told quite frequently by girls who were going into the medical world or the science world or the FBI world or other worlds that I reigned, that they were pursuing those pursuits because of the character of Scully. And I said, 'Yay!'"[52]

While earlier characters like Xena, Buffy, Nikita, Sam Carter, and Dana Scully promoted "girl power," they also perpetuated the racial ideology where the "natural" hero is white, implying that women of color fail to qualify.[53] But with new, more racially diverse characters like Raven Reyes, Quake/Daisy/Skye (*Agents of S.H.I.E.L.D*), and Alex Parrish (*Quantico*), young women will see that being successful in STEM fields is possible for all women, not just Anglo women.[54] Nevertheless, when so few positive stereotypes exist and so few characters are Latinas, creating counter-stereotypes is an important step that can influence women's occupational choices. Studies have shown that adolescents prefer work related to the roles and jobs seen on television.[55] According to Cultivation Theory, stereotypical representations on television can lead to, or cultivate, a more television-like perception of the real world.[56] From a cultivation perspective, young adult viewers' conceptions about occupations may reflect the images they see on television, which according to the research means less important or prestigious jobs.[57] As Nancy Signorielli notes, "if young girls, particularly young girls of color, see limited role models for women of color, there may be fewer reinforced images that would result in maintaining stereotypical notions and developing limiting schemas about occupations."[58]

The analysis of *The 100*'s Raven Reyes suggests a departure from traditionally stereotyped roles for women, and more particularly women of color. Raven is not only an accomplished mechanical engineer, but she is also a woman of color, and that is a rare occurrence on primetime television. Now that she is also permanently disabled, Raven is a member of yet another significant minority group on television. Despite her physical limitations, she remains one of the strongest characters, mentally, physically, and emotionally. Although it could not be completed within the constraints of this essay, analyzing the character's disability is an important next step in the analysis of both race and gender representation on television. Further study into STEM diversity (both on screen and in real life) requires that we move from being gender-focused to analyzing the representation of other minorities. With *The 100* being developed with a young adult audience in mind, could this diverse representation have greater cultural influence? Just as the "Scully Effect" in the 1990s saw the influx of young women pursuing STEM careers, perhaps we are seeing the birth of the "Raven Reyes Effect," where more young women of color and women with disabilities will be empowered to pursue careers in STEM.

NOTES

1. Nancy Signorielli, "Television and Adolescents' Perceptions About Work," *Youth & Society* 24, no. 3 (1993): 314; Suzanne Jeffries-Fox and Bruce Jeffries-Fox, "Gender Differences in Socialization Through Television to Occupational Roles: An Exploratory Approach," *Journal of Early Adolescence* 1, no. 3 (1981): 293–302.

2. Nancy Signorielli and Susan Kahlenberg, "Television's World of Work in the Nineties," *Journal of Broadcasting & Electronic Media* 45, no. 1 (2001): 4.

3. Debra Merskin, "Three Faces of Eva: Perpetuation of the Hot-Latina Stereotype in Desperate Housewives," *Howard Journal of Communications* 18, no. 2 (2007): 134–135.

4. Erica Scharrer et al., "Working Hard or Hardly Working? Gender, Humor, and the Performance of Domestic Chores in Television Commercials," *Mass Communication and Society* 9 (2006): 215–238.

5. Elizabeth Monk-Turner et al., "The Portrayal of Racial Minorities on Prime Time Television: A Replication of the Mastro and Greenberg Study a Decade Later," *Studies in Popular Culture* 32, no. 2 (2010): 101.

6. Dana E. Mastro and Elizabeth Behm-Morawitz, "Latino Representation on Primetime Television," *Journal of Mass Communication Quarterly* 82, no. 1 (2005): 111.

7. Merskin, "Three Faces of Eva," 135.

8. Monk-Turner et al., "The Portrayal of Racial Minorities," 102.

9. *Ibid.*, United States Census Bureau, "Population Estimates, July 1, 2015 (V2015)," QuickFacts United States, accessed October 18, 2016.

10. Jason Rothenberg (creator), *The 100* (The CW: 2014–present).

11. Charles Ramírez Berg, *Latino Images in Film: Stereotypes, Subversion, and Resistance* (Austin: University of Texas Press, 2002), 5–6.

12. Paulus van Horne, "Write Jack Qu'emi Explains the Meaning of 'Latinx,'" *PRI's The World*, June 21, 2016.

13. George Gerbner et al., "Living with Television: The Dynamics of the Cultivation Process," in *Perspectives on Media Effects*, eds. J. Bryant and D. Zillmann, 17–40 (Hillsdale, NJ: Erlbaum, 1986); Ashton Gerding and Nancy Signorielli, "Gender Roles in Tween Television Programming: A Content Analysis of Two Genres," *Sex Roles* 70 (2014): 43–56.

14. Jason Rothenberg, "Earth Skills," *The 100*, season 1, episode 2, directed by Dean White, aired March 26, 2014, on The CW; T.J. Brady and Rasheed Newson, "Murphy's Law," *The 100*, season 1, episode 4, directed by P.J. Pesce, aired April 9, 2014, on The CW; Bruce Miller, "Twilight's Last Gleaming," *The 100*, season 1, episode 5, directed by Milan Cheylov, aired April 16, 2014, on The CW; Akela Cooper and Kira Snyder, "Contents Under Pressure," *The 100*, season 1, episode 7, directed by John F. Showalter, aired April 30, 2014, on The CW; Elizabeth Craft and Sarah Fain, "Day Trip," *The 100*, season 1, episode 8, directed by Matt Barber, aired May 7, 2014, on The CW.

15. Kim Shumway and Kira Snyder, "Unity Day," *The 100*, season 1, episode 9, directed by John Behring, aired May 14, 2014, on The CW; T.J. Brady and Rasheed Newson, "I Am

Become Death," *The 100*, season 1, episode 10, directed by Omar Madha, aired May 21, 2014, on The CW; Jason Rothenberg, "We Are Grounders: Part 2," *The 100*, season 1, episode 13, directed by Dean White, aired June 11, 2014, on The CW.

16. Jason Rothenberg, "The 48," *The 100*, season 2, episode 1, directed by Dean White, aired October 22, 2014, on The CW.

17. Michael Angeli, "Inclement Weather," *The 100*, season 2, episode 2, directed by John F. Showalter, aired October 29, 2014, on The CW.

18. Kira Synder, "Fog of War," *The 100*, season 2, episode 6, directed by Steven DePaul, aired December 3, 2014, on The CW.

19. Bruce Miller, "Space Walker," *The 100*, season 2, episode 8, directed by John F. Showalter, aired December 17, 2014, on The CW.

20. Jason Rothenberg, "Wanheda: Part 1," *The 100*, season 3, episode 1, directed by Dean White, aired January 21, 2016, on The CW.

21. Kim Shumway, "Ye Who Enter Here," *The 100*, season 3, episode 3, directed by Antonio Negret, aired February 4, 2016, on The CW.

22. Charles Grant Craig, "Hakeldama," *The 100*, season 3, episode 5, directed by Tim Scanlan, aired February 18, 2016, on The CW; Charles Grant Craig, "Terms and Conditions," *The 100*, season 3, episode 8, directed by John F. Showalter, aired March 10, 2016, on The CW.

23. Charmaine DeGraté and Javier Grillo-Marxuach, "Fallen," *The 100*, season 3, episode 10, directed by Matt Barber, aired April 7, 2016, on The CW; Kim Shumway, "Nevermore," *The 100*, season 3, episode 11, directed by Ed Fraiman, aired April 14, 2016, on The CW.

24. Justine Juel Gilmer, "Demons," *The 100*, season 3, episode 12, directed by P.J. Pesce, aired April 21, 2016, on The CW.

25. Aaron Ginsburg and Wade McIntyre, "Perverse Instantiation: Part 1," *The 100*, season 3, episode 15, directed by Ed Fraiman, aired May 12, 2016, on The CW; Jason Rothenberg, "Perverse Instantiation: Part 2," *The 100*, season 3, episode 16, directed by Dean White, aired May 19, 2016, on The CW.

26. Gary. D. Keller, *Hispanics and United States Film: An Overview and Handbook* (Tempe: Bilingual Press, 1994), as quoted/paraphrased in Merskin, "Three Faces of Eva," 137.

27. Charles Ramírez Berg, "Stereotyping in Films in General and of the Hispanic in Particular," *Howard Journal of Communications* 2, no. 3 (1990): 294–296.

28. Mastro and Behm-Morawitz, "Latino Representation."

29. *Ibid.*, 125.

30. *Ibid.*, 118.

31. *Ibid.*

32. Melissa Castellanos, "CW's 'The 100' Star Lindsey Morgan Spills on Her Empowering Role, Landing Lead in 'Casa Vita' [Exclusive]," *Latin Post*, April 8, 2015.

33. Mastro and Behm-Morawitz, "Latino Representation," 125.

34. *Ibid.*, 120.

35. *Ibid.*, 121–124.

36. Dana E. Mastro and Bradley S. Greenberg, "The Portrayal of Racial Minorities on Prime Time Television," *Journal of Broadcasting & Electronic Media* 44, no. 4 (2000): 691.

37. Nancy Signorielli, "Minorities Representation in Prime Time: 2000 to 2008," *Communication Review Reports* 26, no. 4 (2009): 323–336.

38. Dana E. Mastro and Riva Tukachinsky, "The Influence of Exemplar Versus Prototype-Based Media Primes on Racial/Ethnic Evaluations," *Journal of Communications* 61, no. 5 (2011): 933.

39. Mastro and Greenberg, "The Portrayal of Racial Minorities," 701.

40. Stacy L. Smith et al., *Gender Roles & Occupations: A Look at Character Attributes and Job-Related Aspirations in Film and Television* (Emmitsburg, MD: Geena Davis Institute on Gender in Media, 2012), 10.

41. *Ibid.*, 13–14

42. Liana Christin Landivar, "Disparities in STEM Employment by Sex, Race, and Hispanic Origin," *American Community Survey Reports*, ACS-24 (Washington, D.C.: U.S. Census Bureau, 2013), 2.

43. *Ibid.*, 5.
44. *Ibid.*
45. *Ibid.*, 15.
46. Castellanos, "CW's 'The 100' Star Lindsey Morgan Spills on Her Empowering Role."
47. Sarah Banet-Weiser, "Girls Rule! Gender, Feminism, and Nickelodeon," *Critical Studies in Media Communication* 21, no. 2 (2004): 119–120.
48. John Schulian and Robert Tapert (creators), *Xena: Warrior Princess* (USA: 1995–2001); Joss Whedon (creator), *Buffy the Vampire Slayer* (WB: 1997–2003); Joel Surnow (creator), *La Femme Nikita* (WB: 1997–2001); James Cameron and Charles H. Eglee (creator), *Dark Angel* (Fox: 2000–2002).
49. There are many studies available on the social and cultural impact of the "tough woman" in popular culture, including Sherrie A. Inness's *Tough Girls: Women Warriors and Wonder Women in Popular Culture* (Philadelphia: University of Pennsylvania Press, 1999) and *Action Chicks: New Images of Tough Women in Popular Culture* (New York: Palgrave Macmillan, 2004); Elizabeth Hills' "From 'Figurative Males' to Action Heroines: Further Thoughts on Active Women in Cinema," *Screen* 40, no. 1 (1999): 38–50; and Martha McCaughey and Neal King's *Reel Knockouts: Violent Women in the Movies* (Austin: University of Texas Press, 2001).
50. Jonathan Glassner and Brad Wright (creators), *Stargate SG-1* (Showtime: 1997–2002, Sci-Fi: 2002–2006); Chris Carter (creator), *The X-Files* (Fox: 1993–2002).
51. J.J. Abrams, Alex Kurtzman and Roberto Orci (creators), *Fringe* (WB: 2008–2013); Donald P. Bellisario and Don McGill (creators), *NCIS* (CBS: 2003–present); Hart Hanson (creator), *Bones* (Fox: 2005–2017); Janet Tamaro (creator), *Rizzoli and Isles* (TNT: 2010–2016).
52. Jennifer Vineyard, "Nearly Everything The X-Files' David Duchovny and Gillian Anderson Said This Weekend," *Vulture*, October 14, 2013.
53. Sherrie A. Inness, *Action Chicks*, 11.
54. Joshua Safran (creator), *Quantico* (ABC: 2015–present); Maurissa Tancharoen, Jed Whedon, and Joss Whedon, *Agents of S.H.I.E.L.D* (ABC: 2013–present).
55. Roberta Wroblewski and Aletha C. Huston, "Televised Occupational Stereotypes and Their Effects on Early Adolescents: Are They Changing?" *Journal of Early Adolescence* 7 (1987): 283–297; Signorielli, "Television and Adolescents."
56. Nancy Signorielli, "Race and Sex in Prime Time: A Look at Occupations and Occupational Prestige" *Mass Communication and Society* 12, no. 3 (2009): 332–352; Gerbner et al., "Living with Television"; Nancy Signorielli and Margaret Lears, "Children, Television and Conceptions About Chores: Attitudes and Behaviors," *Sex Roles* 27, no. 3/4 (1992): 157–170; Signorielli and Kahlenberg, "Television's World of Work in the Nineties."
57. Signorielli, "Race and Sex in Prime Time," 348.
58. *Ibid.*, 334.

Works Cited

Abrams, J.J., Alex Kurtzman, and Roberto Orci. *Fringe*. WB, 2008–2013.
Angeli, Michael. "Inclement Weather." *The 100*, season 2, episode 2. Directed by John F. Showalter. Aired October 29, 2014, on The CW.
Banet-Weiser, Sarah. "Girls Rule! Gender, Feminism, and Nickelodeon." *Critical Studies in Media Communication* 21, no. 2 (2004): 119–139.
Bellisario, Donald P., and Don McGill. *NCIS*. CBS, 2003–present.
Berg, Charles Ramírez. *Latino Images in Film: Stereotypes, Subversion, and Resistance*. Austin: University of Texas Press, 2002.
_____. "Stereotyping in Films in General and of the Hispanic in Particular." *Howard Journal of Communications* 2, no. 3 (1990): 186–300.
Brady, T.J., and Rasheed Newson. "I Am Become Death." *The 100*, season 1, episode 10. Directed by Omar Madha. Aired May 21, 2014, on The CW.

_____. "Murphy's Law." *The 100*, season 1, episode 4. Directed by P.J. Pesce. Aired April 9, 2014, on The CW.
Cameron, James, and Charles H. Eglee. *Dark Angel*. Fox, 2000–2002.
Carter, Chris. *The X-Files*. Fox, 1993–2002.
Castellanos, Melissa. "CW's 'The 100' Star Lindsey Morgan Spills on Her Empowering Role, Landing Lead in 'Casa Vita' [Exclusive]." *Latin Post*, April 8, 2015. http://www.latinpost.com/articles/46589/20150408/cw-the-100-lindsey-morgan-raven-reyes-casa-vita-friday-night-lights.htm.
Cooper, Akela, and Kira Snyder. "Contents Under Pressure." *The 100*, season 1, episode 7. Directed by John F. Showalter. Aired April 30, 2014, on The CW.
Craft, Elizabeth, and Sarah Fain. "Day Trip." *The 100*, season 1, episode 8. Directed by Matt Barber. Aired May 7, 2014, on The CW.
Craig, Charles Grant. "Hakeldama." *The 100*, season 3, episode 5. Directed by Tim Scanlan. Aired February 18, 2016, on The CW.
_____. "Terms and Conditions." *The 100*, season 3, episode 8. Directed by John F. Showalter. Aired March 10, 2016, on The CW.
DeGraté, Charmaine, and Javier Grillo-Marxauch. "Fallen." *The 100*, season 3, episode 10. Directed by Matt Barber. Aired April 7, 2016, on The CW.
Gerbner, George, Larry Gross, Michael Morgan, and Nancy Signorielli. "Living with Television: The Dynamics of the Cultivation Process." In *Perspectives on Media Effects*, edited by J. Bryant and D. Zillmann, 17–40. Hillsdale, NJ: Erlbaum, 1986.
Gerding, Ashton, and Nancy Signorielli. "Gender Roles in Tween Television Programming: A Content Analysis of Two Genres." *Sex Roles* 70 (2014): 43–56.
Gilmer, Justine Juel. "Demons." *The 100*, season 3, episode 12. Directed by P.J. Pesce. Aired April 21, 2016, on The CW.
Ginsburg, Aaron, and Wade McIntyre. "Perverse Instantiation: Part 1." *The 100*, season 3, episode 15. Directed by Ed Fraiman. Aired May 12, 2016, on The CW.
Glassner, Jonathan, and Brad Wright. *Stargate SG-1*. Showtime, 1997–2002; Sci-Fi, 2002–2006.
Hanson, Hart. *Bones*. Fox, 2005–present.
Hills, Elizabeth. "From 'Figurative Males' to Action Heroines: Further Thoughts on Active Women in Cinema." *Screen* 40, no. 1 (1999): 38–50.
Inness, Sherrie A., ed. *Action Chicks: New Images of Tough Women in Popular Culture*. New York: Palgrave Macmillan, 2004.
_____. *Tough Girls: Women Warriors and Wonder Women in Popular Culture*. Philadelphia: University of Pennsylvania Press, 1999.
Jeffries-Fox, Suzanne, and Bruce Jeffries-Fox. "Gender Differences in Socialization Through Television to Occupational Roles: An Exploratory Approach." *Journal of Early Adolescence* 1, no. 3 (1981): 293–302.
Keller, Gary. D. *Hispanics and United States Film: An Overview and Handbook*. Tempe: Bilingual Press, 1994.
Landivar, Liana Christin. "Disparities in STEM Employment by Sex, Race, and Hispanic Origin." *American Community Survey Reports*, ACS-24. Washington, D.C.: US Census Bureau, 2013.
Mastro, Dana E., and Bradley S. Greenberg. "The Portrayal of Racial Minorities on Prime Time Television." *Journal of Broadcasting & Electronic Media* 44, no. 4 (2000): 690–703.
Mastro, Dana E., and Elizabeth Behm-Morawitz. "Latino Representation on Primetime Television." *Journal of Mass Communication Quarterly* 82, no. 1 (2005): 110–130.
Mastro, Dana E., and Riva Tukachinsky. "The Influence of Exemplar Versus Prototype-Based Media Primes on Racial/Ethnic Evaluations." *Journal of Communications* 61, no. 5 (2011): 916–937.
McCaughey, Martha, and Neal King. *Reel Knockouts: Violent Women in the Movies*. Austin: University of Texas Press, 2001.
Merskin, Debra. "Three Faces of Eva: Perpetuation of the Hot-Latina Stereotype in Desperate Housewives." *Howard Journal of Communications* 18, no. 2 (2007): 133–151.
Miller, Bruce. "Space Walker." *The 100*, season 2, episode 8. Directed by John F. Showalter. Aired December 17, 2014, on The CW.

———. "Twilight's Last Gleaming." *The 100*, season 1, episode 5. Directed by Milan Cheylov. Aired April 16, 2014, on The CW.
Monk-Turner, Elizabeth, Mary Heiserman, Crystle Johnson, Vanity Cotton, and Manny Jackson. "The Portrayal of Racial Minorities on Prime Time Television: A Replication of the Mastro and Greenberg Study a Decade Later." *Studies in Popular Culture* 32, no. 2 (2010): 101–114.
Rothenberg, Jason. "Earth Skills." *The 100*, season 1, episode 2. Directed by Dean White. Aired March 26, 2014, on The CW.
———. "The 48." *The 100*, season 2, episode 1. Directed by Dean White. Aired October 22, 2014, on The CW.
———. *The 100*. The CW, 2014–present.
———. "Perverse Instantiation: Part 2." *The 100*, season 3, episode 16. Directed by Dean White. Aired May 19, 2016, on The CW.
———. "Wanheda: Part 1." *The 100*, season 3, episode 1. Directed by Dean White. Aired January 21, 2016, on The CW.
———. "We Are Grounders: Part 2." *The 100*, season 1, episode 13. Directed by Dean White. Aired June 11, 2014, on The CW.
Safran, Joshua. *Quantico*. ABC, 2015–present.
Scharrer, Erica, Daniel D. Kim, Ke-Ming Lin, and Zixu Liu. "Working Hard or Hardly Working? Gender, Humor, and the Performance of Domestic Chores in Television Commercials." *Mass Communication and Society* 9 (2006): 215–238.
Schulian, John, and Robert Tapert. *Xena: Warrior Princess*. USA, 1995–2001.
Shumway, Kim. "Nevermore." *The 100*, season 3, episode 11. Directed by Ed Fraiman. Aired April 14, 2016, on The CW.
———. "Ye Who Enter Here." *The 100*, season 3, episode 3. Directed by Antonio Negret. Aired February 4, 2016, on The CW.
Shumway, Kim, and Kira Snyder. "Unity Day." *The 100*, season 1, episode 9. Directed by John Behring. Aired May 14, 2014, on The CW.
Signorielli, Nancy. "Minorities Representation in Prime Time: 2000 to 2008." *Communication Review Reports* 26, no. 4 (2009): 323–336.
———. "Race and Sex in Prime Time: A Look at Occupations and Occupational Prestige." *Mass Communication and Society* 12, no. 3 (2009): 332–352.
———. "Television and Adolescents' Perceptions About Work." *Youth & Society* 24, no. 3 (1993): 314–341.
Signorielli, Nancy, and Susan Kahlenberg. "Television's World of Work in the Nineties." *Journal of Broadcasting & Electronic Media* 45, no. 1 (2001): 4–22.
Signorielli, Nancy, and Margaret Lears. "Children, Television and Conceptions About Chores: Attitudes and Behaviors." *Sex Roles* 27, no. 3/4 (1992): 157–170.
Smith, Stacy L., Marc Choueiti, Ashley Prescott, and Katherine Pieper. *Gender Roles & Occupations: A Look at Character Attributes and Job-Related Aspirations in Film and Television* (Emmitsburg, MD: Geena Davis Institute on Gender in Media, 2012). http://seejane.org/research-informs-empowers/
Snyder, Kira. "Bitter Harvest." *The 100*, season 3, episode 6. Directed by Dean White. Aired February 25, 2016, on The CW.
———. "Fog of War." *The 100*, season 2, episode 6. Directed by Steven DePaul. Aired December 3, 2014, on The CW.
Surnow, Joel. *La Femme Nikita*. WB, 1997–2001.
Tamaro, Janet. *Rizzoli and Isles*. TNT, 2010–2016.
Tancharoen, Maurissa, Jed Whedon, and Joss Whedon. *Agents of S.H.I.E.L.D*. ABC, 2013–present.
United States Census Bureau. "Population Estimates, July 1, 2015 (V2015)." QuickFacts United States. Accessed October 18, 2016. https://www.census.gov/quickfacts/table/PST045215/00.
Van Horne, Paulus. "Writer Jack Qu'emi Explains the Meaning of 'Latinx.'" *PRI's The World*. June 21, 2016. http://www.pri.org/stories/2016-06-21/writer-jack-quemi-explains-meaning-latinx.

Vineyard, Jennifer. "Nearly Everything The X-Files' David Duchovny and Gillian Anderson Said This Weekend." *Vulture*, October 14, 2013. http://www.vulture.com/2013/10/david-duchovny-gillian-anderson-nycc-paley-center-quotes.html.
Whedon, Joss. *Buffy the Vampire Slayer*. WB, 1997–2003.
Wroblewski, Roberta, and Aletha C. Huston. "Televised Occupational Stereotypes and Their Effects on Early Adolescents: Are They Changing?" *Journal of Early Adolescence* 7 (1987): 283–297.

"We have to know our biology"
Power, Patriarchy and the Body *in* Orphan Black

Lauren Riccelli Zwicky

Social and online media have provided unprecedented possibilities for public conversations of all kinds, and during the last half decade or so, much of that discourse has focused on issues related to gender and sexuality. We find ourselves now at the beginning of a new and important era in the broader history of feminism; within the spheres of both social justice and academia we can identify the emergence of an interest in intersectionality, inclusion, the rights of transgender women and men, and media representation of women's bodies. For better or for worse, "feminism" has become a buzzword. In the arena of pop culture, we've seen public figures such as Beyoncé, Amy Schumer, Tina Fey, and Rashida Jones proudly wear the label "feminist." In the political sphere, issues of transgender bathroom access and women's right to safe, affordable reproductive healthcare have taken center stage. Discrimination and wage equality in the workplace are once again at the forefront of public conversation and educators and professionals are actively attempting to make the STEM fields more accessible to women.

Recently, the hashtags #stemwomen, #stemgirls, #girlswhocode and #womeninscience have emerged. Every corner of contemporary culture evidences this burgeoning attunement to feminist identity politics, and as the number of conversations centered on gender and sexuality taking place on social media has increased, there has been a corresponding explosion of self-consciously feminist cultural products. Although film and television still abound with traditional, problematically monolithic representations of girls and women, we are entering a new golden age of feminist cinema in which an increasing number of films and television shows feature strong, complex, capable women who embody a feminist subjectivity. Films such as *Mad Max: Fury Road* and television programs like Netflix's *Jessica Jones* provide their viewership with examples of female protagonists whose lives are not oriented towards men and relationships and whose knowledge, skills, and capabilities drive the narratives they populate.[1] Perhaps one of the most radical changes even within this burgeoning feminist *oeuvre* is the recent proliferation of filmic representations of women in STEM positions. Not only do we see women emerge as characters focused on their careers, but these female protagonists successfully perform in fields that have hitherto been male-dominated.

The recent series *Orphan Black*,[2] now in its fourth season, features an array of strong, female characters that both singly and collectively resist the stereotypical portrayal of a one-dimensional woman. Especially noteworthy is the fact that *Orphan Black*'s smartest, most knowledgeable, driven character is a female Ph.D. candidate in the field of evolutionary development. Cosima (Tatiana Maslany) is the show's primary voice of authority and we rarely see her consulting male characters for expertise or advice. When confronted with an unfamiliar idea or problem, she researches it on her own and usually arrives at a thoughtful, well-articulated solution. Although all of *Orphan Black*'s women are strong, smart, and capable, Cosima is perhaps the sharpest lens through which to analyze the show's complex and revolutionary sex/gender politics. It is through *Orphan Black*'s representation of Cosima that we come to understand this show's powerful commentary not only on the complexity of female identity, but also on the way in which women's bodies have always been both targets and sites of resistance to patriarchal power.

There is a moment towards the end of *Orphan Black*'s first season when Cosima and her lover Delphine (Evelyne Brochu) examine a lengthy document, a series of encrypted numbers that they've thus far had difficulty understanding. Suddenly, we see a light flicker on in Cosima's eyes. She smiles, looks up at Delphine and announces: "I've got it. It's binary code."[3] This is a key moment not only within the arc of the show's narrative, but also as an illustration of *Orphan Black*'s most critical politics of feminist representation. The general plotline of this speculative fiction series follows a group of women who discover that they are clones created by a team of scientists as part of a research project with connections to both government initiatives and the interests of a private, for-profit company. The women's project becomes one both of uncovering self-knowledge and of resistance. As they engage in a quest to know and understand more about their identities, biology, and purpose, their creators are systematically hunting them down, hoping to regain control. The binary code that Cosima discovers helps to unlock a treasure-trove of information about who they are and where they came from, but also provides their pursuers with a fresh impetus to see their creations safely back within their clutches. Thus, in addition to its function within this show's narrative, Cosima's discovery speaks to some very key aspects of its politics of representation: Cosima (one of at least nine clones, all played by Tatiana Maslany) is a queer, female scientist and although the show's ostensible protagonist is the street-wise clone Sarah Manning, Cosima is an equally important character. While Sarah often seems to be the focal point of the series, Cosima is arguably more of a driving force within its narrative, for it is her discoveries that most effectively add to the body of knowledge this group of clones gains about themselves. Additionally, her background in science, her lesbianism, and her intellect all broaden the kinds of female representations we have traditionally seen on television and in film. She works against the normative notion of female identity as a monolith. She has depth, complexity, and a set of characteristics that draw attention away from mainstream, centric notions of what it means to embody the feminine.

Cosima's discovery also nicely illustrates *Orphan Black*'s politics of bodily representation, illustrating first the way that the female body is always already a target of patriarchal power. This notion comes up again and again in feminist philosophy: that as women we are subject at all times to external gazes, definitions, and delineations. We come into being as subjects in the lower register of a hierarchy of societal power. Since *Orphan Black*'s primary plot centers around a group of women created by a group of (mostly) male scientists, the women function as a living embodiment of the abstract idea of the body as a target of power. However, they also instantiate the extent to which the female body can function as a site of resistance to those very power structures, another critical idea within the broader history of feminist philosophy. At every corner, the clones resist the forces that first created and are now attempting to contain and even in some cases destroy them. They fight back in different ways. Sarah's rebellion largely happens through acts of physical violence whereas Cosima helps her fellow clones through scientific inquiry and knowledge construction. Allison, Helena, and the other clones work alongside Sarah and Cosima, ensuring that at every step the group is functioning smoothly as a team.

Thus, through the way that *Orphan Black* depicts the body as both a target and site of resistance to patriarchal power and through its illustration of a female identity that resists monolithic definition, the series stands as an important feminist cultural product. That all of these ideas are exemplified best by a character who is a *female scientist* renders it even more progressive, for at no other time in history has the issue of women in STEM been more topical or more timely. Andi Zeisler, in her new critical study on women and media aimed at both general and academic audiences, notes that even when we have seen women on film in the past, those representations tend to support and codify pre-existing social structures and stereotypes. She argues: "The aspects of feminism currently given voice in pop culture are the most media-friendly ones, the ones that center on heterosexual relationships and marriage, on economic success that doesn't challenge existing capitalist structures, on the right to be desirable yet have bodily autonomy."[4] Cosima and her fellow clones *do* resist these stereotypical representations and in so doing "re-envision feminism" for twenty-first-century audiences.[5]

Resisting Monolithic Representation: Orphan Black *and Identity*

Perhaps the most grievous wrong perpetrated against women by the media has been its one-dimensional representation of their lived experiences and identities. Time and time again we see limitations placed on female characters that are not equally represented in roles for men. Men on film and television are often complex and their storylines are varied. They might be on a quest for self-discovery; we might watch a boy grow into a man, cheer alongside a male character as he climbs the corporate ladder, or bear witness to the psychological complexity of a soldier acclimating to civilian life after the trauma of war. In contrast, female characters tend to be flat in their characterizations and ancillary in their role within the narrative. Parts for women often focus not on the women themselves, but on their relationships to male characters: they are wives, mothers, girlfriends, and mistresses. They fit into stereotypes such as the "girl next door" or the "controlling mother" or the "dumb blonde." We see a host of films that feature male central characters with a range of topics and plot-lines while women's films more often focus on love, romance, and finding a husband: "The role of a woman in film almost always revolves around her physical attractiveness and the mating games she plays with male characters. Even when the woman is the central character she is generally shown as confused, helpless or in danger, as passive, or as a purely sexual being."[6] The stakes of this kind of representation are high because media, as an institution, has an enormous amount of cultural power. We exist in a world where images of women proliferate on television, on film, in print, and online. When our subjectivities, such as we encounter them, are flat, one-dimensional, and necessarily oriented towards men and male lives, it becomes increasingly difficult for women to see ourselves as capable, complex, and powerful. How many films are there that feature female CEOs? Of that very small number, how many of those CEOs are likeable, interesting, and multi-faceted? If the supposition is true that "films are texts, complex structures of linguistic and visual codes organized to produce specific meanings" then the overwhelming majority of contemporary films construct the idea that there is one possible identity for women today.[7] Thus, one of the key ways that contemporary cultural products can engage, in a very real way, with the politics of feminist representation is to depict complex, multi-faceted female characters. Going beyond that, film and television can depict, in one specific narrative, *a range of female characters*. When we begin to see multiple different potentialities for women we are less willing to accept the kind of flattening stereotypes that suggest that women live in only a small handful of identity boxes.

Orphan Black exemplifies contemporary feminist media in that it is engaged in exactly that project: it both represents the complexity of female identity *and* broadens possible ways of identification by showing a host of strong, female characters who have distinct, differentiated subject positions. Sarah, in the final episode of the second season, during a scene in which all of the clones are gathered together, looks around at all of her "sisters" and observes "God, we're all so different, aren't we?"[8] Indeed, they *are* all individuals in their own right and this representation is extremely important. Examining Cosima in particular, we find a character who revises traditional, dualistic understandings of the self that separate cognition and affect, but we also see a queer woman who derives her sense of self from a variety of characteristics *other* than sexual orientation. She provides a mouthpiece for this line of argumentation time and time again. Even with her lover Delphine, she remains adamant that sexuality isn't her sole defining characteristic.[9] With these kinds of identifications on display, Cosima moves female representation *away* from centric positionality. She re-focuses the spotlight on the margins and makes the argument that women do not have to fit into mainstream norms in order to be intelligent, interesting, beautiful, and worthy of the role of protagonist.

However, Cosima is not the show's sole instance of this type of subjective broadening. Indeed, one of *Orphan Black*'s greatest strengths is the way in which it showcases multiple identities and depicts women who are markedly different in personality, behavior, and life experience coming to know and respect one another and developing the ability to work as a cohesive team. During the second episode of the show's first season Cosima and Allison meet with Sarah to begin to explain to her their history and the danger that they are in. In this scene we see the beginnings of a kind of team building that solidifies the bonds between the clones in spite of their different backgrounds, interests, and abilities. Allison, Cosima, and Sarah occupy different subject positions and initially do not seem to share much in common beyond their genetics. Allison is the most normative of the clones. She is a suburban mother of two, married to a (seemingly) docile, unremarkable man. She could not be more different from Cosima, or indeed Sarah, who at this point in the narrative is still a wary, street smart orphan whose voice, mannerisms, and dress all reveal her working-class upbringing and underprivileged adult life.[10] And yet, the show does not reduce any of these three women to stereotype. Rather, it humanizes each of them, revealing their strengths, weaknesses, and the complexity of their individual personalities.

Orphan Black also revises traditionally monolithic representations of women through the multiform ways in which it resists dualism. The association between femininity and affect, emotion, and the body has a long history within Western civilization; indeed, it is grounded in some of our earliest philosophical traditions. Building on Aristotelian notions of a separately functioning, often at-odds mind and body, Descartes constructed a framework for understanding male and female difference, the echoes of which are still heard today in both intellectual and everyday understandings of the functionality of sex and gender.[11] Not only did he understand the mind and the body as distinct, separate forces, but he also theorized a necessary correlation between the mind and the masculine, and the body and the feminine. One of the critical tasks of feminist philosophers has been not only to systematically dismantle these kinds of misunderstandings and reveal the ways in which the mind and the body, in fact, co-function, but also to illustrate the extent to which women embody both cognitive and affective power and potentiality.[12] The character of Cosima effectively embodies this kind of re-scripting, and I would argue that she does so particularly well because, rather than only presenting a kind of cold, rational, scientific subjectivity, she performs *both* a cognitive and an affectively oriented identity. She is a scientist, a thinker, and a problem solver, but she also possesses emotional intelligence and indeed her sisterly bond with the other clones and her romantic involvement with Delphine both feature prominently within the arc of the show's narrative.

And yet, her romantic or familial attachments in no way make up the only or most interesting facet of Cosima's personality. She is not merely seeking a romantic partner or attempting to perform well in the role of sister. Indeed, she shines the brightest during her moments of scientific discovery. Mid-way through the first season, when Sarah is just beginning to know her history, she wakes one morning with foggy memories of having been subject to some kind of medical experimentation. She seeks out Cosima, who thinks that Sarah has indeed been kidnapped and from marks on her body deduces that Sarah has undergone neurological testing and blood sampling.[13] This information leads to a series of critical breakthroughs and we thus understand that Cosima's position as a scientist is a key part of both her identity and the narrative arc of the series. Indeed, her research is more important than her romantic relationships both in terms of how she embodies her subject position and within the storyline of the show itself. This kind of representation argues that women can function within a narrative as more than romantic figures and it is thus an integral piece of the show's feminist positionality.

Another critical site of subjective broadening in *Orphan Black* is its representation of female sexuality. It is often the case that women on film are represented as the objects of male desire rather than as complex, sexual beings. Women who do enjoy sex tend to be judged for it and are often punished within the narratives that they populate. We haven't come so far from Hester Prynne's scarlet letter as we might think. Men on film (and in life) who enjoy sex, perhaps even with multiple partners, are "ladies' men," "players," and "Don Juans."[14] Meanwhile, women who engage in the very same behavior are slut-shamed. This also translates to what kind of sex scenes we see on film and in television. Foreplay is rare, as is male nudity and male-on-female oral sex. The sexed female body, such as she exists in cinema, is always already objectified and sexualized for a "panoptic male connoisseur."[15] *Orphan Black* resists those kinds of characterizations at every turn and even depicts multiple kinds of transgressive desire. Sarah, while impersonating Beth, enjoys sex with Paul (Dylan Bruce), Beth's monitor. Rachel, another of the clones, also later enjoys having sex with Paul. Allison is shown to be both attracted to her own husband and to the husband of her neighbor, and Cosima engages in a same-sex relationship with Delphine. In each case, the narrative of the show allows the woman to enjoy sex without shame or judgment. It is important too that *Orphan Black* depicts queer desire that also functions as an instance of subjective broadening. It adds to the body of cultural products that normalize homosexuality and provides another instance of *Orphan Black* depicting female identity as complex and varied, as a site of possibility and potentiality. Important also is Cosima's blunt assertion that "my sexuality is not the most interesting thing about me."[16] This sentiment reveals the show's interest in critiquing identity politics, another way in which subjects are pigeonholed. A heterosexual woman can have multiple identifications that define her and yet somehow, a homosexual woman is defined entirely by her queer sexuality. She only "gets" to have that one point of identification; everything else about her is secondary.

Additionally, *Orphan Black*'s interest in historically marginalized identities moves the focal point of the show away from centric subject positions. What we typically see on screen and in print is emphasized femininity: blonde, thin, young, make-up wearing women who embody a current cultural ideal. This is the default, normalized female body that is also docile, affectively rather than cognitively organized, heterosexual, and defined in large part by an external male gaze. The women of *Orphan Black* signal a marked departure from this type: Sarah Manning, the show's ostensible protagonist, although small of frame and normatively beautiful in some ways, has an almost masculine presentation, wears only eye makeup, and is working class. She often punctuates her sentences with the distinctly urban "Oi!" and when we are first introduced to her, everything about her persona depicts this kind of class position.[17] She resists traditional representations of the feminine and in doing so humanizes women of her class background and makes the argument that their stories are worth telling. Cosima also represents traditionally Othered subject positions: she is a lesbian, a scientist, and messily bohemian in her presentation. Neither of these women, or any of the other clones, sexualize themselves. Additionally, there is a transgender clone and Felix (Jordan Gavaris), one of the show's other principle characters, is an openly gay man who engages in relationships that skirt the boundaries of sex work. Both of these characters are sympathetic and the narrative doesn't punish either of them for their transgressive behaviors and embodiments.

Again, *Orphan Black* asks its audiences to consider the humanity of subjects whose identities deviate from the norm. In a world of films and television series that focus on the wealthy, white, powerful elites, this is important. Even in contemporary series that *do* engage with non-traditional subjectivities, it is often the case that the people on display are wealthy and white. *Transparent* and *The L Word* are critical exemplars of this kind of representation.[18] *Transparent*'s narrative focuses on a woman who comes out as transgender in her 60s and *The L Word* showcases the lives of a close-knit group of lesbian and bisexual women in Los Angeles, but in each series we see primarily wealthy, white, thin, middle and upper class characters. They may deviate from the norm in terms of their sexuality, but in every other way they represent dominant subjectivities and "typical" American lives.

Observation and Pursuit: The Body as a Target of Power

Another of the most powerful ways that *Orphan Black* engages with contemporary feminist discourse is its representation of the female body as a target of patriarchal power. The interrelation of power and the body is an important topic within the world of contemporary feminist and queer studies: as Bartkey writes, "Formerly the body was dominantly conceptualized as a fixed, unitary, and primarily physiological reality. Today more and more scholars have come to regard the body as a historical, plural, and culturally mediated form."[19] Thus, we now understand that female bodies have long been subjugated, controlled, and defined by men, and indeed these kinds of regulatory mechanisms construct, bolster, and perpetuate patriarchal social organization. Not only are women oppressed overtly through differential socialization, through the dualistic gendering of intelligence as masculine and emotion as feminine, and through social practices such as relegating women to the domestic spheres of motherhood and household management, but female bodies are also controlled through subtle, subconscious methods.

Because of the systemic nature of patriarchal social organization, women internalize its very values, practices, and norms. To a great extent we absorb the notion that individual identity, self-worth, and merit derive from beauty, maternity, and marriage. Men may access individual success through careers and power, but for women in patriarchal societies what is of importance is the body and its orientation towards men. It is as if "the disciplinary power that inscribes femininity on the body is everywhere and it is nowhere. The disciplinarian is everyone and it is no one."[20] Women do not embrace normative beauty standards and repressive subject positions because they are overtly forced to, but rather because these values have been so "sedimented" into our cultural norms that over time they gain the appearance of not only normalcy, but also a kind of innateness.[21] We come to understand men as inherently powerful and women as inherently weak; men seem predisposed towards intellect, power, and cognition whereas women have every appearance of being "natural" caregivers, better equipped to solve the kinds of problems that require compromise and emotional intelligence. In our contemporary cultural field, "we thus have no direct, innocent, or unconstructed knowledge of our bodies; rather, we are always reading our bodies according to various schemes."[22] As women, we come into being always already targets of power, both overt and covert. *Orphan Black* reveals this in several key ways, beginning with the very origins of the characters themselves. Created as part of a clandestine government operation, their bodies are quite literally targets of power from the very moment of their inception.

Thus, the premise of *Orphan Black* itself engages with the multi-form ways in which the female body comes into being as an always already target of patriarchal power. Cosima, Sarah, and her fellow clones owe their very lives to a covert military operation whose research brought them into being. They are literal creations of a watchful patriarchy; their lives were meant to serve the needs of a governmental power structure through their role as test subjects. The viewers come to know the stakes of this very early on in the narrative of the show. The very first scene in the series depicts the suicide of Beth Childs, one of the cloned women. Sarah Manning, another clone who is as yet unaware of her origins, sees Beth jump in front of a moving train. She then opens Beth's wallet and upon examination of her driver's license, finds that she is staring at what could very well be a photo of her own face: Beth is Sarah's mirror image. Using Beth's cell phone she contacts Cosima, and through a series of conversations Sarah comes to understand not only that she was created as a part of a government experiment, but that the original architects of this project are now hunting their subjects. Thus, both their everyday lives *and* their origins come into focus as targets of an external, patriarchal power. Cosima, because of her doctoral work in evolutionary development, is the best positioned to learn more about the origins and biology of the cloned women and the arc of this show's narrative then is both one of self-discovery and emancipation. The clones actively seek further self-knowledge, but they are also attempting to attain agency and control over their own lives and bodies.[23]

Another critical piece in *Orphan Black*'s representation of the body as a target of power is the monitoring system set in place to keep watch over the clones. Each woman has a monitor, hired to collect daily observational data and to communicate any signs of alarm to the team of scientists. Most noteworthy in this monitoring system is that the monitors are always intimate partners of the clones and in fact are introduced to the clones in order to monitor them. Thus, the clones enter into their romantic partnerships always already as sites of regulation, observation, and control. In a very overt way, this illustrates the clones' lack of agency and independence, but in a more abstract sense it gestures towards the extent to which female sexuality has always functioned as a site of oppression and subjugation. Within the world of *Orphan Black*, we see female clones whose sexual and romantic partnerships are bound up inextricably with the very regulatory body that creates and monitors them. This means that there is an inherent hierarchy of control to each of these relationships and that Cosima, Sarah, Beth, Allison, and the other clones necessarily occupy the disempowered position within it. Indeed, it is shocking to each clone, in turn, when she discovers that her monitor is also her romantic partner. Further, the monitors do develop genuine attachments towards the clones. They are lovers and partners in the truest sense of those words and this constructs incredibly delicate, complex relationships.

It is Cosima, of course, who first discovers not only that the clones are monitored on a daily basis, but that those monitors are their lovers and even in the case of Allison, their husbands. Cosima's own monitor is the beautiful Dr. Delphine Cormier who, if we are to believe her, has never entered into a romantic or sexual relationship with another woman. We aren't privy to any kind of behind-the-scenes discussion between Delphine and Dr. Leekie (Matt Frewer), the head of the Dyad Institute whose research led to the creation of the groups of clones, but we do bear witness to the difficulty Delphine has in exploring her attraction to Cosima. She struggles initially with the transgression that inheres in such acts of same-sex desire and yet she does evidence a markedly knowledgeable (and feminist) understanding of the workings of desire; she notes that sexuality is a spectrum rather than a binary and that both social stigma and bias against same-sex desire only serve to "strengthen and codify" heteronormative social organization.[24] Having verbalized her understanding of the idea that heterosexuality as a dominant position exists in "contradiction of the facts," she seems freer to explore her feelings for Cosima and the two kiss, effectively beginning their romantic relationship.[25] We are not meant to understand their union as one *entirely* dictated by Delphine's status as Cosima's monitor, but we are left to parse out for ourselves the complexity of their power dynamic and the difficulty inherent in such a hierarchical positionality. Again, this representation leads us to a meta-analysis of the necessarily crossed axes of power and sexuality that underpin romantic and sexual relationships.

The most overt way through which *Orphan Black* represents the female body as a target of patriarchal power, however, reveals itself at the end of the first season. In the final episode each of the three primary clone figures, Sarah, Allison, and Cosima, all become targets in a very tangible way. Sarah is arrested and we thus see the female body subject to carceral power. Dr. Leekie visits Allison and, in exchange for answers to her many questions and safety from the group that is hunting the women, offers her a contract. If she agrees to sign away her own bodily rights and agency and submit to additional testing, he will safeguard both Allison and her family. Leekie offers a similar contract to Cosima, only hers also entails the freedom and resources to study herself and her fellow clones. Leekie wants to provide her with a state-of-the-art lab and staff members of her very own at the Dyad Institute. These offers are incredibly lucrative and Cosima argues that in order to protect and understand themselves they "have to know" their "biology."[26] Thus, again we see the complexity of functioning as an always already target of power. We saw with the monitors how the women find themselves in complex relationships whose shifting terrain is difficult to navigate. We saw that power and love can be interpenetrating, and even co-constructing forces. Now, we are presented with another manifestation of the difficulty of navigating power hierarchies in that in order to gain not only protection, but also self-knowledge, the women must sign over their rights to their own bodies. This is an odd sort of paradox for self-knowledge itself is a form of agency, indeed one that the women at this point do not have, *but*, giving Dr. Leekie control over their lives and their bodies seems to wrest from them an arguably greater form of self-control.

Additionally, it is during this episode that Cosima makes another important discovery: the women, the clones, are trademarked. They are "restricted intellectual property" of the Dyad Institute.[27] This revelation happens as a result of figuring out the binary code of their genome, and the knowledge shakes Cosima to her core. Although they are human, because they came into being as part of a scientific experiment, the clones are property of the Dyad Institute. Not only do they owe their existence to an external power force, but they are, by virtue of this copyright, subject to it for the duration of their lives. Their status as intellectual property forms a powerful critique of patriarchy and the various ways that it constructs the female subject as an always already target of regulation and control. Strictly speaking, within patriarchal social organization, there is no way to escape this kind of subjugation. As long as women are oppressed by virtue of sex and gender, they remain targets of power.

Fighting Back: The Body as a Site of Resistance

Orphan Black thus represents the way in which the female body comes into being as an always already target of power, and yet one of its greatest feminist moves is to also illustrate the female body as a site of resistance to such forms of external control. It does so perhaps most markedly through its narrative arc: if roughly half of the show's drama is given over to a depiction of Dyad and the Prolethian Group's efforts to hunt down and capture the clones, the rest of its time is spent representing the women's path towards self-knowledge and their efforts to resist capture. These processes of self-discovery and resistance instantiate a kind of collaborative power termed "intersubjective agency" by contemporary feminist philosophers.[28] "Agency" refers to the ability of an individual to be in control of herself and to act in the manner that she deems fit in any given situation without being acted on by another individual. In most philosophical accounts of agency, it is an individual characteristic. Agents are so because they act alone. However, within the world of contemporary feminist philosophy there is another way to conceptualize agency, called "intersubjective" because according to this model, agents must be able to act in concert with one another. Since we have evolved to live as members of groups both small and large, the ability to collaborate and cooperate with our fellow people is of extreme importance and we are thus *only* fully agentic when we work together successfully.[29] The clones, different as they are, work together very effectively and through doing so are able to harness greater strength than they would on their own.

This process initially is not without friction and while Cosima in particular seems most at ease with her fellow clones, Sarah, Allison, and Helena at times struggle with collaboration. A suburban soccer mom with two young children and a somewhat milquetoast husband, Allison values conformity and propriety. She clashes with both Sarah and Felix in large part because of the difference in their class positions. Allison is protective of her middle-class status and seems judgmental of Sarah and Felix's appearance, behavior, and mannerisms. And yet, they all develop not only the ability to work together, but also a strong bond. Allison and Felix in particular become one of the series' greatest odd couples. It is Allison who teaches Sarah how to shoot a gun while Felix babysits her children.[30] Later Felix rescues Allison when she becomes too inebriated at a party.[31] In each case, we see the clones (and Felix) learn not only to work together effectively, but also to recognize one another's humanity in spite of differences and to understand themselves as a cohesive, even loving group of individuals.

Another key representation of the power of intersubjective agency is the storyline surrounding Helena, perhaps the strangest of the clones. Helena, Sarah's biological twin, was raised in a Ukrainian orphanage and seems to struggle with empathy. She is violent, wild, and of all of the clones has the most difficulty working as part of a team. When she is forcibly impregnated by the Proletheans, the religious group that is hunting the clones, she knows that she must escape. This is a powerful image of the body as a target of power, to be sure, but her flight from the Proletheans, in which she is aided by her fellow clones, illustrates an equally powerful instance of resistance. Her very bodily integrity has been violated and yet she manages to obtain her freedom and to rescue Sarah, who is also being held captive. She kills Sarah's captor and the two leave to rejoin their fellow clones.[32] Neither woman would have had an easy time escaping on her own and we are meant to see, in their collaboration, a representation of the way in which a group functions as more than the sum of its parts.

As always though, Cosima is the primary driving force within the collaboration that is "clone club," as they've termed themselves. She is more even-tempered than Allison, Sarah, or Helena, and not only does she provide the group with scientific knowledge, but she also serves as an affective and relational anchor, maintaining the sense of calm that they need in order to move forward together during difficult times. This is especially interesting in light of the fact that she is suffering from a mysterious lung disorder. Indeed, by the beginning of the second season her respiratory symptoms have worsened and she begins to cough up blood.[33] Yet, she never loses sight of the goals that she and her fellow clones share and we see her at every turn prioritizing the group over her own interests. She truly illustrates the way in which the women are stronger and more agentic as one functioning body than they are individually.

Thus, *Orphan Black* performs a critical, progressive, and important set of cultural tasks in its interest in feminist politics and through its complex representations of the workings of gender, sex, and power. As a series it asks us to not only raise our awareness of the ways in which patriarchy oppresses female subjects, but also provides an account for the ways in which women actively resist that kind of subjugation. In the depth and complexity of its representation it broadens the possibilities for women on film and in so doing sets a contemporary example for girls and women coming into being in this new era of feminist cultural engagement. That all of these important gender-based issues come to the sharpest focus through the character who is actively engaged in a STEM field is of incredible importance and speaks to the increased role that women are playing within the sciences. Even one short decade ago, role models for burgeoning female scientists were few and far between. That we are seeing such an increase in media representation of women in STEM is encouraging and hopefully *Orphan Black* is only one of the first of many films and television shows whose women are intellectually capable, complex, and multi-faceted.

Notes

1. *Mad Max: Fury Road*, directed by George Miller (Warner Brothers: 2015); Melissa Rosenberg (creator), *Jessica Jones* (Netflix: 2015–present).
2. Graeme Manson and John Fawcett (creators), *Orphan Black* (Space and BBC America: 2013–present).
3. Graeme Manson, "Endless Forms Most Beautiful," *Orphan Black*, season 1, episode 10, directed by John Fawcett, aired June 1, 2013, on Space.
4. Andi Zeisler, *We Were Feminists Once: From Riot Grrrl to Covergirl, the Buying and Selling of a Movement* (New York: PublicAffairs, 2016), xv.
5. Ibid., 88.
6. Sharon Smith, "Introduction," in *Feminist Film Theory, A Reader*, ed. Sue Thornham (New York: New York University Press, 1999), 14–15.
7. Ibid.
8. Graeme Manson, "By Means Which Have Never Yet Been Tried," *Orphan Black*, season 2, episode 10, directed by John Fawcett, aired June 21, 2014, on Space.
9. Graeme Manson, "Entangled Blank," *Orphan Black*, season 1, episode 8, directed by Karen Walton, aired May 18, 2013, on Space.
10. Graeme Manson, "Instinct," *Orphan Black*, season 1, episode 2, directed by John Fawcett, aired April 6, 2013, on Space.
11. Rene Descartes, *Discourse on Method and the Meditations* (New York: Penguin, 1968), 150–169.
12. Susan Bordo, *The Flight to Objectivity: Essays on Cartesianism and Culture* (Albany: SUNY Press, 1987), 104–115.
13. Will Pascoe, "Variations Under Domestication," *Orphan Black*, season 1, episode 6, directed by John Fawcett, aired May 4, 2013, on Space.
14. Sandra Bartkey, "Foucault, Femininity, and the Modernization of Patriarchal Power," in *The Politics of Women's Bodies*, ed. Rose Weitz (Oxford: Oxford University Press, 2010), 88.
15. Ibid.
16. Graeme Manson and Karen Walton, "Governed by Sound Reason and True Religion," *Orphan Black*, season 2, episode 2, directed by John Fawcett, aired April 26, 2014, on Space.
17. Graeme Manson, "Natural Selection," *Orphan Black*, season 1, episode 1, directed by John Fawcett, aired on March 30, 2013, on Space.
18. Jill Soloway (creator), *Transparent* (Amazon: 2014–present); Michele Abbott, Ilene Chaiken, and Kathy Greenberg (creators), *The L Word* (Showtime: 2004–2009).
19. Bartkey, "Foucault, Femininity, and the Modernization of Patriarchal Power," 88.
20. Ibid.
21. Judith Butler, *Gender Trouble: Feminism and the Subversion of Identity* (New York: Routledge, 1999), 178–9.
22. Bartkey, "Foucault, Femininity, and the Modernization of Patriarchal Power," 88.
23. Manson, "Instinct."
24. Karen Walton, "Entangled Bank," *Orphan Black*, season 1, episode 8, directed by Ken Girotti, aired on May 18, 2013, on Space.

25. Ibid.
26. Manson, "Endless Forms Most Beautiful."
27. Ibid.
28. Kym McClaren, "Emotional Metamorphoses: The Role of Others in Becoming a Subject," in *Embodiment and Agency*, eds. Sue Cambell, Letitia Meynell, and Susan Sherwin (University Park: University of Pennsylvania Press, 2009), 25–45.
29. Ibid.
30. Graeme Manson, "Variations Under Nature," *Orphan Black*, season 1, episode 3, directed by David Frazee, aired on April 13, 2013, on Space.
31. Pascoe, "Variations Under Domestication."
32. Russ Cochrane, "Governed as It Were by Chance," *Orphan Black*, season 2, episode 4, directed by David Frazee, aired on May 10, 2014, on Space.
33. Ibid.

Works Cited

Abbott, Michele, Ilene Chaiken, and Kathy Greenberg. *The L Word*. Showtime, 2004–2009.
Bartkey, Sandra. "Foucault, Femininity, and the Modernization of Patriarchal Power." In *The Politics of Women's Bodies*, edited by Rose Weitz, 76–97. Oxford: Oxford University Press, 2010.
Berlant, Lauren, and Lee Edelman. *Sex: Or the Unbearable*. Durham: Duke University Press, 2014.
Bordo, Susan. *The Flight to Objectivity: Essays on Cartesianism and Culture*. Albany: SUNY Press, 1987.
Butler, Judith. *Gender Trouble: Feminism and the Subversion of Identity*. New York: Routledge, 1999.
Cochrane, Russ. "Governed as It Were by Chance." *Orphan Black*, season 2, episode 4. Directed by David Frazee. Aired on May 10, 2014, on Space.
Descartes, Rene. *Discourse on Method and the Meditations*. New York: Penguin, 1968.
Fawcett, John, and Graeme Manson. *Orphan Black*. Space and BBC America, 2013–present.
Foucault, Michel. *The History of Sexuality: An Introduction, Volume 1*. New York: Vintage, 1990.
Mad Max: Fury Road. Directed by George Miller. Warner Brothers, 2015.
Manson, Graeme. "By Means Which Have Never Yet Been Tried." *Orphan Black*, season 2, episode 10. Directed by John Fawcett, aired June 21, 2014, on Space.
———. "Endless Forms Most Beautiful," *Orphan Black*, season 1, episode 10. Directed by John Fawcett. Aired June 1, 2013, on Space.
———. "Entangled Bank." *Orphan Black*, season 1, episode 8. Directed by Karen Walton. Aired May 18, 2013, on Space.
———. "Instinct." *Orphan Black*, season 1, episode 2. Directed by John Fawcett. Aired April 6, 2013, on Space.
———. "Natural Selection." *Orphan Black*, season 1, episode 1. Directed by John Fawcett. Aired on March 30, 2013, on Space.
———. "Variations Under Nature." *Orphan Black*, season 1, episode 3. Directed by David Frazee. Aired on April 13, 2013, on Space.
Manson, Graeme, and Karen Walton. "Governed by Sound Reason and True Religion." *Orphan Black*, season 2, episode 2. Directed by John Fawcett. Aired April 26, 2014, on Space.
McClaren, Kym. "Emotional Metamorphoses: The Role of Others in Becoming a Subject." In *Embodiment and Agency*, edited by Sue Cambell, Letitia Meynell, and Susan Sherwin, 25–45. University Park: University of Pennsylvania Press, 2009.
Pascoe, Will. "Variations Under Domestication." *Orphan Black*, season 1, episode 6. Directed John Fawcett. Aired May 4, 2013, on Space.
Rosenberg, Melissa. *Jessica Jones*. Netflix, 2015–present.
Smith, Sharon. "Introduction." In *Feminist Film Theory, A Reader*, edited by Sue Thornham, 1–5. New York: New York University Press, 1999.

Soloway, Jill. *Transparent*. Amazon, 2014–present.
Walton, Karen "Entangled Bank." *Orphan Black*, season 1, episode 8. Directed by Ken Girotti. Aired on May 18, 2013, on Space.
Zeisler, Andi. *We Were Feminists Once: From Riot Grrrl to Covergirl, the Buying and Selling of a Movement*. New York: PublicAffairs, 2016.

"Not everyone's cut out for Hollywood"

"The Iron Ceiling" in Marvel's Agent Carter

LISA K. PERDIGAO

In Joe Johnston's *Captain America: The First Avenger* (2011) and Anthony and Joe Russo's *Captain America: The Winter Soldier* (2014), Agent Margaret "Peggy" Carter (Hayley Atwell) plays a central role in creating the superhero Captain America (Chris Evans) and fights alongside him.[1] In Marvel's *Agent Carter* (2015–2016), Carter returns to the home front after World War II.[2] With *Agent Carter*, the Marvel Cinematic Universe (MCU) expands to the small screen to feature Peggy Carter's backstory as a founder of the Strategic Homeland Intervention, Enforcement, and Logistics Division (S.H.I.E.L.D.). However, unlike the MCU's other origin stories, *Agent Carter* highlights the character's struggle for recognition. Carter is given considerable screen time in the films as more than an accessory to and love interest for Steve Rogers/Captain America; however, when she returns home, she is treated as a secretary within the Strategic Scientific Reserve (S.S.R.), S.H.I.E.L.D.'s antecedent, despite her proven combat record and knowledge of science and technology. Since the MCU is often criticized for casting women in supporting roles rather than as headliners, *Agent Carter* is a remarkable achievement. The story in and of *Agent Carter* emphasizes the gender inequalities present in twentieth and twenty-first-century American society, particularly Hollywood.

Season two of *Agent Carter* offers a change of scenery for the character and series when it moves to Hollywood. In a metafictional turn, Carter's appearance within Hollywoodland highlights what is at work within the series. Where season one depicts the post-war "Iron Curtain" by pitting Carter against Dottie Underwood (Bridget Regan), a formidable Soviet assassin, in season two, the series shifts its focus to depict the "glass ceiling" affecting women in the second half of the twentieth century. Carter's season two opponent, Whitney Frost, born Agnes Cully, (Wynn Everett), is Madame Masque from Marvel comics adapted for the small screen. In Marvel comics, Whitney Frost first appeared in *Tales of Suspense* #98 (1968) and as Madame Masque in *The Invincible Iron Man* #17 (1969). The character wears a golden mask to conceal her disfigurement resulting from exposure to chemicals during a plane crash. While *Agent Carter*'s Whitney Frost does not suffer the same fate, she dons a similar disguise as a Hollywood starlet that conceals a dual identity. Inspired by Hedy Lamarr (born Hedwig Eva Kiesler), *Agent Carter*'s Frost is depicted as the most beautiful woman in film and a groundbreaking scientist.[3] Frost's backstory depicts a series of compromises involving an exchange of her beauty for power that almost masks her genius. When asked if Frost is a genius, fellow Isodyne Energy scientist Dr. Jason Wilkes (Reggie Austin) replies, "I'm a genius. Whitney Frost … she defies categorization."[4] Like Frost, Carter defies categorization: she was a code breaker at Bletchley Park before joining the Special Operations Executive (S.O.E.) and S.S.R. during World War II. And, like her season two antagonist, Carter is revealed to be a complex character that challenges traditional representations of women in STEM, both within the Strategic Scientific Reserve and Hollywood.

Although only Frost is exposed to Zero Matter, Frost and Carter exhibit its associated powers: intangibility and invisibility. Trina Robbins writes that the "plight of most comic book action heroines" in the mid-twentieth century was that "none had ever appeared in her own book, and they were invariably short-lived, rarely lasting for more than three appearances before fading into permanent obscurity."[5] Season two of *Agent Carter* outlines the complexities of sustaining dual identities as comic book action heroines and women in STEM: as Frost's experiments with Zero Matter escalate, her beautiful façade cracks. Frost's depiction in the series is representative of the struggles that Agent Carter faces within both the S.S.R. and the MCU. Frost's statement, "I'm sorry, Agent Carter. Not everyone's cut out for Hollywood," proves to be prophetic for the series.[6] Despite receiving critical acclaim, after the season two finale fittingly titled "Hollywood Ending," *Agent Carter* was cancelled. In its diegesis and exegesis, *Agent Carter* depicts the "Iron Ceiling" for the representation of women in STEM on the small screen.[7]

"The Girl from Cap's Past": Peggy Carter's Origin Story

The transformation of Peggy Carter from Captain America's love interest in *Captain America: The First Avenger* to protagonist of the ABC series can be seen as a radical reimagining of gender tropes in comic books and their contemporary adaptations. Carter was first introduced in *Tales of Suspense* #75 (1966) when Rogers/Captain America awakens in the contemporary world and remembers an unnamed woman from his past:

> [T]here was one *other*! Our lives touched for only a short time—but I've never forgotten her! I can still remember our final date—when she whispered to me, thru trembling lips…. I'll wait till you return, Steve! No matter how long—no matter what happens—I'll wait for you, my darling….[8]

Although he says that he will never forget her, he admits, "that was an eternity ago—in the dead past—the forgotten past."[9] In *Tales of Suspense* #77 (1966), "The Girl from Cap's Past" is given a backstory and an active role during World War II, complicating the earlier depiction of the character as a mere love interest. She plays a more central role in the comic and war, yet her gender is constantly foregrounded in discussions of her place on the front line. When Captain America tells the still-unnamed character, "This isn't *woman's* work," she replies, "I *can't* leave. This war is *everybody's* war…! I was needed … and I answered the call. Just as *you* did, in your own way."[10]

Although Carter asserts the notion of equality in the time of war, saying, "We *both* have to follow orders," she fits Robbins' description of female characters in comics that were "relegated to the role of girlfriend, and their purpose was to be rescued by the hero."[11] In the comics, Carter is cast as the romantic character, asking, "Oh, Cap … Cap…. Will this war never end? Will we never be able to lead *normal* lives? How can we speak of love … when the world is in flames … when I don't even know your *name*?"[12] After leaving Captain America, "The Girl from Cap's Past" is soon captured by the Nazis who believe that "it should not be difficult to learn what [they] wish from one lone female."[13] At the end of the comic, Captain America is left wondering if the mystery woman is alive or dead. Her memory and identity are effectively erased until Captain America sees someone who reminds him of his lost love and it turns out to be her sister.[14]

The television series' resuscitation of Peggy Carter reintroduces the complexities surrounding the character's treatment within the comics. Agent Carter's initial appearance as a ghost-like character—a relic of the past—is indicative of her dichotomous position within and between the Silver Age of Comics (1956–1970) and second-wave feminism (1960–1980).[15] In 1963, Betty Friedan's *The Feminine Mystique* challenged traditional ideas about gender—"the problem that has no name"—and inspired a new wave of feminist theory.[16] In a new introduction to the book published in 1997, Friedan writes,

> Consider the terms of women's new empowerment, the startling changes since that time I wrote about, only three decades ago, when women were defined only in sexual relation to men—man's wife, sex object, mother, housewife—and never as persons

defining themselves by their own actions in society. That image, which I called the "feminine mystique," was so pervasive, coming at us from the women's magazines, the movies, the television commercials, all the mass media and the textbooks of psychology and sociology.[17]

"The Girl from Cap's Past" is representative of the "problem that has no name." Agent Carter informs and shapes the superhero's past; however, she is initially denied a full identity, history, and recurring role in the comics. Carter's history in print and revival as the eponymous character in her own television series highlight the complex ways that gender is reconceived in the twenty-first century, particularly on the front line for women in science.

"Now Is Not the End": Agent Carter Post–Captain America

In the television series' first season, Carter navigates and circumvents antiquated ideas about gender in her work as an S.S.R. agent and founder of S.H.I.E.L.D. While *Captain America: The First Avenger* depicts Carter assisting in Rogers' transformation into a super-soldier, *Agent Carter* emphasizes that its protagonist has skills beyond the battlefield. Returning to the home front after the war, Carter's knowledge of science and technology is instrumental to her work protecting the United States from post-war threats. In season one, Carter helps Howard Stark (Dominic Cooper), who is accused of treason by the U.S. government, clear his name by following the science—the theft and sale of Nitramene by the Soviet science and espionage agency Leviathan. Where the superhero Captain America, a product of science, disappears at the end of the war, Agent Carter persists to challenge ideas about gender in a post-war world.

The pilot episode, "Now Is Not the End," begins with the familiar scene from *Captain America: The First Avenger* when Captain America, sacrificing himself to save the world, says goodbye to Carter. However, where the comics depict a Captain America nostalgic for the woman that he lost, the television series reverses roles: a year after the war, Carter remembers Captain America, the man from *her* past. A montage pairs Carter in quotidian tasks (reading the paper, ironing her clothes, getting dressed, and watering plants) with flashbacks of her active role during the war and in the *Captain America* film. In the opening scene, Carter must adapt to the new environment after the war and after Captain America. Highlighting the gender politics of this new world, Carter's roommate Colleen O'Brien (Ashley Hinshaw) says that ten girls were let go from their jobs because G.I.s were discharged. Colleen says, "I had to show a guy from Canarsie how to use a rivet gun," invoking the iconic image of Rosie the Riveter, an emblematic figure of progressive gender politics during the war.[18] However, while women like Colleen are displaced by men in the workplace, Carter is able to distinguish herself—despite or because of her gender. When Carter walks to work on a busy New York City street, she emerges from a crowd of men wearing dark hats and overcoats, distinct in a red hat and red lipstick. She easily transitions from feminine to masculine spaces, leaving a room of female switchboard operators to enter one populated by male S.S.R. agents.

Agent Carter juxtaposes the World War II contexts of the Marvel comics and the contemporary landscape of the television series. In season one, the radio serial *The Captain America Adventure Program* broadcasts a narrative that recalls and is consistent with the Silver Age Marvel comics. In the radio serial, which Carter dubs "thrillingly realistic," Captain America is the hero and Betty Carver (a "fictionalized" Peggy Carter, voiced by Erin Torpey) is the damsel in distress, a contrast to the twenty-first-century television series' narrative.[19] As the radio announcer (Ralph Garman) reports, "battalion triage nurse Betty Carver tidies up while the men defend their country…," she reflects on her domestic duties, saying, "What a beautiful day to mend these pants. And my new Singer Featherweight 221 sewing machine makes stitching so easy.…"[20] Carver's occupation as a nurse and involvement in chores traditionally assigned to women highlight the ways that the television series reimagines the character. Distracted from her domestic chores by Nazi invaders, the radio serial's Betty cries out, "If only Captain America were here to rescue me," prompting Carter's response, "Who writes this rubbish?"[21] In the episode "Bridge and Tunnel," the radio serial's narrative belies what appears on screen. In the episode, Carter locates suspect Sheldon McFee (Devin Ratray) and a dairy truck containing Nitramene bombs. As Carter enters McFee's house, the radio serial plays in the background, offering a counter-narrative to the television character's actions on screen. The announcer states, "We now return to *The Captain America Adventure Program* in which our hero's defenseless sweetheart finds herself in the clutches of evil," a stark contrast to the scene depicting Carter easily subduing the male character.[22] As "Bridge and Tunnel" concludes, Betty says, "I'm so lucky to have a man as brave and strong as Captain America."[23] The two versions of Agent Carter exist in the same space, juxtaposed in representations on air and on screen.

"Smoke & Mirrors": Agent Carter in Hollywood

While Agent Carter is able to prove her value to the S.S.R. by the end of season one, at the beginning of season two, S.S.R. Chief Jack Thompson

(Chad Michael Murray) attempts to undermine her newfound authority. He sends Carter to the Los Angeles S.S.R. office to assist the newly appointed Chief Daniel Sousa (Enver Gjokaj), Carter's former colleague and love interest, in a case involving a woman frozen in ice. After Sousa asks Thompson for help from the New York office, Thompson replies, "I have just the man for you."[24] Thompson's assignment of the case to Carter is a case of "Smoke & Mirrors" (the title of a later episode in season two). His decision is not based on his assessment of Carter's capability; instead, he seeks to prove that "the S.S.R. can actually function without [her] for a while."[25] However, after arriving in L.A., Carter soon realizes that the murder is not the work of the "lady of the lake" serial killer. After S.S.R. lab tech Dr. Samberly (Matt Braunger) says that the luminescence radiating from the body is caused by "producing the radioisotope in the form of uranium," Carter answers L.A. Homicide Detective Andrew Henry's (Sean O'Bryan) question, "What does that mean?" by replying, "She was near a particle accelerator."[26] The case leads Carter to Isodyne Energy, a "development laboratory dedicated to fuel initiatives in the twentieth century," and the victim's identity: Isodyne scientist Jane Scott. Season two is staged as a struggle for power in and over science— by women. That the backdrop is L.A. is significant. Season two introduces the limits and possibilities of representing women in STEM in Hollywood: they can be either static characters (frozen in ice) or active agents.

In contrast to season one's radio plays, season two offers a metacommentary on *Agent Carter*'s appearance on television with the backdrop of Hollywood. Although Carter is initially reluctant to leave her case in New York, when she arrives in L.A., she immediately appears to adapt to her new surroundings. She appears to welcome the "star treatment": "Miss Carter" is greeted by an assistant, Stark's butler Edwin Jarvis (James D'Arcy), as she disembarks from the plane and immediately puts on red sunglasses. The entire season is framed by the move to Hollywood: the S.S.R. cover is no longer the New York Bell Company office staged with female switchboard operators; instead, it is the Auerbach Theatrical Agency replete with dancing girls. When Carter follows a lead to Isodyne Energy's owner (and Frost's husband), Calvin Chadwick (Currie Graham), Carter admits, "I'm not one for cinema."[27] Yet she quickly adapts to playing a role when she takes on an American accent in an attempt to gather information from Chadwick. Trying to distract Frost, Jarvis claims that he is an agent with an idea for a "spy picture" about a British female agent, in effect, pitching *Agent Carter* for the big screen. In the episode "Better Angels," Stark is working as a director on a film adaptation of Kid Colt comics when Carter and Jarvis appear onset, disrupting the filming. When Stark tells Carter, "I always thought you should be in pictures, Peg," and suggests that she play the role of "wench," she replies, "I'd rather be a cowboy."[28] Stark and Carter engage in a debate about the representation of gender in a mid-twentieth *and* twenty-first-century film industry. After Stark tells her that the audience is not ready for a female cowboy, Carter replies, "But they're ready for a movie based on a comic book. Sounds like a dreadful idea."[29] Season two can be seen as a screen test for the character and series, testing its viability and longevity in Hollywood.

"A means to change the world": Unharnessed Potential

While Carter is resistant to the Hollywood scene, Frost utilizes her role as "America's sweetheart" as a source of power and means to disguise her groundbreaking work in science. Season two expands upon the debates about Carter's role within the S.S.R., which would later become the scientific division of S.H.I.E.L.D., by introducing Frost as the genius behind Isodyne Energy. In the beginning of season two, Frost is underestimated by the men and Carter herself. However, although Carter initially regards Frost as a mere accessory to Chadwick, not a "person of interest," she soon realizes that "things aren't what they seem."[30] The key to the case involving the murder of scientist Jane Scott is Zero Matter. Zero Matter, a "mysterious substance," is identified as more powerful than atomic energy and, according to Dr. Wilkes, "a means to change the world" that is "more dangerous than anything we've ever known."[31] Like Zero Matter, Frost is "far more dangerous than she looks."[32]

Wilke's description of trying to contain Zero Matter that is "always drawing energy into itself" extends to the treatment of its host, Frost, and, more expansively, women. Elizabeth Grosz writes, "As a concept, sexuality is incapable of ready containment: it refuses to stay within its predesignated regions, for it seeps across boundaries into areas that are apparently not its own."[33] Frost embodies this concept: after her exposure to Zero Matter, she transcends the limitations ascribed to women in the mid-twentieth century. Frost appears "uncontainable within any particular sphere or domain," able to "extend the frameworks which attempt to contain [her], to seep beyond their domains of control."[34] After Carter tells Frost that her exposure to Zero Matter has altered her physiology, Frost replies, "Fix me? Why would I want to be fixed? I've never felt more powerful in my entire life."[35] Following the investigation of Scott's murder, Isodyne reports a "containment leak," suggestive of the threat that Zero Matter—as embodied by Frost—represents in the narrative.

Zero Matter is presented as a sign and symptom of the marginalization of women and African Americans during the mid-twentieth century. Wilkes, a male African American scientist, is introduced as a corollary to Frost. Like Frost, Wilkes is a genius, yet he was almost unable to find employment after the war. Frost tells Wilkes, "I simply want to change things for people like us, people that have been ignored, held back, ground up."[36] Frost plays to—and into—Wilkes' own doubts about his position at Isodyne and in post-war American society when she asks, "Do you really believe that Isodyne recruited you because they valued your brilliant mind? You were hired for the same reason that Jane Scott was hired. A woman and a colored man."[37] In "A View in the Dark," Wilkes tells Carter, "it was the war that gave me a real opportunity…. Navy engineer. And then some real, actual scientific work in the weapons propulsion lab."[38] Yet, after the war, out of sixteen companies, Isodyne was the only one to offer him a job. Like Colleen, the Rosie the Riveter character, Wilkes found that he did not have a place in the workforce after the war. Zero Matter, a product of continued atomic testing after the war, is said to "make atomic energy as obsolete as the steam engine."[39] It is indicative of the plights of women and African Americans in post-war American society: obsolescence. However, Zero Matter is suggestive of the power afforded with—and through—invisibility.

Zero Matter and its associated effects can be read as symbolic of the female characters' relative invisibility within comics, film, television, and science. Ruth Watts writes, "In popular parlance, women and science do not appear to go together."[40] Historically, science has been identified as a masculinist pursuit involving the penetration and domination of a "female nature," thus embedding "gendered and sexualized notions of science, and nature, into the discourse of science."[41] It reflects a binary opposition where "man and mind, woman and body, become representationally aligned."[42] However, Lorna Jowett notes that following the second wave of feminism, in the 1960s and 1970s, "the conventions of science came under scrutiny by feminist scholars, who began to reevaluate it as part of our patriarchal society and recognize it as a gendered institution."[43] *Agent Carter*'s representation of Carter's roles as codebreaker and S.S.R. agent and Frost's work with Isodyne reflects a similar reevaluation of the gender constructs at work in post-war society as represented in popular culture.

The "Secret Weapon": Women in STEM

In her roles as scientist and Hollywood actress, Frost is poised between invisibility and celebrity. Watts notes that "few people can name many women scientists beyond Marie Curie" and suggests that the situation is not likely to change anytime soon, citing the "dearth of women among either the top ranks of scientists or even entering some sciences" as well as the "difficulties of even highly reputed female scientists being honoured by their community."[44] In the episode "Better Angels," Sousa informs Carter, "an Okie named Agnes

Cully," "the Heartland's Marie Curie," is Isodyne's "secret weapon."[45] The comparison to Curie punctuates Watts' point about the relative invisibility of most female scientists; however, Sousa's research brings Cully's alternate identity into focus. He is the one to figure out that Whitney Frost is a stage name and that "America's sweetheart is the brains behind Isodyne Energy."[46] Carter recognizes the irony of the situation: "Every eye in the country is on her, and no one sees her."[47] Although the results of Frost's exposure to Zero Matter are remarkably different from Wilkes,' rendering her more corporeal rather than invisible and intangible, here she is seen in similar terms. And, like Wilkes, her invisibility is a source of power, a byproduct and symbol of Zero Matter itself.

Frost's résumé reads like Hollywood icon Hedy Lamarr's who was reportedly the "most beautiful woman in Hollywood" and a genius.[48] Frost was, as Sousa notes, an inventor and "then some": her work "put Isodyne on the map during the war."[49] Like Lamarr who patented a radio guidance system for torpedoes during the war, Frost is reported to have worked on radio frequency modulators that were employed by the Allies to send coded messages during the war, ironically connected to Carter's work decoding Axis messages at Bletchley Park. On another front, Frost faces a similar struggle to Lamarr and other "golden goddesses" of the silver screen as the industry turns to younger actresses, looking for a "fresh face."[50] Notably, after debuting in American films with *Algiers* (1938), Lamarr capitalized on her beauty in provocative roles before her final film appearance in *The Female Animal* (1958) where she plays an aging Hollywood actress.[51] In "Better Angels," while the director worries about the lines on Frost's face that makeup and lighting do not seem to hide, the actress' exposure to Zero Matter mars her "picture-perfect" face, reflecting the tension between the character's dual identities.[52]

"Fragmented Identity": The Masked Woman

Although *Agent Carter*'s Whitney Frost is never identified as Madame Masque from Marvel comics, the mask motif is central to the character's composition. Julia Round writes that the mask motif "reveal[s] the gothic notion of fragmented identity at the basis of the superhero genre," a "constitutive otherness, where marginalized elements define the text and apparent unity is maintained only by processes of exclusion and opposition."[53] The Madame Masque persona is incorporated in the staging of the series. Frost is often positioned before a mirror in her dressing room at home where two pairs of masks hang on the wall and stand directly in front of the mirror. The masks are foregrounded in the shots and in the mirrored reflections. Lisa Gotto writes that the mask "brings the unknown into recognition and the unrepresentable to representation"; it is a "means of covering as well as of uncovering," a "presence of absence" that "reveals what it hides" and "hides what it reveals."[54] Whitney Frost's connections to—and background as—Madame Masque inform the narrative of *Agent Carter*.

Like Marvel comics' Peggy Carter, Whitney Frost/Madame Masque is a product of 1960s culture and can be viewed as a reflection of the "feminine mystique" that Friedan describes. Her identity is continually shaped by the men in her life: her real father, Count Luchino Nefaria, her adopted father Byron Frost, fiancé Roger Vane, S.H.I.E.L.D. agent Jasper Sitwell, Tony Stark/Iron Man, and the villainous Midas. Frost is considered to be the "girl who has everything" and "one of the so-called 'beautiful people'" before her accident.[55] Her upbringing, away from her real father and crime family, gives her a "respectable façade." When Frost appears in *The Invincible Iron Man* #1 (1968), she appears as a damsel in distress calling for help before she is saved by Sitwell, who affectionately dubs her his "beautiful burden."[56] However, Frost quickly demonstrates that she is only playing a role; when she is alone in her apartment, she thinks, "I failed to find *Tony Stark*, but *Jasper Sitwell* may do as well … *he'll* be even *more* vulnerable to my charms."[57] Her master plot involves reclaiming her "rightful place as the Big M, head of the Maggia," and she uses her sexuality to achieve that goal. Once she reclaims that role, she announces, "in doing so, [she] *more* than fulfilled all Count Nefaria might have expected of a son."[58]

However, the loss of her beauty resulting from the plane crash changes Frost's sense of her identity. The mask highlights her "constitutive otherness," "marginalization," and "exclusion" within the comics that contrasts the male superheroes. Where Iron Man's "*power*, all his much-vaunted *invincibility*," "lies in the secrets of his incredible *costume*," Madame Masque's costuming betrays a vulnerability that comes to be identified with women, suggestive of the "naturalized" role that Grosz describes when she writes, "Female sexuality and women's powers of reproduction are the defining (cultural) characteristics of women, and, at the same time, these very functions render women vulnerable, in need of protection or special treatment, as variously prescribed by patriarchy."[59] After being told "how *emotional* women are" and to "*stop* that sentimental whimpering and *listen*" in her formative years, it is not surprising that Frost is susceptible to the ostensibly "invincible" male superhero who asks her, "Is it so unusual for a man to help a woman…? And I'd bet there's *quite* a woman behind that mask."[60] The powerful Madame Masque character is unable to defeat Stark/Iron Man, convincing herself, "You can hide your *features*, Madame Masque, but not your *emotions*. Not even *Midas'* wrath can make you slay a man who, if only for an *instant* … made you feel like a *woman* again."[61]

"I bet you're real pretty when you smile": Adopting the Mask

While *Agent Carter*'s Whitney Frost does not share the Marvel Comics character's history, her origin story reveals a similar conditioning about gender roles, particularly in relation to her awareness of her intelligence and beauty. In "Smoke & Mirrors," a young Agnes Cully (Ivy George) is criticized for not smiling at her "Uncle Bud" (Chris Mulkey) when she is busy repairing a broken transistor radio. Uncle Bud tells her, "I bet you're really pretty when you smile" while her mother, Willa Cully (Samaire Armstrong), reminds her, "I told you to be sweet."[62] Although Cully exhibits genius, her mother tells her, "No one cares what's inside your head," and her beauty is the "only thing that's gonna get [her] anywhere in this world."[63] Later, her mother waves a rejection letter in front of the teen Cully (Olivia Welch), saying, "You really think that that fancy science program is gonna take a girl? It doesn't matter how smart you are. You're stuck here. Same as me."[64]

Frost rejects her mother's words, only to find her power—at least initially—exactly as she had prescribed. Cully is able to escape her hometown in Broxton, Oklahoma, but she ends up following her mother's advice when she is approached by Ned Silver (Andrew Carter), "talent agent to the stars," outside of a Montgomery, Alabama, movie theater in 1934.[65] He repeats Uncle Bud's lines when he says, "You know, I bet you're real pretty when you smile."[66] The episode shows the continuous role that Cully/Frost has played throughout the years: Frost's husband Chadwick asks her to wear the white dress "with the neckline" for a photo shoot, telling her, "That's my beautiful girl."[67] Karin E. Westman writes that in popular media "To be recognized and accepted as intellectually brilliant frequently depends on a physical brilliance, a beauty underwritten by cultural norms of Western aesthetics."[68] Frost uses this false dichotomy to her advantage, reappropriating Silver's words that she can be "whatever [she] want[s]" in Hollywood to a resignified purpose.[69] Yet she nonetheless remains unable to fully rewrite her role; she sticks to the script.

"Smoke & Mirrors" exposes the illusory nature of gender constructs, those "naturalized" roles that shaped Frost and Carter and persist in postwar society. In the beginning of the episode, a young Peggy Carter (Gabriella Graves) plays the role of a knight saving a fair maiden from a dragon, challenging her depiction in the comics and radio serial aired in season one. However, she is told by her mother (Carole Ruggier) that "she's going to have to start behaving like a lady."[70] In Bletchley Park, in 1940, Carter is newly engaged when another "proposal" comes her way: she is asked to join the Special Operations Executive (S.O.E.), a "new war division spearheaded by Winston Churchill himself."[71] Carter thinks that she is being recruited as a codebreaker but learns that she will be trained in "espionage, sabotage, guerrilla tactics" specifically because she is a person who "won't be drawing attention walking down the street."[72] Being a woman guarantees a certain amount of invisibility.

Although Carter is an "exceptional codebreaker," she does not recognize or realize her "great potential," saying, "I don't believe that I'm meant to be in the field" and "I'm simply not cut out for that kind of work."[73] The crosscutting between the flashbacks to 1940 and the present day in 1947 highlights precisely how well suited the character is to "that kind of work." Friedan describes the self-imposed limits on the mid-twentieth-century woman, writing that

> no matter how much she had wanted that husband, those children, that split-level suburban house and all the appliances thereof, which were supposed to be the limits of women's dreams in those years after World War II, she sometimes felt a longing for something more.[74]

Carter's brother Michael (Max Brown), a soldier on the front line during World War II, had recommended his sister for the program, knowing that she would want more than the traditional narrative prescribed for her. The editing in "Smoke & Mirrors" highlights what Friedan describes. After news of Michael's death reaches the Carter family home in Hampstead, England, where Carter is trying on her wedding dress, one "proposal" is exchanged for another: Carter leaves a wedding dress on a dress form and an engagement ring on the table as she leaves home to begin training.

"Code Pink": Undermining the Patriarchy

Sandra Harding's comment that "women have been more systematically excluded from doing serious science than from performing any other social activity except, perhaps, frontline warfare" is suggestive of what is at work in *Agent Carter*: the front line is relocated from war time to a post-war society that remains regressive in its ideas about women's roles in the mid-twentieth century.[75] The two women, Frost and Carter, are pitted against the patriarchy that attempts to limit women to prescribed roles. Grosz writes,

> Patriarchal oppression [...] justifies itself, at least in part, by connecting women much more closely than men to the body and, through this identification, restricting women's social and economic roles to (pseudo) biological terms. Relying on essentialism, naturalism, and biologism, misogynist thought confines women to the biological requirements of reproduction on the assumption that because of particular biological, physiological, and endocrinological transformations, women are somehow *more* biological, *more* corporeal, and *more* natural than men.[76]

The antagonist of season two is not only Frost; more broadly conceived, it is the Arena Club where "women aren't allowed."[77] Described as having both a "hidden door" and "secret area," the setting of the Arena Club highlights its political function as the meeting place of the Council of Nine.[78] The Club and Council are steeped in the tradition of the "boys' network," where men are afforded the power to change the world; those that gather there are the "men that keep the world spinning."[79] Both Frost and Carter find themselves at odds with the Arena Club and its politics. However, where Frost is able to take control of the Club by force, after literally consuming half of the male board members with Zero Matter, Carter's methods are more subversive. In "Better Angels," Stark helps Carter gain access to the Club by bringing his bevy of women to the site. When Arena Club host Torrance calls out, "Code Pink," signaling the presence of the women and requesting reinforcement to remove them, he identifies the threat that women represent to the patriarchy more generally.

Not surprisingly, the characters learn that the S.S.R. is colluding with the Arena Club, illustrating a unified front against gender equality. As the aptly named Vernon Masters (Kurtwood Smith), a member of the War Department working with the Council, grooms his protégé Thompson for a prominent position within the "club," he capitalizes on Thompson's fears about Carter, who is "quite the independent thinker," and his own loss of control.[80] Masters tells him, "This Carter woman is disobeying your direct orders. Now, if you want to impress the people in this room, climb the only ladder that counts, you can't let a female subordinate make an ass out of you like this."[81] His plans involve "destroy[ing] the very idea of her," and he asks Thompson to "Discredit, disgrace, and subdue her," making her work "invalid."[82] Where the end of the era of Rosie the Riveter is announced in the series' pilot episode, the patriarchy appears determined to counter the emerging and evolving feminist movements by the end of its second season. Both Frost and Carter foretell changes to the old order. When Frost tells the remaining members of the Council, "This is about power…. The kind of power that could bring the world to its knees," she highlights a threat to the patriarchy, particularly as she stands before the now-seated remaining Council members.[83] When Masters warns, "a tidal wave is coming," threatening the dangers to Carter and her S.S.R. colleagues of being branded Communists, he also suggests the changing tide of gender politics, the second wave of feminism, another "rising tide."[84]

"Hollywood Ending": Agent Carter's Last Act

In "The Edge of Mystery," Frost tells Carter, "Such a pity that two accomplished women should be standing on opposite sides," and Carter replies, "Yes, you're such a staunch defender of the sisterhood," highlighting the similarity and fundamental difference between the two women and their causes.[85] Where Frost is "led by her own innate need for power," Carter continues the work that is fundamental to the S.S.R., and later S.H.I.E.L.D.'s vision, protecting the home front. Ultimately, the episode "Hollywood Ending" offers an ambiguous conclusion to season two and the series, reintroducing rather than resolving questions about Carter's place within Hollywood and the MCU. The final confrontation with Frost is set in Stark Pictures' 180-acre studio lot, against an artificial backdrop. The depiction of a "fissure" between worlds extends beyond the immediacy of Zero Matter to indicate what is at work in the series. The "rising tide" is figured into this landscape, and the two women are both struggling to harness and contain the power that is unleashed.

It is obvious that "Hollywood Ending," despite the suggestion of finality in the episode title, was not meant to be the series'—and character's—last act. At the end of the series, Carter appears to have been given "one compelling reason to stay" in L.A. rather than returning home to New York City, and, at the episode's end, she and Sousa are locked in a "Hollywood kiss" (initiated by Carter) with Doris Day's "Oh, but I Do," the final song on her *Hooray for Hollywood* (1958) album, playing.[86] Yet a final scene resists closure: Thompson, about to return to New York City, is shot by an anonymous man as Day's song continues. Frost's comment that Agent Carter is not "cut out for Hollywood" is prescient for the series. Currently, *Agent Carter*, unlike the other Marvel properties, is not available for streaming on Netflix or Hulu. Despite Agent Carter's struggle to remain visible, the politics of the MCU direct the future of the series.

Season two debates about women's visible and invisible roles within society—from science to Hollywood—extend beyond the limits of television narrative, particularly the miniseries format that *Agent Carter* follows. Although the cancellation of *Agent Carter* tells one story, the central roles that executive producers Tara Butters and Michele Fazekas, writers Sue Chung and Lindsey Allen, and director Jennifer Getzinger play in the series' second season tell another, signaling changing ideas within Hollywood and the comics industry. Jowett writes,

> The increasing number of real women working in science, coupled with feminist challenges to its historical construction, have undoubtedly affected representations of women scientists on television, though these remain limited to some extent by the constraints of the popular (especially romance) and of generic conventions (action, science fiction, horror).[87]

Agent Carter, the character and series, goes some way in "reshaping science," serving as a foundation not only for S.H.I.E.L.D. but for women like *Marvel's Agents of S.H.I.E.L.D.*'s computer hacker and agent Skye/Daisy Johnson (Chloe Bennett) and the scientific division's Jemma Simmons (Elizabeth

Henstridge).[88] Despite its premature ending, *Agent Carter* introduces a new beginning for the MCU with a legacy that extends beyond the printed page to inform and shape the MCU on the small screen.

Notes

1. *Captain America: The First Avenger*, directed by Joe Johnston (2011; Burbank: Buena Vista Home Entertainment, 2015), Blu-ray; *Captain America: The Winter Soldier*, directed by Anthony Russo and Joe Russo (2014; Burbank: Walt Disney Studios Home Entertainment, 2014), DVD.

2. Christopher Markus and Stephen McFeely (creators), *Agent Carter* (ABC: 2015–2016).

3. *Agent Carter* executive producer Tara Butters explained to *Cinema Blend*, "I think we've changed the look of her a bit obviously.... We've made her an actress, which is very Hedy Lamarr. She was a '40s siren actress who was also a scientific genius, so that's part of what we're mining with this character." Marisa Lascala, "Who Is Whitney Frost on 'Agent Carter'? Marvel Comics Fans Know Her as Madame Masque," *Bustle*, January 19, 2015.

4. Sue Chung, "Smoke & Mirrors," *Agent Carter*, season 2, episode 4, directed by David Platt, aired February 2, 2016, on ABC.

5. Trina Robbins, "The Great Women Superheroes," in *The Superhero Reader*, eds. Charles Hatfield, Jeet Heer, and Kent Worcester (Jackson: University Press of Mississippi, 2013), 54.

6. Lindsey Allen, "The Atomic Job," *Agent Carter*, season 2, episode 5, directed by Craig Zisk, aired February 9, 2016, on ABC.

7. "The Iron Ceiling" is the fifth episode of season 1, which features Dottie Underwood's backstory and connection to the Marvel Black Widow character. Jose Molina, "The Iron Ceiling," *Agent Carter*, season 1, episode 5, directed by Peter Leto, aired February 3, 2015, on ABC.

8. Stan Lee, *Tales of Suspense* #75 (New York: Marvel Comics, 1966). *Captain America* #1 (1941) introduces a female agent X-13 who assists in Operation Rebirth and a female FBI agent Betty Ross who falls in love with Captain America. In *Captain America* #66 (1947), the renamed Betsy Ross appears as Captain America's sidekick Golden Girl. Decades later, Lieutenant Cynthia Glass is introduced in *The Adventures of Captain America* #1 (1991) as another variation on the character who played a role in Captain America's genesis as superhero. The MCU's Peggy Carter appears to be an amalgam of these earlier characters.

9. Ibid.
10. Stan Lee, *Tales of Suspense* #77 (New York: Marvel Comics, 1966).
11. Robbins, "The Great Women Superheroes," 54.
12. Ibid.
13. Ibid.
14. Originally, Peggy Carter's "double" is her sister; however, the comics attempt to rectify the time lapse by rewriting the character as Carter's niece.
15. The silver age of comics follows the golden age of comics (1938–1950), which introduced superheroes such as Superman (1938) and Captain America (1941). The Silver Age precedes the Bronze Age (1970–1985) and Modern Age (1985–present).
16. Betty Friedan, *The Feminine Mystique* (New York: Norton, 1997), 57.
17. Ibid., 18.
18. Christopher Markus and Stephen McFeely, "Now Is Not the End," *Agent Carter*, season 1, episode 1, directed by Louis D'Esposito, aired on January 6, 2015, on ABC.
19. Eric Pearson, "Bridge and Tunnel," *Agent Carter*, season 1, episode 2, directed by Joe Russo, aired on January 6, 2015, on ABC.
20. Ibid.
21. Ibid.
22. Ibid.
23. Ibid.

24. Brant Englestein, "The Lady in the Lake," *Agent Carter*, season 2, episode 1, directed by Lawrence Trilling, aired on January 19, 2016, on ABC.
25. *Ibid.*
26. *Ibid.*
27. *Ibid.*
28. Jose Molina, "Better Angels," *Agent Carter*, season 2, episode 3, directed by David Platt, aired on January 26, 2016.
29. *Ibid.*
30. *Ibid.*
31. Eric Pearson and Lindsey Allen, "A View in the Dark," *Agent Carter*, season 2, episode 2, directed by Lawrence Trilling, aired on January 19, 2016, on ABC.
32. Sue Chung and Eric Pearson, "Life of the Party," *Agent Carter*, season 2, episode 6, directed by Craig Zisk, aired on February 16, 2016, on ABC.
33. Elizabeth Grosz, *Volatile Bodies: Toward a Corporeal Feminism* (Bloomington: Indiana University Press, 1994), viii.
34. *Ibid.*, xi.
35. Allen, "The Atomic Job."
36. Brandon Easton, "Monsters," *Agent Carter*, season 2, episode 7, directed by Metin Hüseyin, aired on February 16, 2016, on ABC.
37. Easton, "Monsters."
38. Pearson and Allen, "A View in the Dark."
39. *Ibid.*
40. Ruth Watts, *Women in Science: A Social and Cultural History* (London: Routledge, 2007), 1.
41. *Ibid.*, 32.
42. Grosz, *Volatile Bodies*, 4.
43. Lorna Jowett, "Lab Coats and Lipstick: Smart Women Reshape Science on Television," *Geek Chic: Smart Women in Popular Culture*, ed. Sherrie A. Innes (New York: Palgrave, 2007), 31–32.
44. Watts, *Women in Science*, 1.
45. *Ibid.*
46. Molina, "Better Angels."
47. *Ibid.*
48. Executive producers Tara Butters, Michele Fazekas, and Chris Dingess said, "Inspired by Hollywood icons like Hedy Lamarr and Lauren Bacall, we knew we needed an actor who was classically glamorous and fiercely intelligent. Wynn is both, and we're thrilled to watch her bring this formidable character to life." Natalie Abrams, "Marvel's Agent Carter," *Entertainment Weekly*, October 9, 2015.
49. Molina, "Better Angels."
50. *Ibid.*
51. Like Lamarr, Frost is credited with being the studio's "top earner" by 1938. Chung, "Smoke & Mirrors."
52. Molina, "Better Angels."
53. Julia Round, "Fragmented Identity: The Superhero Condition," *International Journal of Comic Art* 7, no. 2 (2005): 365–366.
54. Lisa Gotto, "Fantastic Views: Superheroes, Visual Perception, and Digital Perspective," in *Superhero Synergies: Comic Book Characters Go Digital*, ed. James N. Gilmore and Matthias Stork (Lanham, MD: Rowman & Littlefield, 2014), 42–43.
55. Archie Goodwin, *The Invincible Iron Man* #8 (New York: Marvel Comics, 1968).
56. Archie Goodwin and Gene Colan, *The Invincible Iron Man* #1 (New York: Marvel Comics, 1968).
57. *Ibid.*
58. *Ibid.*
59. *Ibid.* Grosz, *Volatile Bodies*, 14.
60. Archie Goodwin, *The Invincible Iron Man* #17 (New York: Marvel Comics, 1969).
61. *Ibid.*

62. Chung, "Smoke & Mirrors."
63. *Ibid.*
64. *Ibid.*
65. *Ibid.*
66. *Ibid.*
67. *Ibid.*
68. Karin E. Westman, "Beauty and the Geek: Changing Gender Stereotypes on the Gilmore Girls," *Geek Chic: Smart Women in Popular Culture*, ed. Sherrie A. Inness (New York: Palgrave, 2007), 12.
69. Chung, "Smoke & Mirrors."
70. *Ibid.*
71. *Ibid.*
72. *Ibid.*
73. *Ibid.*
74. Friedan, *The Feminine Mystique*, 8.
75. Watts, *Women in Science*, 1.
76. Grosz, *Volatile Bodies*, 14.
77. Molina, "Better Angels."
78. Chung, "Smoke & Mirrors."
79. Chung and Pearson, "Life of the Party."
80. Chung, "Smoke & Mirrors."
81. Chung and Pearson, "Life of the Party."
82. *Ibid.*
83. *Ibid.*
84. Chung, "Smoke & Mirrors."
85. Brant Englestein, "The Edge of Mystery," *Agent Carter*, season 2, episode 8, directed by Metin Hüseyin, aired on February 23, 2016, on ABC.
86. Chris Dingess, "Hollywood Ending," *Agent Carter*, season 2, episode 10, directed by Jennifer Getzinger, aired on March 1, 2016, on ABC.
87. Jowett, "Lab Coats and Lipstick," 44.
88. *Ibid.*

Works Cited

Abrams, Natalie. "Marvel's Agent Carter." *Entertainment Weekly*, October 9, 2015. http://www.ew.com/article/2015/10/09/agent-carter-whitney-frost-season-2-spoilers.

Allen, Lindsey. "The Atomic Job." *Agent Carter*, season 2, episode 4. Directed by Craig Zisk. Aired February 9, 2016, on ABC.

Captain America: The First Avenger. Directed by Joe Johnston. 2011. Burbank: Buena Vista Home Entertainment, 2015. BluRay.

Captain America: The Winter Soldier. Directed by Anthony Russo and Joe Russo. 2014. Burbank: Walt Disney Studios Home Entertainment, 2014. DVD.

Chung, Sue. "Smoke & Mirrors." *Agent Carter*, season 2, episode 4. Directed by David Platt. Aired February 2, 2016, on ABC.

Chung, Sue, and Eric Pearson. "Life of the Party." *Agent Carter*, season 2, episode 6. Directed by Craig Zisk. Aired on February 16, 2016, on ABC.

Dingess, Chris. "Hollywood Ending." *Agent Carter*, season 2, episode 10. Directed by Jennifer Getzinger. Aired on March 1, 2016, on ABC.

———. "A Little Song and Dance." *Agent Carter*, season 2, episode 9. Directed by Jennifer Getzinger. Aired on February 23, 2016, on ABC.

Easton, Brandon. "Monsters." *Agent Carter*, season 2, episode 7. Directed by Metin Hüseyin. Aired on February 16, 2016, on ABC.

Englestein, Brant. "The Edge of Mystery." *Agent Carter*, season 2, episode 8. Directed by Metin Hüseyin. Aired on February 23, 2016, on ABC.

———. "The Lady in the Lake." *Agent Carter*, season 2, episode 1. Directed by Lawrence Trilling. Aired on January 19, 2016, on ABC.

Goodwin, Archie. *The Invincible Iron Man* #8. New York: Marvel Comics, 1968.
_____. *The Invincible Iron Man* #17. New York: Marvel Comics, 1969.
Goodwin, Archie, and Gene Colan. *The Invincible Iron Man* #1. New York: Marvel Comics, 1968.
Gotto, Lisa. "Fantastic Views: Superheroes, Visual Perception, and Digital Perspective." In *Superhero Synergies: Comic Book Characters Go Digital*, edited by James N. Gilmore and Matthias Stork, 41–56. Lanham, MD: Rowman & Littlefield, 2014.
Grosz, Elizabeth. *Volatile Bodies: Toward a Corporeal Feminism*. Bloomington: Indiana University Press, 1994.
Jowett, Lorna. "Lab Coats and Lipstick: Smart Women Reshape Science on Television." In *Geek Chic: Smart Women in Popular Culture*, edited by Sherrie A. Innes, 31–48. New York: Palgrave, 2007.
Lascala, Marisa. "Who Is Whitney Frost on 'Agent Carter'? Marvel Comics Fans Know Her as Madame Masque." *Bustle*, January 19, 2015. http://www.bustle.com/articles/136114-who-is-whitney-frost-on-agent-carter-marvel-comics-fans-know-her-as-madame-masque.
Lee, Stan. *Tales of Suspense* #75. New York: Marvel Comics, 1966.
_____. *Tales of Suspense* #77. New York: Marvel Comics, 1966.
Markus, Christopher, and Stephen McFeely. *Agent Carter*. ABC: 2015–2016.
_____. "Now Is Not the End." *Agent Carter*, season 1, Episode 1. Directed by Louis D'Esposito. Aired on January 6, 2015, on ABC.
Molina, Jose. "Better Angels." *Agent Carter*, season 2, episode 3. Directed by David Platt. Aired on January 26, 2016, on ABC.
_____. "The Iron Ceiling." *Agent Carter*, season 1, episode 5. Directed by Peter Leto. Aired February 3, 2015, on ABC.
Pearson, Eric. "Bridge and Tunnel." *Agent Carter*, season 1, episode 2. Directed by Joe Russo. Aired on January 6, 2015, on ABC.
Pearson, Eric, and Lindsey Allen. "A View in the Dark." *Agent Carter*, season 2, episode 2. Directed by Lawrence Trilling. Aired on January 19, 2016, on ABC.
Round, Julia. "Fragmented Identity: The Superhero Condition." *International Journal of Comic Art* 7, no. 2 (2005): 358–369.
Watts, Ruth. *Women in Science: A Social and Cultural History*. London: Routledge, 2007.
Westman, Karin E. "Beauty and the Geek: Changing Gender Stereotypes on the Gilmore Girls." In *Geek Chic: Smart Women in Popular Culture*, edited by Sherrie A. Inness, 11–30. New York: Palgrave, 2007.

A Bad Case of the Feels
Emotion Versus Reason on Blindspot

Erin Nicholes

Women characters on television crime dramas over the past 50 years draw a timeline for American women's progress. The busty, badged damsels with libidos who starred as TV detectives in the 1970s reflect the women's liberation movement. The crime-fighting females of the 1980s who could juggle sex lives, sleuthing, and sorting laundry reflect the workplace equality movement.[1] Current TV crime dramas reflect a modern women's issue: underrepresentation in the sciences, technology, engineering, and math. The past two decades have seen an increasing number of women at the head of television crime labs on prime time shows such as *CSI*, *NCIS*, and most recently *Blindspot*, which first aired on NBC in 2015.[2]

While women scientists have become common on TV crime dramas, the characters have little in common with mainstream American women. *CSI*, which premiered in 2000 on CBS, was among the first shows to put a woman at the head of a crime lab with scientist Sara Sidle (Jorja Fox). A skilled scientist who is particularly sensitive to victims of domestic violence, Sara Sidle is an antisocial character who prefers corpses to live people. She rarely smiles. Her wardrobe is limited to dark slacks and white shirts under her lab coat. She wears no makeup. In contrast, *NCIS* offers an equally brilliant character in Abby Sciuto (Pauley Perrette). She is more personable and fashionable than Sara Sidle, but in a quirky, gothic sense. She typically wears black clothing, heavy eye and lip makeup, and chokers, and her inky black hair is often divided in pigtails. While Fox and Perrette's characters are among those who establish women as scientists, they also establish women scientists as unusual; they are not characters with whom average viewers can relate.

Blindspot pushes back against a characterization of women scientists as awkward, eccentric geniuses who should be heard but not seen through the character of Agent Patterson (Ashley Johnson). Agent Patterson is a 20-something FBI scientist with girl-next-door looks and exceptional smarts. She has a polished appearance; her shoulder-length blonde hair is smooth, her lip-gloss is shiny, and her mascara is barely there. Cardigans and collared shirts are her fashion staples, and she often leaves her lab coat open to reveal her preppy style. She smiles often, speaks with enthusiasm about fingerprints and DNA, and is eager to please her bosses. She analyzes evidence by day, and goes out for drinks with the girls at night. Through this accessible, everyday-woman character, *Blindspot* creates a new role model for women in STEM.

Yet, while *Blindspot* breaks down some gender barriers in STEM and calls attention to difficulties women face in STEM workplaces, the show reinforces other stereotypes about women and emotion. Agent Patterson, whose first name is never used—not even by her friends and her boyfriend—works as hard, is as dedicated to her job, and makes as many sacrifices for the public good as her male coworkers. She consistently matches the men on her FBI team in mental and physical stamina, and ups the ante with well-placed mascara and lip gloss. Her character is a positive role model, except for one thing: she mismanages her emotions to her detriment. Smart as she is, Patterson neglects her emotions at work, fails to use reason under emotional stress, and struggles to balance her work and romantic lives. Ultimately, *Blindspot* reflects real struggles for women in male-dominated professions, who are in the difficult position of trying to break gender stereotypes and barriers while being both their authentic selves and respected professionals.[3] However, the show sends the message that physical obstacles are more easily cleared than emotional obstacles for women who want to succeed as scientists.

Agent Patterson as a Role Model

Blindspot breaks down gender barriers for women in STEM and criminal justice with characters who can match men in hand-to-hand-combat, sleuth work, and science. The first episode begins with a woman (played by Jaimie Alexander), who is later called "Jane," emerging from a bag in Times Square in New York City.[4] She is nude, frightened, lacks a memory, and is covered head-to-toe in tattoos. Despite appearing as a damsel in distress, she possesses a hidden criminal agenda and secret combat skills. She is sent to Agent Patterson's FBI team after a tattoo across her shoulders references one of the team's agents, Kurt Weller (Sullivan Stapleton), who is a rustically handsome, verbally gruff, and physically fierce crime-fighter. In addition to agents Weller and Patterson, the all-star FBI team includes a contemplative African American male agent named Edgar Reade (Rob Brown), a spirited Latina field agent who is also a computer whiz named Tasha Zapata (Audrey Esparza), and a fiercely loyal homosexual Black woman who runs the New York Office of the FBI, named Bethany Mayfair (Marianne Jean-Baptist). The capable team is confounded by Jane's tattoos until Patterson emerges from her lab in the second episode, "A Stray Howl."[5] She recognizes the body art as a set of puzzles that provide clues for preventing crimes related to government corruption.

Agent Patterson represents an encyclopedic definition of a scientist who possesses a wealth of knowledge in everything from biology to technology. Her signature genius, though, is in solving puzzles. Encryption, cryptography, ciphers, and other message-concealing methods are within her area of rich expertise. She reports to her team with breathless excitement about logic grid puzzles and geometric puzzles such as tangrams. When she combines her puzzle-solving gifts with her knowledge about computers, art, writing, and people in general, she is a powerful scientific character. For example, she can quickly decipher computer passwords and decrypt codes to stop hackers. She can explain ambiguity in the results of DNA tests by using algebra. Most importantly, where others see ink on Jane's body, Agent Patterson recognizes hidden messages. She is the key that unlocks the clues that the FBI needs to stop devastating crimes.

When Agent Patterson steps into view wearing her white lab coat in "A Stray Howl," she steps up as a pop-culture role model for women in STEM, which is sorely needed, according to research focusing on young women and TV characters. In "Criminal Justice 'Hollywood Style': How Women in Criminal Justice Professions Are Depicted in Prime Time Crime Dramas," Kimberly A. DeTardo-Bora argues that "for many college students, television is a source of knowledge, and the information presented in crime dramas can be easily misconstrued."[6] A young woman watching crime dramas in the early 2000s, such as *CSI*, for example, may perceive scientists as either white males, or quirky women with masculine qualities and poor social skills. Low recruitment and retention rates for women in STEM has been linked to a lack of role models.[7] Agent Patterson fills the void as a role model for young women interested in science.

Specifically, Agent Patterson's niche as a role model is in her physical appearance and personality traits. She is not the first woman on television to run a crime lab, but she is among few to maintain an appearance and characteristics that align with the image of mainstream American femininity. Her character sends the message that a woman can be both exceptionally smart and deeply sensitive as well as approachably attractive and widely respected. *Blindspot* plays up those character traits while playing down Agent Patterson's sexuality, strengthening her character as a role model. Dawn H. Currie, in

"Decoding Femininity: Advertisements and Their Teenage Viewers," argues that young girls are subjected to images in magazine ads that portray adult femininity as emphasizing beauty and heterosexuality: "Taken at face value, the representations in women's magazines seem to imply that we become women naturally through domestic and sexual roles."[8] In addition, other researchers have found that while there are many conceptualizations of masculinity, the conceptualization of femininity is often limited to behaviors and appearances that are submissive to, and intended to be desirable to, men.[9] Agent Patterson fits the commonly projected image of American femininity in her attractiveness and her heterosexuality, and in her submissiveness to men. It may seem counterintuitive that someone who plays into a stereotype could be breaking gender barriers at the same time. Compared with the women TV scientists before her, though, Agent Patterson's character makes the argument that every girl who has science skills or excels at math is a candidate for a career in STEM, regardless of her ability to interact socially or her fashion sense.

In the world of women's fashion, Agent Patterson's style would best be described as sophisticated-preppy; her clothes play up her femininity, speak to her strong cerebellum, and downplay her sexuality. She often wears subtly patterned, neutral-toned sweaters and shift dresses over collared shirts. She leaves the top button of her shirt undone only a few times, and only once in season one is she pictured in something other than work clothes: she exercises in the FBI gym wearing a sweatshirt and sweatpants. She is attractive, but almost in protest to the Victoria's Secret version of sexy. Her professional outfits look pulled together, but they also allow her intellect to be the quality that stands out the most. For example, in "Bone May Rot," she wears a blue and white floral button-down under a royal blue cardigan while explaining the results of a tooth analysis to Agent Weller.[10] In "Swift Hardhearted Stone," she wears a navy blue cardigan over a sky-blue button-down shirt and striped trousers as she fires a gun at members of a crime family who are trying to abduct a little girl.[11] Her preppy appearance is in sharp contrast to the women detectives in 1980s crime dramas whose flowing hair and loosely secured cleavage took center stage during shootouts and chases. Agent Patterson's body is covered by high necklines and low hemlines. For most of season one, she is in a committed heterosexual relationship with another scientist, but their love scenes are limited to kisses. Agent Patterson's character seems to strategically divert attention away from female sexuality, and towards other characteristics associated with femininity.

Specifically, *Blindspot*, emphasizes Agent Patterson's sensitivity, compassion, and nurturing. She appears approachable and endearing from the beginning, and her dialogue is peppered with lines that ensure her coworkers are not put off by her smarts. The acknowledgment that her intelligence might be intimidating to others serves as evidence that she is more socially aware than the women TV scientists before her. In "Eight Slim Grins" she expresses compassion and sincerity when Jane walks into her lab, brokenhearted that she has not been allowed to go out on a call regarding one of her tattoos with the team. She tries to relate Jane's situation to a tangram, which is a geometric puzzle: "This team has been one shape for a very long time, and you're a new piece, and we're just trying to find out how you fit into all this," she says comfortingly, lightly touching Jane's arm, "We're going to find our new shape; it's just going to take a second."[12]

Later, Agent Patterson's character displays nurturing behaviors. She is presented as maternal in "Swift Hardhearted Stone," volunteering to accompany a little girl named Maya Ahmadi (Oona Laurence) to a safe house to protect her from members of a crime family: "I'll go," Agent Patterson volunteers during a debriefing with fellow agents. "Why do you want to go?" Agent Mayweather replies skeptically. "I just … I like cottages," Agent Patterson stammers, and then adds softly and sincerely, "I just … I want to help Maya."[13] In that episode, she fiercely protects Maya by gunning down the men who have been sent to abduct her. Her physical closeness and contact to other characters who need comforting, her tone of voice, and her choice of words all feel distinctly nurturing and feminine.

Agent Patterson's femininity challenges the prevailing pop-culture projection of the female scientist and creates a new role model for young women, while her physical representation does the same for scientists in general, who are associated with a less-attractive image than other professions. One study of grade schoolers' drawings of scientists, veterinarians, and teachers found that "students made clear distinctions: drawing teachers as most attractive and largely female, and scientists as most often male and least attractive. Aspects of the drawings suggest that scientists do have an 'image problem' among children."[14] Agent Patterson's appearance may attempt to address that perception issue.

By expanding the image of women scientists, Agent Patterson becomes a strong role model. If scientists are perceived as being unattractive, quirky, or marginal, the career path is less appealing to young people than if the image of the scientist is broader and more colorful, some research suggests. Previous television scientists, such as Abby Sciuto and Sara Sidle, have been quirky, eccentric, disassociated from femininity, and socially awkward. It's difficult for a typical college-aged woman to see herself playing that role. Stereotypes can impact the way people envisions themselves in professional positions.[15] Agent Patterson's character, though, is someone with whom many typical twenty-somethings can relate. She cares about what both her clothes and the quality of her work say about her. She nurtures lab results and a budding romantic relationship. She solves puzzles by day, and goes out for drinks with the girls at night. In "Persecute Envoys," Agent Patterson joins Jane and Agent Zapata at a bar for shots and small talk.[16] When she gets a text-message from her ex-boyfriend, with whom she has recently parted ways, she becomes sad. Zapata teasingly tells her: "Don't be the sad girl at the bar looking at her phone," and gesturing to the bartender she adds, "another round."[17] The scene would likely be recognizable to many women viewers in their twenties.

While Agent Patterson pushes back against stereotypes about women in STEM, she plays into persistent stereotypes about women in criminal justice, particularly emotional stereotypes. Despite the advancements of women cops on TV, many still struggle to balance their emotional needs with the demands of their jobs, according to DeTardo-Bora. Agent Patterson breaks the mold for a woman scientist, but fits the mold for a woman detective. As DeTardo-Bora writes, "stereotypical images of women as subordinate, nurturing, affectionate, and sexually attractive still prevail. However, compared to their male counterparts, female characters were equally assertive, self-confident, and competitive."[18] Patterson is assertive, confident, and competitive in her lab, but she also displays the feminine qualities described above, in particular subordination. She speaks with youthful energy and emotional investment with regard to science: "The human tooth is a gold mine of information," she says with enthusiasm and a smile in "A Stray Howl."[19] Yet, her scenes with her coworkers are marked by efforts on Agent Patterson's part to not make waves, to avoid alienating people with her intelligence, and to suppress her emotions. She is especially submissive when it comes to men. For example, in "Cede Your Soul," Agent Patterson confronts Agent Weller about a tattoo on Jane's body that matches an FBI case file.[20] He dismisses and suppresses her concerns, and she submits. This fits right into stereotypes about women as subordinates.

Agent Patterson and Emotion

Agent Patterson and other women on *Blindspot* mismanage their emotions and reinforce harmful stereotypes described by Melissa M. Sloan, who argues that American women's work opportunities are limited by the belief that women are more emotional than men.[21] Her research found that women tend to express more positive emotions such as happiness in the workplace, while men express more negative emotions such as anger.[22] That holds true on *Blindspot*, where women's mismanagement of emotions is primarily displayed through suppression and denial of negative emotions such as fear, anger, anxiety, grief, and shame. The female characters either try to ignore their emotions, or are completely incapacitated by them. The tattooed main character, Jane, tries to fight her way through her fear by helping the FBI follow her tattoos, but ultimately vacillates between bravely taking down bad guys, and crumpling up to cry in corners. With the exception of her interactions with suspects, Agent Patterson rarely utters an assertive word at work, even when her male supervisor is barking at her. Moreover, halfway through the first season, her mismanagement of emotion puts her in grave danger. She allows her love life and her professional life to intertwine, and nearly loses her life. Agent Patterson's subordinate position as well as her emotional and romantic issues weaken her position as a role model.

Agent Patterson is most strikingly submissive to Agent Weller. Almost as quickly as Agent Patterson establishes herself as a dominant scientist, she steps into the role of submissive woman. Agent Weller is terse and unappreciative when giving Agent Patterson directives and receiving scientific reports. In "A Stray Howl," Agent Patterson explains to Weller and other agents, with excitement, that she has found a clue hidden in a cipher in one of Jane's tattoos. Weller expresses impatience, and says sarcastically, "OK, just pretend that we're not you."[23] Rather than standing up to him, she continues to maintain a cheerful disposition, allows him to interrupt her, and diverts her gaze rather than looking him in the eyes. She matches Sloan's description of a woman who is more likely to emphasize happiness than anger at work: "As women are often in lower status positions in the workplace than men, they tend to be subject to job conditions that necessitate different types of emotion management (that is, the control of their emotional expressions)."[24] In only two instances in season one does Agent Patterson express aggression: once to a teenage girl who is a computer hacker, and then to a male crime suspect who is in FBI custody. Both of those people became the subject of her ire after criticizing her knowledge as a scientist.

Agent Weller is a gruff character, and he speaks to Agent Patterson and a young male agent in a similar manner. However, the male agent meets him with more resistance. In "A Stray Howl," Agent Reade challenges Weller's decision to allow Jane to accompany the FBI team on the investigation. "Blindly following her tattoos is reckless," challenges Reade, who is a stern critic of the decision to let Jane participate in her tattoo investigation.[25] "I don't think you recognize how important she is," Weller returns, more mildly than before.[26] "It's a little early to make that call, don't you think," Reade fires back.[27] Weller replies gently and with restraint, "No, the most important thing to do is stop [the criminal], so, can you go join Patterson and find me a lead? Thank you."[28] When the men on the show stand up to Agent Weller, they weaken his dominant position and his posturing. Yet, he typically tells Patterson what to do, rather than asking her the way he does with Agent Reade.

A young woman considering a STEM career could see the relationship between agents Weller and Patterson as evidence supporting a harmful stereotype that STEM work environments are unfriendly to women. The idea is rooted in fact; according to one study, nearly half of women who leave STEM jobs leave their careers because of workplace hostility: "condescension and belittlement, long hours and unclear work objectives were common reasons for leaving."[29] The study, which surveyed 3,700 women with degrees from 230 different universities, shows that a significant number of women interested in STEM careers never enter the field because of the perception that workplaces are "inflexible and unsupportive of women."[30] Additionally, hiring practices, funding, and journal reviewing in STEM all discriminate against women. Science journals are less likely to publish work by women scientists whose first names sound feminine, which *Blindspot* may acknowledge by never giving Agent Patterson a first name.[31] The interaction between Agent Patterson and Weller draws attention to STEM work environments as being difficult for women.

Blindspot also presents Agent Patterson as someone who can't seem to strike a balance between her romantic life and work, further reinforcing the notion that STEM workplaces are unfriendly to women. Women scientists often feel they have to choose between relationships and work, and Agent Patterson's character plays out that struggle on screen. She has a boyfriend, David (Joe Dinicol), who is also a scientist. In the middle of season one, in the episode "Sent on Tour," their relationship reaches a crossroads. He suggests they move in together, saying, "I should have my own key. I sleep here every night; we basically already live together; shouldn't we make it official?"[32] She becomes uncomfortable and asks for space to think it over. Instead of backing off, David attempts to win her over by becoming involved with solving a puzzle tattoo that she brought home from work, but didn't intend to share with him. He tells her, "Sometimes you just have to take a leap," but she responds by saying, "I'm just not built that way."[33] Agent Patterson resists his help, but he insists, and follows the tattoo clues to the Brooklyn Historical Society. He shares what he has learned with Agent Patterson, who discovers a code hidden inside of a book at the society. They collaborate and Agent Patterson cracks the code, revealing concealed communication between Russian spies. In her victorious state, she accepts David's offer to move in and they kiss. Seconds later, they are caught in the Brooklyn Historical Society by Agent Mayfair. David is taken into custody and Agent Patterson is nearly fired for allowing a civilian to see classified photos. When he is released, she breaks up with him, saying, "I can't do this…. This job, I love this job, and it takes all of me and I can't be…"[34] David interjects, "Happy?" and Patterson replies, "Distracted."[35] Her conflict sends the message that it isn't possible for women to have both relationships and careers as scientists.

Agent Patterson fails to demonstrate sound management of her emotions when she allows David to become involved in her work. She explicitly asks for more time to weigh the pros and cons of moving in together: "I would like to talk about this later," she says in her apartment.³⁶ She draws a firm boundary and tells him not to get involved with her work: "I'm serious David, you have to stop," she says during a phone conversation from work, after he calls her from the Brooklyn Historical Society.³⁷ She also tells him that she would rather solve the puzzle in her lab, where she has high-tech software that could help speed things up. Despite her sound reasoning, Agent Patterson allows him to help with puzzle, gets caught up in the emotion of solving it, and then decides they should move in together after all. The emotional decision to allow David to help her with the puzzle contradicts Agent Patterson's reason, and reinforces the notion that even the smartest women will submit to emotional pressure. David's interference in the case has another problematic implication for women in STEM, who struggle to receive credit for their work. Instead of receiving accolades for solving the case, Agent Patterson finds herself at the center of a debacle because of an emotional decision that she made to let David help, even though she didn't need anyone's assistance.

In the episodes that follow, Agent Patterson fails to balance emotion with reason in her response to a tragedy, further weakening her position as a potential role model for women in STEM. After breaking up with her boyfriend, Agent Patterson stays in contact with him through text messages. Two episodes later, in "Authentic Flirt," David hides a message for her by rearranging the letters in a café sign. She sees the message, and they meet. He wants to get back together, but she reminds him that she has "these obligations."³⁸ He continues to try to win her over by returning to the Brooklyn Historical Society for more clues. He witnesses a Russian spy putting another code into a book, follows her, and is shot to death. Throughout the next several episodes, Agent Patterson's coworkers urge her to take time off; Agent Mayfair tells her, "I've been where you are, and I dealt with it in the same way. It worked, for a while. The longer you run from this, the more it will hurt when it catches you. And trust me. It will catch you."³⁹ And it does, several episodes later in "Many Telepathic Lookouts."⁴⁰ Agent Patterson discovers a scavenger hunt that David left for her before he died. She conjures him up in her imagination, and they embark on the scavenger hunt together. It leads her to an antique store where she is abducted by a paranoid man. She ends up escaping and runs through the woods barefoot before Agent Weller rescues her. At the end of the episode, the imaginary David encourages her to find someone new, suggesting she consider dating the FBI psychiatrist: "It's almost like I'm the manifestation of your subconscious," he tells her.⁴¹ The episode is marked by bizarre and reckless behavior by Agent Patterson that is apparently the result of her not dealing with David's death proactively. However, she expresses an unwillingness to take time off because she was needed at work. The episode again reinforces the notion that there isn't room in STEM careers for women to meet both their emotional needs and the demands of the job.

Agent Patterson's responses to her boyfriend and his death also reinforce outdated notions that women think with their feelings, not their heads. *Blindspot* suggests that even smart, driven women cannot overpower the need for love and affection, and will put reason aside and make emotional decisions when under pressure. In contrast, the show's men manage to maintain emotional distance from their work even though they face the same kinds of situations. That difference is actually a cornerstone of *Blindspot*'s plot. In the first episode, Agent Weller suspects that Jane is actually his childhood friend who was abducted when he was 10, and for whom he has been searching his whole life. In "A Stray Howl," Agent Patterson confirms Jane's identity as the missing girl, Taylor Shaw, with a series of DNA tests. However, in "Eight Slim Grins," Agent Patterson presents new evidence from a test on Jane's tooth enamel that reveals she was born in sub-Saharan Africa, which contradicts the DNA evidence that she is Taylor Shaw. Weller refuses to acknowledge the contradiction. When he is confronted by his boss, Agent Mayfair, he denies and dismisses the contradiction and his emotional attachment to the situation and instead tries to apply logic, "The DNA Match was 99.9 percent," he argues boldly and gruffly, "the law treats DNA as ironclad, so why don't we? [...] This has nothing to do with what I want; her DNA is Taylor's DNA—end of story."[42] The differences between his and Agent Patterson's responses to emotional situations give power to stereotypes that men and women think differently.

There may be a reality behind Agent Patterson's difficulty in managing her emotions as a woman scientist. Rhoton suggests that women in real-world STEM careers are pressured to disassociate with femininity and adopt masculine qualities in order to survive the workplace: "Some women who adopt this practice do so as a way of coping with a male-dominated climate, facilitating their acceptance into the culture. Others do so simply because they believe that it is the appropriate professional behavior."[43] A woman scientist like Agent Patterson who retains feminine qualities, such as physical attractiveness and social-emotional connection might actually be ostracized not only by men in the field, but by other woman scientists. Rhoton interviewed women in STEM positions for the study, and found that the women distanced themselves from other women and from qualities deemed feminine as part of workplace culture. The women reported that they preferred the company of male friends, for example, and described other women as overly emotional.[44] Other research suggests women may feel cultural pressure to act more masculine because of the work demands of science itself—methodical, unemotional, competitive, assertive behaviors are deemed masculine.[45] However, the pressure to draw a clear line between being a woman and being a scientist causes divisions amongst women, specifically those who want to retain, or even bring, feminine qualities to the job.[46]

The show reflects those confusing tensions for female scientists, or for those aspiring to be female scientists, who want to be seen as both capable and feminine. Sloan's research about controlling anger and happiness at work suggests that women in powerful positions are expected to express themselves in a manner most consistent with male emotional style—including expressing anger and aggression when appropriate.[47] Patterson does not express herself according to "male emotional style"; although she is in a position of power as an FBI agent and a scientist who provides the team with necessary information, she does not assert herself through anger or aggression. Meanwhile, her attempts to suppress other, feminine modes of emotional expression fall short. Moreover, *Blindspot* also reinforces negative stereotypes about women by contrasting Patterson with men, such as Agent Weller, who express few feelings even in intensely emotional situations.

Conclusion

Agent Patterson is a strong role model for women in STEM because she is both feminine in appearance and characteristics, and maintains her genius. She brings both bold brainpower and subtle beauty to a world where women who want to succeed are often forced to choose between being feminine and being scientists. Agent Patterson is sociable, approachable, and comfortable in her own skin, which happens to be typically feminine. She can solve puzzles, analyze fingerprints, and interpret computer codes—and look good doing it. Research shows that men, women, and even children do not associate the image of a scientist with someone like Agent Patterson.[48] *Blindspot* attempts to reconcile the images of a typical scientist and a typical woman in a way that could appeal to a college-age woman considering a career in STEM. In that way, *Blindspot* breaks down gender barriers for women.

However, Agent Patterson's position as a role model is weakened by her mismanagement of emotion. She fails to manage her emotions because she tries to pretend they don't exist at work while also making questionable choices in emotional situations. She claims that her job doesn't leave enough flexibility in her life for a relationship. While some of these qualities could be attributed to any twenty-something woman, or any twenty-something in general, they are of particular sensitivity when it comes to Agent Patterson as a role model for women in STEM. *Blindspot* recognizes issues that promote mismanagement of emotion for women in STEM, such as discrimination and workplace hostility, but does little to challenge those stereotypes because it does not portray a lab as a safe workplace for a woman. Additionally, Agent

Patterson gives power to archaic stereotypes of women as weaker, less intellectually capable, and less emotionally stable than men. Alas, *Blindspot*'s Agent Patterson would be a stronger role model for women in STEM if she managed her feelings as effectively as she manages her lab.

NOTES

1. Tsilia Romm, "The Stereotype of the Female Detective Hero on Television: A Ten Year Perspective," *Studies in Popular Culture* 9, no. 1 (1986): 94–95.
2. Anthony Zuiker (creator), *CSI: Crime Scene Investigation* (CBS: 2000–2015); Donald P. Bellisario and Don McGill (creators), *NCIS* (CBS: 2003–present); Martin Gero (creator), *Blindspot* (NBC: 2015–present).
3. Laura A. Rhoton, "Distancing as a Gendered Barrier: Understanding Women Scientists' Gender Practices," *Gender and Society* 25, no. 6 (2011).
4. Martin Gero, "Pilot," *Blindspot*, season 1, episode 1, directed by Mark Pellington, aired September 21, 2015, on NBC.
5. Martin Gero, "A Stray Howl," *Blindspot*, season 1, episode 2, directed by Mark Pellington, aired September 28, 2015, on NBC.
6. Kimberly A. DeTardo-Bora, "Criminal Justice 'Hollywood Style': How Women in Criminal Justice Professions Are Depicted in Prime-Time Crime Dramas," *Women & Criminal Justice* 19, no. 2 (2009): 166.
7. Sarah D. Herrmann et al., "The Effects of a Female Role Model on Academic Performance and Persistence of Women in STEM Courses," *Basic and Applied Social Psychology* 38, no. 5 (2016): 258.
8. Dawn H. Currie, "Decoding Femininity: Advertisements and Their Teenage Readers," *Gender and Society* 11, no. 4 (1997): 455.
9. Mimi Schippers, "Recovering the Feminine Other: Masculinity, Femininity, and Gender Hegemony," *Theory and Society* 36, no. 1 (2007).
10. Christina M. Kim, "Bone May Rot," *Blindspot*, season 1, episode 4, directed by Karen Gaviola, aired October 12, 2015, on NBC.
11. Christina M. Kim, "Swift Hardhearted Stone," *Blindspot*, season 1, episode 20, directed by Rob Seidenglanz, aired May 2, 2016, on NBC.
12. Eoghan Mahony and Martin Gero, "Eight Slim Grins," *Blindspot*, season 1, episode 3, directed by Steve Shill, aired October 25, 2016, on NBC.
13. Kim, "Swift Hardhearted Stone."
14. Susan C. Losh, Ryan Wilke, and Margareta Pop, "Some Methodological Issues with 'Draw a Scientist Tests' Among Young Children," *International Journal of Science Education* 30, no. 6 (2008): 773.
15. Sylvia C. Nassar-McMillan, Mary Wyer, Maria Oliver-Hoyo, and Jennifer Schneider, "New Tools for Examining Undergraduate Students' STEM Stereotypes: Implications for Women and Other Underrepresented Groups," *New Directions for Institutional Research* 2011, no. 152 (2011): 87.
16. Chelsey Lora, "Persecute Envoys," *Blindspot*, season 1, episode 8, directed by Marcos Siega, aired November 9, 2015, on NBC.
17. Ibid.
18. DeTardo-Bora, 153.
19. Gero, "A Stray Howl."
20. Alex Berger, "Cede Your Soul," *Blindspot*, season 1, episode 6, directed by Rob Hardy, aired October 26, 2015, on NBC.
21. Melissa M. Sloan, "Controlling Anger and Happiness at Work: An Examination of Gender Differences," *Gender, Work, and Organization* 19, no. 4 (2012): 370.
22. Ibid.
23. Gero, "A Stray Howl."
24. Sloan, "Controlling Anger and Happiness at Work," 372.
25. Gero, "A Stray Howl."

26. Ibid.
27. Ibid.
28. Ibid.
29. "Workplace Hostility Drives Women from STEM," *Women in Higher Education* 20, no. 5 (2011): 3.
30. Ibid.
31. Catherine Hill, Christianne Corbett, and Andresse St. Rose, *Why So Few? Women in Science, Technology, Engineering and Mathematics* (Washington, D.C.: AAUW, 2010), 24.
32. Chris Pozzebon, "Sent on Tour," *Blindspot*, season 1, episode 7, directed Steve Shill, aired November 2, 2015, on NBC.
33. Ibid.
34. Ibid.
35. Ibid.
36. Ibid.
37. Ibid.
38. Katherine Collins, "Authentic Flirt," *Blindspot*, season 1, episode 9, directed by David McWhirter, aired November 16, 2015, on NBC.
39. Martin Gero, "Cease Forcing Enemy," *Blindspot*, season 1, episode 11, directed by Rob Seidenglanz, aired February 29, 2016, on NBC.
40. Rachel Caris Love, "Mans Telepathic Loyal Lookouts," *Blindspot*, season 1, episode 17, directed by Jeff T. Thomas, aired April 11, 2016, on NBC.
41. Ibid.
42. Mahony and Gero, "Eight Slim Grins."
43. Rhoton, "Distancing as a Gender Barrier," 698.
44. Ibid.
45. Ibid.
46. Ibid.
47. Sloan, "Controlling Anger and Happiness at Work," 372.
48. Losh et al., "Some Methodological Issues."

Works Cited

Bellisario, Donald P., and Don McGill. *NCIS*. CBS, 2003–present.
Berger, Alex. "Cede Your Soul." *Blindspot*, season 1, episode 6. Directed by Rob Hardy. Aired October 26, 2015, on NBC.
Collins, Katherine. "Authentic Flirt." *Blindspot*, season 1, episode 9. Directed by David McWhirter. Aired November 16, 2015, on NBC.
Currie, Dawn H. "Decoding Femininity: Advertisements and Their Teenage Readers." *Gender and Society* 11, no. 4 (1997): 453–477.
DeTardo-Bora, Kimberly A. "Criminal Justice 'Hollywood Style': How Women in Criminal Justice Professions Are Depicted in Prime-Time Crime Dramas." *Women & Criminal Justice* 19, no. 2 (2009): 153–168.
Gero, Martin. *Blindspot*. NBC, 2015–present.
_____. "Cease Forcing Enemy." *Blindspot*, season 1, episode 11. Directed by Rob Seidenglanz. Aired February 29, 2016, on NBC.
_____. "Pilot." *Blindspot*, season 1, episode 1. Directed by Mark Pellington. Aired September 15, 2015, on NBC.
_____. "A Stray Howl." *Blindspot*, season 1, episode 2. Directed by Mark Pellington. Aired September 28, 2015, on NBC.
Herrmann, Sarah D., Robert Mark Adelman, Jessica E. Bodford, Oliver Graudejus, Morris A. Okun, and Virginia S.Y. Kwan. "The Effects of a Female Role Model on Academic Performance and Persistence of Women in STEM Courses." *Basic and Applied Social Psychology* 38, no. 5 (2016): 258–268.
Hill, Catherine, Christianne Corbett, and Andresse St. Rose. *Why So Few? Women in Science, Technology, Engineering and Mathematics*. Washington, D.C.: AAUW, 2010.

Kim, M. Christina. "Bones May Rot." *Blindspot*, season 1, episode 4. Directed by Karen Gaviola. Aired October 12, 2015 on NBC.
_____. "Swift Hardhearted Stone." *Blindspot*, season 1, episode 20. Directed by Rob Seidenglanz. Aired May 2, 2016, on NBC.
Lora, Chelsey. "Persecute Envoys." *Blindspot*, season 1, episode 8. Directed by Marcos Siega. Aired November 9, 2015, on NBC.
Losh, Susan C., Ryan Wilke, and Margareta Pop. "Some Methodological Issues with 'Draw a Scientist Tests' Among Young Children." *International Journal of Science Education* 30, no. 6 (2008): 773–792.
Love, Rachel Caris. "Mans Telepathic Loyal Lookouts." *Blindspot*, season 1, episode 17. Directed by Jeff T. Thomas. Aired April 11, 2016, on NBC.
Mahony, Eoghan, and Martin Gero. "Eight Slim Grins." *Blindspot*, season 1, episode 20. Directed by Steve Shill. Aired May 2, 2016, on NBC.
Nassar-McMillan, Sylvia C., Mary Wyer, Maria Oliver-Hoyo, and Jennifer Schneider. "New Tools for Examining Undergraduate Students' STEM Stereotypes: Implications for Women and Other Underrepresented Groups." *New Directions for Institutional Research* 2011, no. 152 (2011): 87–98.
Pozzebon, Chris. "Sent on Tour." *Blindspot*. season 1, episode 7. Directed by Steve Shill. Aired November 2, 2015, on NBC.
Rhoton, Laura A. "Distancing as a Gendered Barrier: Understanding Women Scientists' Gender Practices." *Gender and Society* 25, no. 6 (2011): 696–716.
Romm, Tsilia. "The Stereotype of the Female Detective Hero on Television: A Ten Year Perspective." *Studies in Popular Culture* 9, no. 1 (1986): 94–102.
Schippers, Mimi. "Recovering the Feminine Other: Masculinity, Femininity, and Gender Hegemony." *Theory and Society* 36, no. 1 (2007): 85–102.
Sloan, Melissa M. "Controlling Anger and Happiness at Work: An Examination of Gender Differences." *Gender, Work, and Organization* 19, no. 4 (2012): 370–391.
"Workplace Hostility Drives Women from STEM." *Women in Higher Education* 20, no. 5 (2011): 3.
Zuiker, Anthony. *CSI: Crime Scene Investigation*. CBS, 2000–2015.

Femininity and Forensics
Silent Witness *and the Representation of the Female Pathologist*

LAURA FOSTER *and* HELEN MCKENZIE

The forensic pathologist dissects the dead body to uncover the cause of death, and operates within a unique profession that bridges medicine, laboratory research, and detection. The role of the pathologist involves crime scene analysis, conducting post-mortems, working alongside the police, interacting with the victim's grieving relations for formal identification, examining medical history and test results, and delivering findings in court. In popular culture, the forensic pathologist is, in many ways, a contradictory signifier. In peering into the darkened recesses of the decaying body, the pathologist has come to embody social anxieties about the nature of death. At the same time, however, pathologists are scientists, representative of logic and reason; in tending to the human corpse, they mitigate our fears of the unknown and offer the reassurance found in knowledge.

In recent years, television drama has recuperated the forensic pathologist, who has emerged from the gloomy margins of the plotline to become the central protagonist. This essay focuses on the UK television series *Silent Witness* (1996–present), a forensic drama featuring, as its lead protagonists, a team of pathologists.[1] Now entering its twentieth series, BBC's *Silent Witness* has enjoyed consistently high viewing figures and has won a number of awards.[2] As Heather Nunn and Anita Biressi point out, the show "is knowing, self-reflexive, and deliberately complicated at a time when TV drama is accused [...] of crude simplicity."[3] In a society in which women make up only 14.4 percent (as of August 2015) of the STEM workforce, *Silent Witness* is also revolutionary in terms of its female lead.[4] First broadcast in 1996, *Silent Witness* was one of the earliest programs to feature a female forensic pathologist, initially Professor Sam Ryan (Amanda Burton, 1994–2004), followed by Dr. Nikki Alexander (Emilia Fox, 2004–present).

The on-screen female forensic pathologist is a development of the female detective, and made possible by earlier TV crime dramas.[5] ITV's *Prime Suspect*, for instance, features Detective Chief Inspector Jane Tennison (Helen Mirren), described by Nunn and Biressi as "an ambitious woman trying to succeed within a chauvinistic culture."[6] Indeed, Deborah Jermyn argues, "The impact of *Prime Suspect*'s evocation of gender and realism and its contribution to the "reinvention" of TV crime drama has been internationally resonant; it has become a genre that can now be carried by female leads and routinely figures explicit descriptions and images of forensics that would have been unheard of on prime-time TV in the era before."[7] *Silent Witness* is indebted to *Prime Suspect* in its construction of Professor Sam Ryan, a senior female pathologist and quasi detective.[8] Like Tennison, Ryan is a high-ranking woman working in a male-dominated profession.

As mentioned, in the UK, the gender divide within the STEM workforce is substantial; Stephanie Spurr points out that "gender stereotypes imposed by society have created both perceived and concrete barriers for women."[9] There is, however, an increasing move towards redressing this gender imbalance. At the forefront of the push to integrate women into the UK STEM workforce is WISE, a campaign to promote women in science, technology and engineering. WISE is working towards achieving the initial goal of increasing the proportion of female professionals within the STEM workforce to 30 percent.[10] There is a similar picture of gender imbalance within the broad range of pathology disciplines, including forensic pathology.[11] In 2015, the Royal College of Pathologists published, for the first time, their Medical Workforce Planning Report.[12] Within it they examine the gender divide that exists in the profession: in November 2013, the College identified 62 consultant forensic pathologists in the UK, of whom only 15 were female and 47 were male.[13] The report considers how the profession will change in the future in terms of gender; as they note, the profession is predominantly made up of an older male workforce approaching retirement and "a younger, increasingly female, workforce is being appointed."[14]

Silent Witness reflects this trend towards greater female representation in the STEM workforce. While much criticism has focused on the significance of Professor Sam Ryan in relation to gender politics, substantially less attention has been paid to Dr. Nikki Alexander, who enters *Silent Witness* in series 8, in the wake of Sam Ryan's departure.[15] In her examination of Sam, Sue Turnbull positions her within the "generic trope" of "the forensic scientist as the empathetic champion of the voiceless victim."[16] Like Sam, Nikki acts as an empathetic advocate for those who have been silenced, even in the case of predominant opposition, and both women stand as strong, successful female professionals against a male-dominated and traditionally patriarchal system. Developing her discussion, Turnbull notes that Sam offers viewers a "strong, no nonsense female lead whose short hair and brusque manner make no concessions to feminine 'niceness.'"[17] Despite their similarities, Nikki Alexander is, in many ways, constructed differently to her predecessor Sam Ryan, including, and interestingly, the feminine "niceness" she embodies. In the construction of Nikki's character, scientific rationale, professionalism, and a voice for the victim are fused with a more openly sympathetic and warm approach and, in contrast to Sam's somber suits, determinedly feminine clothing and mannerisms. In her late-twenties when she arrives in series eight (2004), Nikki offers an identifiable figure for a younger generation of female viewers.

Silent Witness consciously engages with, and undermines, stereotypes of the female scientist. In one episode, "Body of Work" (series 10, 2006), a senior female pathologist, speaking at a conference, describes the skillset needed to succeed in this line of work. According to her, pathologists must have "a monogamous commitment to our profession, attention to detail, objectivity, and good sense of smell"; pathology, she declares, is "an art as much as a science."[18] In a later conversation between Nikki and her colleague, Dr. Harry Cunningham (a key protagonist, played by Tom Ward), Harry refers to the speaker as "an old prune with no children and no friends and little obvious social life."[19] Significantly, Harry's remarks are focused on his conjectures about the private life of this female pathologist. His comment, though intended as a joke, draws attention to the popular stereotype of the older female scientist as a dour spinster, and to the representation of STEM subjects as somehow "unfeminine." In particular, his comment about her lack of children, intended as an insult, emphasizes the public scrutiny placed upon the bodies and private lives of successful women. Indeed, contemporary culture continues to judge women by whether or not they have children, suggesting that a failure to give birth indicates a want of proper femininity. For example, in September 2016, the *Sunday Times* faced criticism for publishing a list of "childless" Members of Parliament; no male politicians were included on this list.[20]

Nikki stands in opposition to the stereotype of the female pathologist as an unfeminine spinster. Resolutely feminine in her dress and demeanor, she has a social life and numerous romantic affairs alongside her successful career. *Silent Witness* provides Nikki with a backstory that serves to both accentuate her achievements and make her a sympathetic character. Viewers learn that, when Nikki was eleven, her father abandoned her and her mother, leaving them in financial straits. Similar to numerous literary and on-screen female detectives who lack family support, Nikki was effectively orphaned after the death of her mother.[21] Nikki had to struggle to overcome financial and personal issues, as well as the gender prejudice facing women in STEM subjects, making her career as a successful pathologist all the more impressive.

The show is ambivalent in its representation of the family unit: in the lives of the team and in the multiple cases they investigate, biological families are shown to be fragmented and unstable, and are frequently characterized by violence. While Nikki is deserted by her father, Harry's father is revealed to have been a domestic abuser. Even Professor Leo Dalton (William Gaminara), a central protagonist who is portrayed as a likeable figure and worthy of the viewer's respect, is not, perhaps, represented as an ideal father figure; he lives and works in London while his wife and daughter are a three-and-a-half hour drive away in Sheffield.[22] If *Silent Witness* is equivocal about the genetic family, it represents a positive version of team work; Dr. Nikki Alexander, Dr. Harry Cunningham, and Professor Leo Dalton form a pseudo-family, supporting each other both professionally and personally. Significantly, Lindsay Steenberg suggests that in forensic TV drama the relationship between colleagues is a way in which "abject horrors of murdered bodies and wound culture are mediated."[23] In *Silent Witness*, the affectionate relationships between the three protagonists provide constancy and a support network that counteracts the chaos of crime, violence, and death. This formula provides a reassuring stage upon which *Silent Witness* can explore contemporary social anxieties and, pertinently, issues of gender and misogyny.

This essay focuses on the period spanning series 8 to 15 (2004–2012), which features the core team of Leo, Harry, and Nikki. Specifically, it examines the figure of Nikki Alexander, suggesting that this construction of a woman scientist offers female viewers a likeable and identifiable role model. This period charts Nikki's professional and personal development, from her initial appointment until her establishment as a successful and high-ranking female forensic pathologist. Firstly, this essay explores the representation of Nikki's negotiation of empathy and science. It then examines the instability of forensic evidence and the divisive and implicitly gendered narratives that this evidence yields in order to explore the construction of the female pathologist in *Silent Witness*.

Empathy and Emotion

Nunn and Biressi argue that, with the figure of Sam Ryan, *Silent Witness*, "breaks new ground in the complexity of its construction of feminine subjectivity and its erosion of the boundaries between the professional and emotional."[24] This also holds true for Nikki, whose rational approach and scientific expertise are balanced with empathy for the victim and respect for the dead.

Her more openly compassionate approach is accentuated by a recurring trope that sees Nikki paired with brash and apparently unfeeling police inspectors who interpret empathy as misplaced or distracting. In the episode "Choices" (series 9, 2005), one of her first as a fully-fledged pathologist at the Lyle Centre, Nikki's empathetic approach to the discovery of the body of a homeless young woman is placed in tension with the more dismissive attitude of the police inspector.

During the course of an investigation into gang-related shootings, Nikki uncovers the body of a woman, Lisa, in a derelict building. The case is unrelated to the shootings and the male police inspector is openly frustrated by the dead "junkie" that he is now "stuck with."[25] Despite the signs that someone else was present at Lisa's death, the officer is eager to close the case in order to return to "more important work"; as he insists, "she's a smackhead, she was out of it, she just collapsed."[26] The later scene of the post-mortem stages the conflict between Nikki and the officer; her view that "every life is important" is juxtaposed with the officer's opinion that some lives "are more important than others."[27] Presented with these two value-laden judgments about the body of a woman marginalized by society, the viewer is implicitly aligned with Nikki and her more sympathetic worldview.

The cutting room is not only a metaphorical stage on which such conflicts play out, but a literal one as well. Nunn and Biressi discuss the historical connection between the dead body and popular entertainment, and point out that "*Silent Witness*' presentation of the corpse through staged scenes melds science, sensational crime, and theatricality."[28] The laboratory is overlooked by a gallery from which fellow pathologists and police officers can observe the post-mortems. Lucy Kay argues that "the autopsy room is a form of panopticon where the pathologist has the power of the gaze over the dead body but is simultaneously—and significantly as a woman—the object of the gaze of other characters and the viewers."[29] This idea of the cutting room as panopticon is particularly evident in this scene: as Nikki carries out the post-mortem on Lisa's body, her work and behavior are overseen by Leo's disciplinary gaze. Still holding a dissection knife, Nikki confronts the police officer about his overt disrespect for the body; as she does so, however, Leo interrupts her, ordering, "that is enough! Just get back to work, will you!"[30] This unusual show of dominance temporarily disrupts the established dynamics of the team. Though Leo's anger is due to grief following the sudden death of his wife and daughter, it demonstrates the potential for the workplace to be regulated by oppressive, and gendered, hierarchies of power.

In a later scene, Leo exaggerates Nikki's actions, accusing her of "running around the cutting room waving a scalpel" at the police officer and "mouthing off like some silly schoolgirl."[31] These unfair and, importantly, gendered criticisms emphasize how, as a young female pathologist in a male-dominated workplace, Nikki's professionalism is repeatedly placed under scrutiny. The viewer, positioned with Nikki, feels a sense of injustice at these remarks. When she responds that she was "challenging [the officer's] attitude" because "he has absolutely no empathy with the victim," Leo insists, "He's right! You shouldn't get emotionally involved."[32] Both Leo and the officer construct emotional involvement as something subversive and, implicitly, feminine. Although affected by the criticism, Nikki's belief in the importance of acknowledging the humanity of the victim is uncompromised. Significantly, her approach and values eventually influence the behavior of the police officer. Lisa's best friend, Emma (Alice O'Connell), also a heroin addict, is revealed to have covered up Lisa's dead body after an accidental overdose. Rather than criminalize Emma, however, the officer takes her to a rehabilitation unit. As Nikki says to him, "secretly you're glad you're giving her the chance."[33] Ultimately the episode endorses Nikki's more sympathetic approach to her work, demonstrating the value of empathy and its humanizing effect. In depicting the police officer offering this young woman another chance at life, *Silent Witness* suggests the potential for social redemption and mitigates the bleak social outlook embodied in the concurrent gang-shooting storyline.

The tension between the female pathologist's emotional response to her cases and logical reasoning, implicitly coded as masculine, is played out most overtly in the episode "Cargo" (series 10, 2006). The case centers upon the wreckage of a boat found along the Thames, which is revealed to have been illegally transporting migrant workers. Attending the scene of the crash, Nikki's eye is caught by a doll lying on the bank, signaling the presence of a child on the boat. As time passes and the search for the little girl, Ying (Kim Dang), yields nothing, everyone but Nikki gives up hope of her being found alive. When Nikki insists to the investigating detective that "there is still a chance," he responds, "You need to be realistic. We have to shift our resources."[34] Repeatedly in this episode, Nikki's insistence that they continue to search is constructed by her male colleagues as unrealistic and illogical.

Despite the grim statistics about Ying's likelihood of survival, the viewer is emphatically placed on Nikki's side in her mission to find the girl. Flashes of a child's eye recur through the episode, growing in length until the viewer is shown Ying, still alive and waiting to be found. In an effort to save Ying, Nikki is shown working through the night analyzing seaweed found on the boat. Later, as Nikki carries out a post-mortem on a person believed to have been on the boat, the team realizes that the body is infected with a deadly virus. Nikki pushes to be allowed to continue the post-mortem despite the personal risk, indicating her willingness to prioritize the life of an innocent child. In the eyes of her male colleagues, Nikki's emotional connection to the case clouds scientific rationality and represents a dangerous blurring of professional and personal boundaries. But, as the first episode closes, viewers are shown the longest picture of Ying yet: she is sitting in the dark and turning the handle of a toy music box. Constructing the search for Ying as a race against time, the viewer wills Nikki to keep fighting in the knowledge that the child can still be rescued.

Unusually for Nikki, as the case progresses she is steps outside the parameters of the legal system by unofficially interrogating a man who was arrested on suspicion of being on the boat and who claims his name is "Dexter" (Patrice Naiambana). While normally adamant that the rules of the legal and justice systems must be upheld, Nikki is here willing to compromise those principles to find the child. Nikki's conflicts with bureaucracy, in the form of the police and "Dexter's" lawyer, suggest a subtle criticism of British rules and regulations. Restricted by an unyielding system of strict stipulations, it is Nikki who repeatedly reminds those connected to the case of the six-year-old girl whose life is at stake. She successfully appeals to the lawyer for an unofficial interview with "Dexter" by asking him to imagine his own daughter in Ying's situation. Then, in an "off the record" conversation with "Dexter" at the police station, she conjures for him an image of the child being smuggled, "in crates, in the back of vans, huddled under wet tarpaulin, cold, scared, not knowing why this was happening."[35] Nikki's emotional appeal to him to consider the innocence of the lost little girl resonates enough for him to later privately admit to her his presence on the boat. In the episode's closing scene, when the search is escalated, Nikki finds the child alive. Her fusing of rationality and emotion, coupled with a willingness to fight the system, is thus ultimately endorsed and shown to have value. Across the series, the female pathologist's ability to draw upon both empathy and science is fundamental to the resolution of the investigation.

Dissident Narratives

Silent Witness explores the complexity and instability of evidence that must be read by the forensic pathologist. In each episode the pathologist is charged with piecing together the narrative behind a body. Repeatedly, however, the evidence spawns multiple interpretations and yields doubt rather than certainty. This issue of the divergent narrative of death comes to the forefront in a politicized case of sudden infant death in the episode "Paradise Lost" (series 15, 2012). The dissident voice in question is a female voice: in a courtroom scene, pathologist Helen Karamides (Pooky Quesnel) gives evidence that a baby died from natural causes, while Leo, President of the Institute of Pathologists, asserts that this is a case of shaken baby syndrome. Despite being the leading pediatric specialist, Karamides' narrative is found less convincing by the judge than the masculine narrative given by Leo. Foregrounding gender politics, Nikki compares the professional attack upon Karamides, her former mentor, to a "witch-hunt," asserting, "Ever since Helen Karamides started challenging the triad, they [the Institute of Pathologists] have been out to get her."[36] Nikki constructs here the sense of a male-dominated profession closing ranks on a woman who fails to conform to the prevailing opinion. In a later conversation with Karamides, Leo claims, "the judicial system depends on us for a consistent judgment. We can't debate our differences of opinion in open court. We have to speak with one voice."[37] In this instance at least, the "one voice" is unquestionably a male voice. Leo's belief in his duty to provide a "consistent judgment" promotes an ideology that marginalizes dissident viewpoints within the profession. Frequently, however, *Silent Witness* covertly works to unsettle the dominant, and implicitly male, "one voice," instead endorsing the contradictory narratives commonly vocalized by Nikki. In placing the act of reading evidence under scrutiny, *Silent Witness* dramatizes how social ideology influences interpretation.

In the episode "Double Dare" (series 11, 2007), in particular, scientific narratives of forensics are shown to be tied to cultural narratives of gender. The episode draws attention to the demonization of women who deviate from society's standards of femininity and foregrounds contemporary culture's latent misogyny. The case at the heart of the episode concerns a young woman, Anna Holland (Cara Horgan), who was implicated four years earlier in the death of another woman, a wife and mother of two. Seventeen-year-old Anna had "dared" her boyfriend, Drage (Nick Court), to kill the next person they saw. Drage's involvement in the brutal stabbing of Paula Colebrook (Victoria Kruger) is unambiguous, but the extent of Anna's participation is uncertain. At trial, Nikki's interpretation of the blood splatter evidence cast Anna as a bystander in the murder, in contradiction with the prosecution's narrative that she took an active role in the stabbing. Though found innocent of murder, Anna is unquestionably guilty in the eyes of the police, the media, and the public. The dissident narratives at the heart of this contentious case provide a stage on which to explore gender stereotypes.

The episode opens four years later as Anna, now living in a safe house under police protection, prepares to go abroad. However, she and her police escort are attacked as they leave the house. The car in which they flee subsequently crashes and explodes, leaving one woman (identified as Anna) dead and the other critically injured and hospitalized. The popular attitude towards Anna Holland is immediately established by the words of DI Glynn (Danny Midwinter), the investigating officer, as he welcomes Nikki to the scene: "Got a real treat for you this morning, Dr. Alexander. Fried to a crisp."[38] Nikki's professional evaluation of the body contrasts with Glynn's venomous disrespect for the corpse; interrupting Nikki's examination, he insists, "Now you listen to me. Anna Holland finally got what was coming to her[....] Roasting in hell."[39]

Interestingly, the language used by the media, the police, and the public constructs Anna Holland as a modern-day witch. Someone graffiti sprays "the witch is dead" onto Anna's mother's garage door and Jason Colebrook (Paula's bereaved husband, played by Wayne Foskett) is portrayed reading aloud a fairy tale about an evil witch to his son.[40] After Anna was found not guilty of murder in court, Colebrook had apparently declared that he would like to "cut her open with a knife and rip out her black, evil heart."[41] Colebrook's reference to her "black" heart suggests an idea of Anna as pathologically diseased. Moreover, his words draw upon imagery of the post-mortem, suggesting a desire to punish the transgressive woman through laying open her sinful body to public scrutiny. The mode of Anna's death also feeds into the construction of her as a witch: Anna has apparently been burnt alive, a punishment historically meted out to women accused of witchcraft. Importantly, *Silent Witness* subtly undermines this projection of Anna. In response to Glynn's repeated jibes at Anna's suffering, Nikki reminds him that Anna was "a free young woman with every right to live a normal life."[42] Answering another police officer's over-interested question as to whether Anna was stabbed through the heart, Harry's sarcastic response is, "Yeah, yeah, but it didn't kill her. She just woke up on the slab."[43] Here, Harry mockingly subverts society's malicious narrative representing Anna as a witch or vampire.

Throughout the case Nikki must contend with Glynn's domineering and verbally aggressive manner. When Leo announces his intention to perform Anna's post-mortem, Glynn interjects, "they just don't want you making the same mistakes, love."[44] The term "love" is employed here as an insult, intended to belittle and patronize Nikki. His hostility towards her, which stems from his belief that her interpretation of evidence let Anna "get off with murder," manifests in increasingly sexist comments designed to disempower her.[45] Nikki insists upon retaining responsibility for the case and, as she analyzes the corpse in the cutting room, her own body is simultaneously analyzed by the male gazes of Glynn, Harry, and another police detective. Overlooking Nikki in the viewing gallery, Glynn says laughingly, "She's by far the best-looking pathologist I've ever met"; he then claps Harry on the back saying, "You're a lucky guy working here."[46] This calculated bawdiness is designed to undermine Nikki's professional identity and her reading, and reduce her to a sexualized body. Moving closer to the glass screen in anticipation, Glynn declares, "Never much liked post-mortems, but I'm so looking forward to this one."[47] His words are laced with innuendo; he looks forward to seeing Anna's dead body cut open, but also, implicitly, to watching Nikki's living body. As Glynn speaks, a reflection of Nikki examining the body is caught in the glass screen; this reminder of her professionalism interrogates the male gaze and counteracts Glynn's attempt to diminish her to sexual object.[48]

The episode draws attention to the media's demonization of women who step outside expected gender parameters. Anna, already Othered by her demonstrable interest in gothic subculture (evident in her clothing and how she has decorated her bedroom), "dares" Drage to commit a violent act and, in doing so, transgresses proper models of feminine behavior. Not only does she seemingly instigate a murder, but her crimes are also rendered more heinous by the fact that the victim, as a wife and mother, conformed to conventional ideologies of gender. As Jason Colebrook will later say, "a woman stabbing a woman" is worse than a man stabbing a woman because "you'd imagine, wouldn't you, that some protective instinct would kick in!"[49] Colebrook draws on culturally ingrained stereotypes about the nature of women; Anna's criminality is accentuated by her transgression of cultural narratives of femininity.

As she did for Lisa in "Choices," Nikki stands up for a disempowered woman who has been demonized by society. In publicly defending Anna at trial four years previously, Nikki became aligned with her in the public imagination and, in turn, implicitly criminalized. Owing to her role in Anna's successful defense team, Nikki is subsequently blamed by the police for the injuries sustained by the fellow officer who was with Anna. When Nikki is shown being mobbed by hostile reporters, *Silent Witness* dramatizes the aggression of the media and its role in constructing a narrative of guilt. In the face of such intense public scrutiny, Leo covertly withdraws his support for Nikki's interpretation of the original evidence in Paula Colebrook's murder, telling her that it now seems "more questionable."[50] Glynn's aggressive behavior, the media pressure, and Leo's lack of support result in Nikki starting to doubt her own convictions; she begins to imagine an alternative narrative in which Anna is killed because she confessed to her full role in the stabbing. Despite his role in provoking doubt, Leo warns Nikki that altering her reading of the evidence "could have serious implications for your career."[51] The episode thus stages the potential professional and personal ramifications of an interpretation that diverges from popular opinion.

Ultimately, Nikki is proven correct in her reading of the case and learns to trust in her own judgment. The discovery of multiple other female murder victims leads to Drage's confession that Anna was not involved in the killing. Nikki's sympathetic chat with Anna's mother about her daughter's childhood allows Nikki to recognize a distinguishing feature of the hospital patient that identifies her as Anna. This final revelation, Nikki's discovery that the dead body is not Anna Holland, but that of the police officer protecting her, serves to further undermine and criticize Glynn's attitude: the glee he took in watching the dissection of the charred body was actually directed at his colleague.

Anna Holland's survival overturns Glynn's, and the public's, construction of Anna Holland and, in doing so, draws attention to and critiques society's tendency to demonize women.⁵² However, misogynistic attitudes are seemingly so engrained that, despite the rewriting of Anna's narrative, Glynn continues to believe implicitly in her guilt. As he says about Anna at the episode's close, "she'll get what's due."⁵³ In Glynn's opinion, Anna's words in "daring" Drage make her as culpable as if she had committed the physical act of murder.

Nikki's support for those marginalized by society frequently places her in tension with the media, the police, and with culturally constructed stereotypes. In the episode "Voids" (series 13, 2010), however, her professional readings of a cadaver and the crime scene isolate her from her colleague and friend, Harry. This episode focuses upon a complex and divisive case in which Bridget Flannery (Josephine Butler) is found dead in a pool of blood at the bottom of the stairs. Nikki, now an established expert in staircase falls, accompanies Harry to the scene out of professional interest. Significantly, Nikki and Harry read the scene, and later the body, in opposition: while Harry concludes that Bridget is the victim of a brutal attack by her husband, controversial writer Tom Flannery (John Lynch), Nikki argues that the injuries are just as likely to be the result of an accidental fall.

Harry and Nikki's competing readings of the evidence draw attention to the complexity of a narrative that explains death.⁵⁴ Nikki's interpretation is, in part, informed by her intuition at the crime scene. As she observes to a dismissive Harry, "I can't shake the utterly unscientific impression that [Flannery's] shock's for real."⁵⁵ Harry presents his version of events as the only rational, scientific, and reliable explanation and, in doing so, represents Nikki's reading as illogical, emotive, and biased.⁵⁶ By refusing to moderate her dissident interpretation of evidence to accord with that of her male colleague, Nikki lays herself open to accusations of unprofessional behavior and dishonesty. *Silent Witness*, however, positions the viewer with Nikki, drawing attention to, and criticizing, these attacks upon her professionalism. From the very moment that Nikki and Harry arrive at the crime scene, the camera follows Nikki's gaze as she observes the chaotic handling of the case, including a dog with blood on its paws and a policewoman wiping blood off her shoes. When Nikki later agrees to work with Flannery's defense team, she is seen laying down her ground rules; she is "no liar for hire," and insists that, in recording her evidence, she "won't change anything to suit. Not a word, not a comma."⁵⁷ Such moments repeatedly testify to Nikki's integrity and prioritization of the truth in her building of a narrative.

Harry's frustrations with Nikki's refusal to conform ignite when he returns to the crime scene for a final evaluation, only to find Nikki there first. He aggressively questions not only her interpretation, but also her personal motivations; as he declares, "Nikki against the world once more[....] You love this, don't you? Here you come, the knight in shining armor, bloody but unbowed. It's like a little Jane Eyre fantasy made flesh."[58] Harry reads Nikki's alignment with a male suspect as an act of selfish martyrdom, borne of an inherently contrary nature that reaps pleasure in standing against the system and popular opinion. By invoking the idea of Nikki enacting a "Jane Eyre fantasy," Harry constructs her as reveling in her position of outsider; simultaneously, his words also attempt to infantilize Nikki, reducing her to the stubborn little girl at the opening of Charlotte Brontë's 1847 novel *Jane Eyre*. Nikki, Harry implies, deliberately fails to see reason, because to do so means to relinquish her outsider status. Crucially, however, it is Harry's professional identity, not Nikki's, that is subverted in this episode. Harry is unable to accept the validity of another interpretation, or the inherent instability of evidence. Unable to control his emotions, Harry storms from the room, leaving the viewer united with Nikki, as she continues to assess the crime scene.

Significantly, the Flannery episode overtly draws attention to the frequent impossibility of providing a consistent interpretation. Unable to reconcile their differences in opinion, both Nikki and Harry are asked to present their readings of the evidence at Bridget Flannery's inquest. In response to Nikki's production of files that demonstrate her painstaking research, Harry comments, "I don't have Dr. Alexander's flair for theatre, so I've left most of my files at home."[59] As Alison Byerly points out, "Theatricality represents a false show that historically has been associated with the feminine."[60] By invoking Nikki's "flair for theatre," Harry implicitly undermines her professional judgment and casts doubt on her reliability. Ironically, he demonstrates his own theatricality to the viewer when he draws a laugh from the court audience at Nikki's expense. When Harry then fails to corroborate Nikki's memory of seeing a policewoman wiping blood from her shoes, he further challenges her version of events in front of the courtroom. For a viewer, however, who has witnessed the chaos of the crime scene alongside Nikki and knows her version to be true, Harry's words act to subtly subvert his own character. Nevertheless, Harry's success in obstructing Nikki's version in court is evident when the distressed sister of the deceased woman accuses Nikki of "twisting and distorting and showing off."[61] The masculine version of events has succeeded in rendering Nikki's interpretation of the evidence unsubstantiated and affected.

Harry expresses his frustration through numerous verbal snipes. When it is revealed that there are errors in both of their narratives, Harry is unable to admit his own failings and places the blame entirely upon Nikki. In suggesting she was "paid by the word," he attacks her professional identity and equates her with a tabloid journalist.[62] Given Nikki's refusal to change "not a word, or a comma," this accusation seems particularly unjust to the viewer.[63]

He subsequently demands, "What was it about [Flannery]? Tell me. Seriously, what was it? Did he remind you of your father?"[64] Nikki's version of events, Harry implies, is colored by unresolved emotional issues or a susceptibility to the charms of an older man, and her professional judgment is therefore inconstant and unreliable. In light of the alignment between Nikki and the viewer, these personal attacks and innuendoes serve only to emphasize her professionalism in the face of Harry's unprofessional and increasingly sexist behavior.

Although Nikki's reading of Flannery's emotions at the start of the episode is implicitly correct, the episode ends by casting doubt as to the "truth" of the case; it is left unresolved as to whether Bridget died as a result of an accident or, as is implied, a deliberate act by her stepdaughter. The lack of complete resolution to the case draws attention to the impossibility of ever truly discovering the whole truth, an issue ever faced by the pathologist. This absence of a definitive narrative places significance on the ways in which the case has been read both emotionally and professionally. While dramatizing the instability of evidence, the episode implicitly endorses Nikki over Harry, placing trust in the female pathologist and her professional integrity, and subverting gender stereotypes.

Conclusion

In *Silent Witness*, the figure of the pathologist encompasses the role of scientist, detective, and therapist. This complex representation of pathologists and the cases they investigate allows the series to examine a diverse range of contemporary issues and cultural anxieties. The pathologist, represented in *Silent Witness* as a reassuring and likeable figure, mediates the horror of violence and the threat of death. Though the series knowingly represents the gendered politics and struggles Nikki encounters, it ultimately works to empower and endorse this female pathologist.

Importantly, *Silent Witness* occupies a prominent place in the increasing move towards representing women successfully working in STEM occupations.[65] The stereotype of the female pathologist as an "old prune" is, in this series, shown to be outdated and inaccurate. Repeatedly, *Silent Witness* positions Nikki as the heroine of the narrative and, in doing so, offers viewers a professional pathologist who is highly successful, yet decisively feminine. The series continues to be progressive in terms of its diverse representation of women scientists. Series 16 (2013) saw the arrival of Clarissa Mullery (Liz Carr), the female forensic examiner who performs the laboratory testing vital to the investigations, and who also uses a wheelchair. As a particularly efficient scientist with a quiet sense of authority, she further develops

Silent Witness's inclusive approach to representing women in STEM subjects on TV.

Undoubtedly, a substantial gender divide remains in STEM professions. In her research into the experiences of female STEM professors, Colette Fagan notes that "obstacles to their advancement included deeply rooted issues of unconscious bias and gendered expectations about men and women."[66] At the same time, organizations such as Athena SWAN (established in 2005 by female academic scientists) and UKRC (UK Resource Centre for Women in Science, Engineering and Technology) have grown over the last couple of decades and offer hope for redressing this gender imbalance.[67] Significantly, the organization Women in Science in Australia draws attention to the importance of role models in the push to change gendered constructions of STEM professions; as the scientists Marguerite Evans-Galea and Michelle Gallaher point out, it is "absolutely crucial [...] for today's successful women in science to inspire the potential women in science of tomorrow[....] We must ensure that our children see women science professionals as 'the norm.'"[68] It is this essay's contention that *Silent Witness* plays a part in normalizing women scientists in the popular imagination. In its representation of Nikki Alexander, *Silent Witness* offers young women a positive female scientist with whom to identify.

NOTES

    1. Nigel McCrey (creator), *Silent Witness* (BBC: 1996–present).

    2. Each "series" consists of between four and six episodes, each divided into two parts lasting sixty minutes, allowing *Silent Witness* to have complex plots. The program has been consistently popular with audiences. In 2015, the *Mirror* reported that viewing figures had topped 6.33 million (Alistair McGeorge, "*Silent Witness* Dominates Ratings with Over 6 Million Viewers on BBC One," *Mirror*, January 14, 2015). It has also won multiple industry awards including, significantly, Best TV Drama at the European Science TV and New Media Awards in 2013.

    3. Heather Nunn and Anita Biressi, "Silent Witness: Detection, Femininity, and the Post-Mortem body," *Feminist Media Studies* 3, no. 2 (2003): 197.

    4. "Women in the UK STEM Workforce," *WISE: A Campaign to Promote Women in Science, Technology and Engineering*, September 7, 2015. WISE draws upon information published in the Office for National Statistics' Labour Force Survey April–June 2015.

    5. For a discussion of the development of the female detective, see Lucy Kay, "Frills and Thrills—Pleasurable Dissections and Responses to the Abject: Female Pathology and Anthropology in *Déjà Dead* and *Silent Witness*," *Mortality* 7, no. 2 (2002): 159–161.

    6. Lynda La Plante (creator), *Prime Suspect* (ITV: 1991–2006); Nunn and Biressi, "Silent Witness," 194. For a more detailed examination of the significance of the character of DCI Jane Tennison and *Prime Suspect* in television culture, see Susan Sydney-Smith, "Endless Interrogation," *Feminist Media Studies* 7, no. 2 (2007): 189–202; Charlotte Brunsdon, "Television Crime Series, Women Police, and Fuddy-Duddy Feminism," *Feminist Media Studies* 13, no. 3 (2013): 375–394; Deborah Jermyn, *Prime Suspect* (London: Palgrave Macmillan, 2010); Deborah Jermyn, "Women with a Mission: Linda La Plante, DCI Jane Tennison and the Reconfiguration of TV Crime Drama," *International Journal of Cultural Studies* 6, no. 46 (2003): 46–63.

    7. Jermyn, "Women with a Mission," 48–49.

8. For a more detailed examination of the history of women in crime drama, the gradual alterations of stereotypes, and the connection between *Prime Suspect*, *Silent Witness*, Tennison and Ryan, see Nunn and Biressi, "Silent Witness." See also Brunsdon, "Television Crime Series." Since the establishment of *Silent Witness*, more UK TV shows have featured female detectives. For example, *Vera* (ITV: 2011–present), *Line of Duty* (BBC: 2012–present), *Scott and Bailey* (ITV: 2011–present), and *Happy Valley* (BBC: 2014–present).

9. Stephanie Spurr, "A United Front," *International Innovation* 194 (2015): 2.

10. WISE tracks progress towards the goal of a critical mass of women working in the UK STEM workforce (30 percent) through the Labour Force Survey, which gives a gender breakdown for different occupations. See "Women in the UK STEM Workforce."

11. Pathology includes over nineteen specialties; forensics constitutes only a small percentage of the pathology profession but has by far the greatest public presence through television programs such as *Silent Witness*. "What Is Pathology?" *The Royal College of Pathologists*, accessed June 17, 2017.

12. "First Annual Medical Workforce Report: 2015," *The Royal College of Pathologists*, August 10, 2015.

13. Figures provided in August 2016 correspondence with the Workforce Department at the Royal College of Pathologists.

14. "First Annual Medical Workforce Report: 2015," section 5.1.

15. Nunn and Biressi, "Silent Witness"; Kay, "Frills and Thrills"; Robin Nelson, "Performing (Wo)Manoeuvres: The Progress of Gendering in TV Drama," in *Frames and Fictions on Television: The Politics of Identity Within Drama*, eds. Bruce Carson and Margaret Llewellyn-Jones (Exeter: Intellect 2000), 62–74.

16. Sue Turnbull, *The Crime Drama* (Edinburgh: Edinburgh University Press, 2014), 131.

17. Turnbull, *The Crime Drama*, 132. Robin Nelson points out that, in *Silent Witness*, "Ryan's 'male professionalism' is stressed" and that "Amanda Burton performs Sam Ryan with an intensely private quality which suggests determined control of an inner pain." Nelson, "Performing (Wo)Manoeuvres," 66, 69.

18. Rhidian Brook, "Body of Work," *Silent Witness*, series 10, episode 3, directed by Martyn Friend, aired July 31, 2006, on BBC One.

19. Brook, "Body of Work."

20. Mandy Rhodes, "Nicola Sturgeon: 'If the miscarriage hadn't happened, would I be first minister now? I'd like to think yes,'" *Sunday Times*, September 4, 2016.

21. Nunn and Biressi discuss Dr. Sam Ryan's loss of her father. Nunn and Biressi, "Silent Witness," 200.

22. After his wife and daughter's deaths, Leo feels great regret and guilt for working away: "I should never have gone to London. I should never have been away. I was working all the time Cassie was growing up. I was never there." Tony McHale, "Ghosts," *Silent Witness*, series 9, episode 1, directed by Richard Signy, aired July 25, 2005, on BBC One.

23. Lindsay Steenberg, *Forensic Science in American Popular Culture: Gender, Crime and Science* (New York: Routledge, 2013), 90. Steenberg refers specifically to the relationship between Seeley Booth and Temperance Brennan in American forensic drama *Bones*.

24. Nunn and Biressi, "Silent Witness," 195.

25. Doug Milburn, "Choices," *Silent Witness*, series 9, episode 2, directed by Andy Hay, aired August 1, 2005 on BBC One.

26. Ibid.

27. Ibid.

28. Nunn and Biressi, "Silent Witness," 200.

29. Kay, "Frills and Thrills," 162.

30. Milburn, "Choices." Lucy Kay suggests that the surgical knife is perhaps "seen by male police officers as holding the symbolic potential for castration." Kay, "Frills and Thrills," 159.

31. Milburn, "Choices."

32. Ibid.

33. Ibid.

34. Doug Milburn, "Cargo," *Silent Witness*, series 10, episode 1, directed by Michael Offer, aired July 16, 2006, on BBC One.

35. *Ibid.*

36. Stephen Davis, "Paradise Lost," *Silent Witness*, series 15, episode 3, directed by Edward Bennett, aired on April 15, 2012, on BBC One. This conflict between Karamides and the Institute of Pathologists had, and continues to have, particular contemporary resonance. In 2011, *The Times* published an article on three female pathologists challenging the reliability of the "triad," three symptoms that are widely believed to point to a diagnosis of shaken baby syndrome (Camilla Cavendish, "Is Shaken Baby Syndrome a Myth?" *The Times*, April 13, 2011). In September 2014, *The Telegraph* reported that one of these female neuropathologists was facing a "police witch hunt" (Angela Levin and Laura Donnelly, "Shaken Baby Expert Faces 'Witch Hunt,'" *The Telegraph*, September 14, 2014).

37. Davis, "Paradise Lost."

38. Michael Crompton, "Double Dare," *Silent Witness*, series 11, episode 4, directed by Maurice Phillips, aired on September 17, 2007, on BBC One.

39. *Ibid.*

40. *Ibid.*

41. *Ibid.*

42. *Ibid.*

43. *Ibid.*

44. *Ibid.*

45. *Ibid.*

46. *Ibid.*

47. *Ibid.*

48. Framed by their position at the screen, the three men represent an inversion of the gendered trope of the window in costume drama. As Julianne Pidduck suggests, "the recurring moment of the woman at the window captures a particular moment of feminine stillness, constraint and longing" (Julianne Pidduck, "Of Windows and Country Walks: Frames of Space and Movement in 1990s Austen Adaptations," *Screen* 39, no. 4 [1998]: 381–400). In this scene, it is the men who are static, while Nikki inhabits the professional and scientific space of laboratory.

49. Crompton, "Double Dare."

50. *Ibid.*

51. *Ibid.*

52. For a detailed examination of a real-life example of a woman victim criminalized for the actions of a man, see Janine Mary Little, "Jill Meagher CCTV," *Feminist Media Studies* 15, no. 3 (2015): 397–410.

53. Crompton, "Double Dare."

54. Martin Willis also discusses this episode and the potential for the body to yield multiple narratives of death. Martin Willis, "The Narrative Body in Contemporary Medical and Crime Drama: Dissecting the Flaws in Foucault's Medical Gaze," paper presented at "Cops on the Box: Crime Drama on Contemporary UK Television Screens," University of Glamorgan, March 18, 2013.

55. Ed Whitmore, "Voids," *Silent Witness*, series 13, episode 2, directed by Thaddeus O'Sullivan, aired on January 14, 2010, on BBC One.

56. Steenberg suggests that "the expertise of the female investigator incorporates more traditionally feminine forms of knowledge, such as intuition, to form a hybrid forensic intuition." Steenberg, *Forensic Science*, 63.

57. Whitmore, "Voids."

58. *Ibid.*

59. *Ibid.*

60. Alison Byerly, *Realism, Representation, and the Arts in Nineteenth-Century Literature* (Cambridge: Cambridge University Press, 1997), 55.

61. Whitmore, "Voids."

62. *Ibid.*

63. *Ibid.*

64. *Ibid.*
65. The trend towards representing women working as pathologists is being repeated in other TV crime dramas. In ITV's *Midsomer Murders*, for instance, 2011 saw the arrival of the character of Dr. Kate Wilding as replacement for Dr. George Bullard, the resident pathologist. Following the departure of Wilding in 2016, another woman, Dr. Kam Karimore, takes over the position.
66. Colette Fagan, "Positions of Power: Closing the Gender Gap in Academic Leadership," *International Innovation* 194 (2015): 96.
67. "Athena SWAN Charter," *Equality Challenge Unit*, accessed June 17, 2017; "Welcome to the UK Resource Centre for Women in SET," *UK Resource Centre for Women in Science, Engineering and Technology*, accessed June 17, 2017.
68. Margarite Evan-Galea and Michelle Gallaher, "Interview of Women in Science Australia Marguerite Evans-Galea and Michelle Gallaher," *International Innovation* 194 (2015): 16. In a study commissioned by UKRC researchers demonstrated the need for "more diverse, less stereotyped, representation" of women in TV dramas. They found that "positive comment [from interviewees] focused on issues such as demonstrating how a female scientist deals with working in a 'male chauvinist' workplace, showing team work and demonstrating the excitement of science. Some programmes (such as *Silent Witness*) have been strikingly successful in this way of portraying scientists." Joan Haran, Mwenya Chimba, Grace Reid, and Jenny Kitzinger, *Screening Women in SET: How Women in Science, Engineering and Technology are Represented in Films and on Television* (Project Report) (UKRC and Cardiff University, 2008), 85–86.

WORKS CITED

"Athena SWAN Charter." *Equality Challenge Unit*. Accessed June 17, 2017. http://www.ecu.ac.uk/equality-charters/athena-swan/.
Brook, Rhidian. "Body of Work." *Silent Witness*, series 10, episode 3. Directed by Martyn Friend. Aired July 31, 2006, on BBC One.
Brunsdon, Charlotte. "Television Crime Series, Women Police, and Fuddy-Duddy Feminism." *Feminist Media Studies* 13, no. 3 (2013): 375–394.
Byerly, Alison. *Realism, Representation, and the Arts in Nineteenth-Century Literature*. Cambridge: Cambridge University Press, 1997.
Davis, Stephen. "Paradise Lost." *Silent Witness*, series 15, episode 3. Directed by Edward Bennett. Aired on April 15, 2012, on BBC One.
Cavendish, Camilla. "Is Shaken Baby Syndrome a Myth?" *The Times*, April 13, 2011. http://www.thetimes.co.uk/tto/health/child-health/article2982782.ece.
Crompton, Michael. "Double Dare." *Silent Witness*, series 11, episode 4. Directed by Maurice Phillips. Aired on September 17, 2007, on BBC One.
Evan-Galea, Margarite, and Michelle Gallaher. "Interview of Women in Science Australia Marguerite Evans-Galea and Michelle Gallaher." *International Innovation* 194 (2015): 16–17.
Fagan, Colette. "Positions of Power: Closing the Gender Gap in Academic Leadership." *International Innovation* 194 (2015): 96–97.
"First Annual Medical Workforce Report: 2015." *The Royal College of Pathologists*, August 10, 2015. https://www.rcpath.org/resourceLibrary/first-annual-medical-workforce-report—2015.html.
Haran, Joan, Mwenya Chimba, Grace Reid, and Jenny Kitzinger. *Screening Women in SET: How Women in Science, Engineering and Technology are Represented in Films and on Television* (Project Report). UKRC and Cardiff University, 2008. http://orca.cf.ac.uk/17535/1/report_3_haran.pdf.
Jermyn, Deborah. *Prime Suspect*. London: Palgrave Macmillan, 2010.
_____. "Women with a Mission: Linda La Plante, DCI Jane Tennison and the Reconfiguration of TV Crime Drama." *International Journal of Cultural Studies* 6, no. 1 (2003): 46–63.
Kay, Lucy. "Frills and Thrills: Pleasurable Dissections and Responses to the Abject: Female

Pathology and Anthropology in *Déjà Dead* and *Silent Witness*." *Mortality* 7, no. 2 (2002): 155–170.
La Plante, Lynda. *Prime Suspect*. ITV: 1991–2006.
Levin, Angela, and Laura Donnelly. "Shaken Baby Expert Faces 'Witch Hunt.'" *The Telegraph*, September 14, 2014. http://www.telegraph.co.uk/news/health/news/11094379/Shaken-baby-expert-faces-witch-hunt.html.
Little, Janine Mary. "Jill Meagher CCTV." *Feminist Media Studies* 15, no. 3 (2015): 397–410.
McCrey, Nigel. *Silent Witness*. BBC: 1996–present.
McGeorge, Alistair. "*Silent Witness* Dominates Ratings with Over 6 Million Viewers on BBC One." *Mirror*, January 14, 2015. http://www.mirror.co.uk/tv/tv-news/silent-witness-dominates-ratings-over-4977749.
McHale, Tony. "Ghosts." *Silent Witness*, series 9, episode 1. Directed by Richard Signy. Aired July 25, 2005, on BBC One.
Milburn, Doug. "Cargo." *Silent Witness*, series 10, episode 1. Directed by Michael Offer. Aired July 16, 2006, on BBC One.
_____. "Choices." *Silent Witness*, series 9, episode 2. Directed by Andy Hay. Aired August 1, 2005, on BBC One.
Nelson, Robin. "Performing (Wo)Manoeuvres: The Progress of Gendering in TV Drama." In *Frames and Fictions on Television: The Politics of Identity Within Drama*, edited by Bruce Carson and Margaret Llewellyn-Jones, 62–74. Exeter: Intellect, 2000.
Nunn, Heather, and Anita Biressi. "Silent Witness: Detection, Femininity, and the Post-Mortem Body." *Feminist Media Studies* 3, no. 2 (2003): 193–206.
Pidduck, Julianne. "Of Windows and Country Walks: Frames of Space and Movement in 1990s Austen Adaptations." *Screen* 39, no. 4 (1998): 381–400.
Rhodes, Mandy. "Nicola Sturgeon: 'If the miscarriage hadn't happened, would I be first minister now? I'd like to think yes.'" *Sunday Times*, September 4, 2016. http://www.thetimes.co.uk/article/nicola-sturgeon-if-the-miscarriage-hadnt-happened-would-i-be-first-minister-now-id-like-to-think-yes-07m3btgck.
Spurr, Stephanie. "A United Front." *International Innovation Magazine* 194 (2015): 2.
Steenberg, Lindsay. *Forensic Science in American Popular Culture: Gender, Crime and Science*. New York: Routledge, 2013.
Sydney-Smith, Susan. "Endless Interrogation." *Feminist Media Studies* 7, no. 2 (2007): 189–202.
True-May, Brian. *Midsomer Murders*. ITV: 1997–present.
Turnbull, Sue. *The Crime Drama*. Edinburgh: Edinburgh University Press, 2014.
"Welcome to the UK Resource Centre for Women in SET." *UK Resource Centre for Women in Science, Engineering and Technology*. Accessed June 17, 2017. http://www.setwomenstats.org.uk.
Willis, Martin. "The Narrative Body in Contemporary Medical and Crime Drama: Dissecting the Flaws in Foucault's Medical Gaze." Paper presented at "Cops on the Box: Crime Drama on Contemporary UK Television Screens," University of Glamorgan, March 18, 2013. http://www.academia.edu/2969744/The_Narrative_Body_in_Crime_and_Medical_Television_Drama_Dissecting_the_Flaws_in_Foucaults_Gaze.
"What Is Pathology?" *The Royal College of Pathologists*. Accessed June 17, 2017. https://www.rcpath.org/discover-pathology/what-is-pathology.html.
Whitmore, Ed. "Voids." *Silent Witness*, series 13, episode 2. Directed by Thaddeus O'Sullivan. Aired on January 14, 2010, on BBC One.
"Women in the UK STEM Workforce." *WISE: A Campaign to Promote Women in Science, Technology and Engineering*, September 7, 2015. https://www.wisecampaign.org.uk/resources/2015/09/women-in-the-stem-workforce.

When the Woman Cuts
The Figure of the Female Medical Examiner on CSI: Miami *and* Crossing Jordan

CARY M.J. ELZA

"I get all worked up about things. I care too much about my case and it gets me in trouble. That's why my life is a disaster half of the time. I've got no editor in my brain."
—Dr. Jordan Cavanaugh, *Crossing Jordan*[1]

On NBC's *Crossing Jordan* (2001–2007), tough-talking, rule-breaking medical examiner (M.E.) Jordan Cavanaugh (Jill Hennessy), a good-looking female with an ambiguously gendered name, terrorizes a fictional Boston M.E.'s office with her relentless drive to find justice for the victims who end up on her autopsy table.[2] Meanwhile, in the TV land version of Miami, Alexx Woods (Khandi Alexander), another assertive, attractive forensic pathologist with a similarly androgynous name, reads the clues on victims' dead bodies and shares her findings with the team on *CSI: Miami* (2002–2012).[3] From Dr. Kay Scarpetta, who made her first appearance in Patricia Cornwell's novels in 1990, to Dr. Jill Brock on *Picket Fences* (1992–1996), to Dr. Dana Scully on *The X-Files* (1993–2002), to Dr. Temperance Brennan on *Bones* (2005–2017), female medical examiners have become familiar figures in the media since the early 1990s, especially on TV.[4]

Crossing Jordan and *CSI: Miami* are examples of what many critics have discussed as an overall proliferation of crime investigation series on television, which, as Elayne Rapping writes in *Law and Justice as Seen on TV*, relates to an "increasingly intense focus on crime and criminals as major issues in American society."[5] Rapping discusses the ways in which this trend is linked to the airing of live-televised criminal trials and the visibility of alarmist depictions of criminality on TV. Rather than looking at media representations as a mirror or a window to society, however, it's important to view televisual representations as playing a vital, at times even generative, role in how Americans see and judge the relevance of social, cultural, and political issues. The tension between actual problems in society and the ways problems play out on TV becomes a valuable tool of inquiry, if media are seen as fundamental to our understanding of the world around us. With this in mind, the popularity of criminal investigation shows such as the franchises *CSI* and *Law and Order* should be examined for their production and reproduction of a culture of fear, hyperbole, and vindictiveness with regard to criminality.

Rapping and other critics often cite a deep-seated American need to see good triumph over evil, which, beginning in the 1990s, is part of an increasing conservatism that led to the victims' rights movement. In a nutshell, victims' rights advocates favor tougher punishment for criminals and the increasing visibility, in the media and in court cases themselves, of the victims of violent crime. Some argue that this greater visibility of victims—which many critics allege narrows the term "victim" to the point where it refers *only* to white, middle-class subjects of violence—has also resulted in a national emphasis on revenge, passionate emotions, and even the disregard of law.[6] Even as early as 1992, the *Boston Globe* traced the origins of the victims' rights movement, alleging that while Mothers Against Drunk Driving sowed the seeds for victims' rights in 1980:

> It was during the presidential election campaign of 1988 that crime victims became a real political force. Those who had suffered at the hands of Willie Horton, a convicted murderer who assaulted a Maryland couple while on furlough from a Massachusetts prison, told and retold their stories in campaign stops for George Bush. Their personal tragedies hit a public nerve in an electorate feeling vulnerable to violence and frustrated by a court system widely perceived as unresponsive.[7]

The article points out that victims' rights have become an arena in which tears are used as manipulative weapons. The close relationship of political strategy to planned emotional response in audiences, which existed at the very outset of the victims' rights movement, points to a vital link between television, ideology, and the depiction of crime, as will be brought out further in this essay. Rapping notes that with regard to the victims' rights movement, "television has played an especially important role, because, as a visual, dramatic medium, it has the power to forge larger-than-life images of human suffering and to elicit strong emotional responses which are in keeping with the rhetoric of victims' rights."[8] This is especially true, she notes, in the context of televised court cases, which have standardized emotional sensationalism in the depiction of criminal proceedings. Although I will discuss the victims' rights movement and its role on TV in more depth later, it's worth mentioning at the outset of this essay as a factor existing alongside the popularity of criminal investigation series in the 2000s.

Jordan Cavanaugh and Alexx Woods are capable, attractive, educated women, one white (Jordan), one Black (Alexx), who dissect dead bodies for a living and, as each narrative insists, are experts in what they do. As its name suggests, *Crossing Jordan* revolves primarily around the figure of Jordan, with a regular ensemble supporting cast. On *CSI: Miami*, Alexx is a member of an ensemble cast, and enjoys a smaller amount of screen time during her six seasons on the show. Apart from several episodes where she has a more pronounced storyline, she usually appears only during crime scene exams or while conducting autopsies. Unlike Jordan, who exemplifies the expanded job description of investigators on TV (Jordan is an M.E., but goes rogue to track down criminals, or assists her cop friends), Alexx leaves the field investigation to the rest of her CSI team.[9] Both Jordan and Alexx, though, play vital roles in the narrative structure of these criminal series. After all, the crime begins with the body.

This essay explores how these depictions of female medical examiners on TV, which rely upon gendered images of mediation and containment, work with the trend of the victims' rights movement to maintain the control of the criminal justice system. A vital element of these criminal series is the autopsy scene, and the figure of the medical examiner who "translates" the signs on the dead body into clues that can be used for further investigation. The act of autopsy is a vexed one in American society, and has been the subject of public fascination for centuries. Not as much attention has been paid, however, to the figure of the medical examiner, especially the female M.E., whose recent proliferation in print, in film, and especially on television makes her worth a closer look. I will first discuss the performance of autopsy and Alexx and Jordan as sexualized and maternalized figures who mediate and translate, speaking for the dead and giving voice to the voiceless. I then look at how the female pathologist is a figure who "worries responsibly," a phrase first coined by Janice Radway in *Reading the Romance* to refer to the feminist researcher, who "worries responsibly" about what other women consume in popular culture. The phrase was taken up again by Charlotte Brundson in the context of soap opera and feminist criticism. Brundson's contribution facilitates a discussion of the widespread feminization/soap opera-fication of many science/criminal/court shows, and TV drama in general. Finally, I take into account the ways in which the texts of *Crossing Jordan* and *CSI: Miami* control and contain the female M.E., through images of supervision and the trope of "making it personal." The figure of the female M.E. fulfills gender-specific functions, which helps account for the proliferation of this figure in the media, but with great power and specialized skill comes an ideological need, under dominant culture, to hold that power in check.

Death and the Maiden, or, the Performance of Autopsy and the Female M.E.

Elizabeth Klaver notes in *Sites of Autopsy in Contemporary Culture* that "when the performance of autopsy, whether medical or literary/cultural, is considered in terms of the Western academy, it seems to rely largely on the work of radically distinguishing subject from object in the service of humanist inquiry. One must regard the cadaver as a *thing* in order to 'violate' it."[10] Performing an autopsy means violating a corpse in two ways: visually, with the "penetrating gaze" of the medical eye, which seeks to find answers by "reading" or "listening to" the body, and physically, with medical implements which penetrate and, according to some cultures, desecrate the wholeness of the body. The person conducting the autopsy is simultaneously in a position of great power, because of her specialized skills, invasive manipulations, and ability to read the body, as well as danger, because as a subject regarding a recently deceased subject, her own subjecthood, or mortality, becomes viscerally apparent. Klaver cites Michel de Certeau's contention in *The Practice of Everyday Life* that a "split between the subject and object [...] was necessary for a positivist medical science to proceed. [...] The dead body had to become strictly classified as other, clearly objectified on some other side, helped along by alienating constructions of class and criminality."[11] These alienating constructions were available in the early modern days of autopsy by virtue of the fact that bodies for dissection were often supplied post-execution; the criminality of the corpse would be class-inflected, providing a social distance from the educated anatomists working on the body. From a psychoanalytic standpoint, Julia Kristeva addresses this split in terms of "abjection"; Barbara Creed explains Kristeva's notion of the abject as something that "threatens life" and must be "propelled away from the body and deposited on the other side of an imaginary border which separates the self from that which threatens the self. Although the subject must exclude the abject, the abject must, nevertheless, be tolerated for that which threatens to destroy life also helps to define life[...]. The ultimate in abjection is the corpse."[12] The corpse, the abject object, must be tolerated because it holds key answers in a struggle between law and order, life and death. The corpse on TV must be tolerated and addressed because the criminal narrative revolves around the presence of a dead body and the question of who killed it and why.

The same process of Othering is at work today, in several ways. First, the corpse, the "ultimate in abjection,"[13] contrasts the living, sexualized image of the female forensic pathologist. The act of cutting open a dead body carries a taboo association, because of the double penetration of the gaze and the physical implements of dissection. In addition to this, as Klaver notes, while "the potential for a sexually charged display is all too imminent," given the structural norms of an autopsy (the body is unclothed, prone, subject to manipulation and penetration), this potential is "prohibited in a culture where the dead body *must be desexualized* at all costs. After all, in the United States, having sex with a corpse is considered one of the great defilements and a crime punishable by a lengthy prison term."[14] And, Klaver continues, in the context of media representations of autopsy, this desexualization is even more vital, given network regulations on partial and full nudity. Forensic pathology on television must walk a fine line, as the nude but concealed body, "attracting and repulsing at the same time," depends on the presence of the medical examiner to mitigate the possible whiff of necrophilia. In part, this process of Othering occurs through visual representation.[15] Klaver refers to the emphasis on the pallid color of the corpse in paintings as far back as the seventeenth century, which contrasted the flesh tones of the examiner conducting the autopsy. This is equally true for television depictions of corpses—gray, ashy skin, bluish lips, and closed eyes are visual conventions for bodies on TV, even if they've just died.

On television, the female M.E.'s sexiness mediates the horror of the corpse. Both Jordan and Alexx are good-looking and attractive to the opposite sex. Their conventionally gendered physical attractiveness helps to contain the horror of the dead body by providing a stark visual contrast. Well-cut V-neck scrubs cover their bodies while they work on autopsies, and outside the lab each tends to wear semi-casual, close fitting tees that show off thin and desirable physiques. Alexx in particular is highly sexualized through costume. The show's setting in Miami can, to a certain extent, account for the sleeveless, low-cut tops she often wears, but one would think the heat might preclude heavy eye makeup and long, glamorous hair. Jordan's appearance is less overtly made-up, but narrative clues suggest her desirability; secondary characters often hit on Jordan, and her sexuality has come up as a major topic of discussion in more than one episode.[16] The sexual objectification of Alexx and Jordan, conventional for network television, enables the Othering and desexualization of the dead body, prone and naked on the autopsy slab.

In addition to the Othering that takes place through desexualization, the corpse is also identified as Other through its powerlessness. At the moment of death, the corpse transforms into a victim, a thing, through the removal of its capacity for agency. Its inability to act contrasts the actions of the M.E., whose manipulation of the body for the purposes of helping the victim demonstrates specific physical skills, associated with nurturing and the maternal. Kristeva's theory of the abject helps to demonstrate how the visceral, hands-on manipulation of the corpse might be associated with a mother-child relationship. Creed writes that in the Freudian pre-symbolic, "the subject's first contact with 'authority' is with the maternal authority when the child learns, through interaction with the mother, about its body: the shape of the body, the clean and unclean, the proper and improper areas of the body."[17] If the mother brings order to the disorderly, acts as an authority in making sense of the chaotic body as the child enters the symbolic, then it is the maternal role of the female M.E. to bring final order to the body after the subject has *exited* the symbolic. The inability of the corpse to perform for itself, and its reliance upon an outside figure for the final cleanliness of the body, suggests its construction as an infantilized Other in relation to the female M.E.'s maternal role.

As audiences watch scenes of autopsies on television, this mother-child relationship has another dimension. As Creed writes, images of the abject "are central to our culturally/socially constructed notions of the horrific," since,

> on the one hand, these images of bodily wastes threaten a subject that is already constituted, in relation to the symbolic, as "whole and proper." Consequently, they fill the subject—both the protagonist in the text and the spectator in the cinema—with disgust and loathing. On the other hand they also point back to a time when a "fusion between mother and nature" existed; when bodily wastes, while set apart from the body, were not seen as objects of embarrassment and shame.[18]

On both *Crossing Jordan* and *CSI: Miami*, Jordan and Alexx are associated not only with the ultimate in the abject, the corpse, but also in the substances that come along with it—blood, stomach contents, organs. At least one autopsy scene per episode, and often two or three, reaffirms the M.E.'s close physical contact with the abject. Overhead shots occasionally reveal fully opened torsos, the M.E. bent over them, plastic gloves covered with the victim's blood. They open up bodies, manipulate internal organs, find answers, then reorder the bodies, sew them up, and enable their final rest. While "historically, it has been the function of religion to purify the abject," Creed argues that with the breakdown of traditional ritual comes the need to seek purification through other cultural forms, such as through the role of the abject in popular horror films.[19] Through the final revisitation of the pre-symbolic maternal association with the abject, what we might call a post-symbolic reordering, Alexx and Jordan, as female forensic pathologists, perform a maternal function that identifies the corpse as infantilized Other.

And as a voiceless, immobile entity, the corpse is powerless—it depends on the medical examiner to ensure that its message (cause of death) is received. In addition to being desexualized in part through the sexualization of the female coroner, and being marked as powerless by the maternal actions of the female M.E., the corpse, usually the victim of a violent crime, is often marked by class, race, gender, or the intersection of two or more of these markers. This may work in a way that emphasizes the corpse's poverty, questionable career choices ("life on the street"), or tolerance of discrimination, or may skew to the opposite direction, pointing to the corpse's wealth and privileges. In either case, the race, class, and gender characteristics of the victim feed into the extent to which the female M.E. will form a point of (dis)identification with the body. Often the corpse was powerless in life: prostitutes, the elderly, young runaways, or children are common examples of this on both shows. *CSI: Miami* tends to depict autopsies of young, attractive club girls, presented as tragic, naïve victims of predatory men. Jordan autopsies the mentally ill, teenage drug addicts, and victims of domestic abuse, among others. In the case of the pathetic and victimized prior to death, Othering takes place when the corpse's situation is shown to be non-normative, and thus theoretically preventable. In addition, the body can be marked as Other by its own transgressions, if the victim—usually male—committed a crime that led to its death. The victim in this case might be wealthy, or seem "normal," but investigation reveals dark secrets. Both shows use this device, and as Alexx even remarks after one of these cases during season one, "Truth is, nobody really knows anyone."[20] The class, race, gender, and crime-marked Othering in which both shows engage situates the corpses in socially-marginalized, powerless positions that assure their dependence on the female M.E. to act as their voices.

Televisual representations of autopsy suggest that aside from the obvious medical training required, the forensic pathologist must be patient, willing to listen, and even nurturing—qualities coded feminine by dominant society. Both Jordan and Alexx show their willingness to listen by speaking to the bodies they dissect. Alexx does this most frequently—she talks to dead bodies at least once an episode and calls them pet names like "sweetheart" and "honey," drawing attention to the nurturing function of her character. In a first season episode, for example, she asks a deceased blonde coed found on the beach during spring break, "How's this happen, sugar? All you wanted was a week of fun and sun, hanging out with your friends."[21] She not only addresses the corpse, but also tells it that she knows its motivations, that she understands and is ready to listen. The frequency with which Alexx talks soothingly to dead bodies contributes to her characterization as a maternal figure. Jordan, too, speaks to the dead, but not as often; when she does, her tone is casual, sometimes even addressing the corpse as a living being. During a second season episode, she says to a dead woman's body, "It looks like you're the only one around here I can talk to."[22] Her empathetic willingness to treat the corpse as a subject, rather than an object, goes a long way towards restoring past subjecthood and decoding the clues the body provides. Both shows also frequently refer to corpses "telling" the investigators who the killer is. In one episode involving the death of a priest, Alexx asks his body, "What can you tell us, Father, about who did this to you?" while on *Crossing Jordan*,

Jordan responds to another character's question about a woman's cause of death with: "Let's hope she tells us."[23] Klaver writes that "because we are reluctant, or perhaps powerless, to withdraw being and agency even from a *dead person*, being and agency are reassigned though a vocal tropology as compensation for the objectification of the 'subject' as material for study, as 'object' to violate."[24] She goes on to suggest that the metaphor of hearing and listening replaces the act of reading signs on the body, giving the body some kind of honorary agency in the process of autopsy. To listen and talk to a body, therefore, is to respect its past as a human being and its subjecthood, and to evince a desire to find out where it comes from and what its story is. This implies that all corpses have something to say, and the value of the female M.E. lies in her willingness to listen and translate.

"Worrying Responsibly" on TV

As noted above, the figure of the female medical examiner is worth studying especially because she provides a mediating framework in which the stories of the dead can be told on television. Through her sexualization, her maternalization, and her ability to act as a sympathetic conduit for the voices of victims, she makes the experience of witnessing autopsy manageable for the television audience. In her role as mouthpiece for the dead, the powerless, she adopts a position of concern and advocacy for the victim. This humanistic, victim-oriented behavior makes her a figure who "worries responsibly." Referring to her 1984 study of female romance novel readers, Radway writes:

> Although I tried very hard not to dismiss the activities of the Smithton women [the subjects of her study] and made an effort to understand the act of romance reading as a positive response to the conditions of everyday life, my account unwittingly repeated the sexist assumption that has warranted a large portion of the commentary on the romance. It was still motivated, that is, by the assumption that someone ought to worry responsibly about the effect of fantasy on women readers.[25]

Charlotte Brundson, too, uses this phrase in order to show how the feminist critics in the 1940s and the 1970s took up the position of the responsible worrier, again and again—the worrier is the feminist who investigates whether women's genres such as soap opera are really "bad objects" to be reviled, or celebrations of femininity, or a release valve, or sources of community-building, or any combination of the above. The worrier seeks to protect the weakest members of society and gives them a voice, yet in doing so, often unwittingly reproduces the dominant structures of patriarchy. We can see this figure in both Alexx and Jordan, who each show presents as nurturing to victims.

Aside from the psychoanalytic relationship that the female forensic pathologist has to motherhood articulated above, both characters have more overt maternal roles in their respective narratives. Motherhood defines Alexx in particular. Her tendency to talk to victims and call them pet names speaks to this, of course, but the series goes further to establish her nurturing background. Viewers first learn that she has children in the first season episode "Broken," where a little girl is kidnapped, molested, and murdered in a Chuck E. Cheese–type establishment. The scene where Alexx autopsies the girl begins with Alexx on the phone, telling one of her kids not to feed potato chips to the cat, and "no TV tonight, have Dad read you a story."[26] She's clearly distressed at the small child on her table. At the end of the episode, Alexx sits on the floor of a bedroom in her house, reading a story to her two kids. The mise-en-scène is very fuzzy and comfortable looking, with a fluffy rug and a sun-drenched room, yet as Alexx hugs her children to her tight, she says "I want to tell you guys about bad people."[27] Home and motherhood are presented as a haven for Alexx, and she continues to define herself by her family throughout the series, to the extent that she quits her job after her son becomes implicated in one of the department's cases.[28] Her attempts to balance the demands of family and work are ultimately depicted as futile; in order to properly care for her family, or as she puts it, "spend more of my time taking care of the living," she must give up her job.[29]

Jordan's maternal role is less clear, as she represents the expanded job description that characterizes the protagonists of many criminal investigation shows today: she performs autopsies, but she also works with her police friend Woody to chase down criminals. Jordan is presented as a toughie, a loose cannon, and her nurturing role is less overt than Alexx's. Yet time and time again she is put into situations that reveal her maternalism. In a first season episode, for example, "Someone to Count On," she comes to the defense of and provides a refuge for a fourteen-year-old African American girl wrongly accused of killing her mother.[30] During "Family Ties," an episode in which a baby is found with a dead woman in a car, Jordan goes to great lengths to find out to whom the baby belongs, to the point where the police officer investigating the case with her insists that the answers just aren't there. Instead of admitting defeat, Jordan doesn't rest until she uncovers the truth. At the end of the episode, she cradles the orphaned baby and asks her colleague Dr. Garrett Macy, "Ever wonder what kind of mother you'd make?"[31] Her flirtation with motherhood is clear here, but less obvious maternal leanings, in the guise of the drive to protect victims, are part of Jordan's overall character. While the narrative of *CSI: Miami* specifically defines Alexx as a mother, Jordan is far more closely associated with the role of victim. We learn as the series progresses that Jordan's mother was killed when she was ten, and the killer remains at large. She has a rocky relationship with her father, a retired police officer, in part because of the unsolved murder. As a result, Jordan's drive to find justice for victims is linked both to her nurturing side and a desire to avenge her mother's death. This combination of revenge and emotion ties the role of the female M.E., whose family and past circumstances figure into her tendency to worry about victims and her drive to help, to the influence of the victims' rights movement on TV.

What Rapping calls the "criminalization of American life" is linked to the melodramaticization of criminal TV, and gender is inextricably tied up with both of these.[32] The victims' rights movement is an important social element existing alongside the format changes in TV dramas, including the effects of soap opera melodrama and the dramatic televising of court cases. Among other scholars, Robin Nelson asserts, "the interweaving of different narrative strands developed in soap has become TV drama's model form."[33] Complicated, long-running storylines, an emphasis on characters' backstories and psychological motivations, and a lack of narrative closure all can be attributed to the soap format's influence on television in the 1990s and early 2000s. *CSI: Miami* and *Crossing Jordan* exemplify the increasing soap-ification of TV drama: while a novice viewer might be able to follow the primary storyline of a given episode (like many other dramas since the 1990s, *CSI: Miami* and *Crossing Jordan* juxtapose single-episode storylines with wider narrative arcs), a full grasp of the episode's developments requires devoted viewing. And on both shows, characters' pasts are revealed gradually throughout the series, while past experiences and traumas inform their actions. TV drama's "close-up on personal relationships, largely to the exclusion of broader environments and subjects [...] locates the measure of experience in the individual and equates proximity with sincerity," Nelson notes.[34] This refers to both the physical shot of the close-up, and a broader move towards delving into the personal lives of characters on dramatic shows.[35] The conventions of TV drama today rely upon a more emotive, closer, more personal mode than in the past, one that demands closer identification from viewers, and a more engaged audience. The melodramaticization of TV drama, thanks to its historical roots in the soap opera and "women's genres," is inextricably coded feminine, as is, I think, the victims' rights movement.

The Cost of "Making it personal"

TV crime dramas in general share much in common with the victims' rights movement. As Glen Creeber puts it, serials in the 1990s and 2000s began to "offer examples of a new relationship between politics and the self (meaning that political issues are now increasingly centered convincingly around the domain of personal and private interaction) [...] 'soap opera' techniques [...] have now become the very means by which 'radical' and 'progressive' drama is frequently conceived and constructed for a contemporary audience."³⁶ Creeber puts "radical" and "progressive" in quotes for good reason: the depiction of political issues through the lens of the private and personal fills a hegemonic function in TV drama. The individualization and personalization of suffering and tragedy is part of a depoliticizing process; a focus on the individual story threatens to undercut any critique of the problems of the larger system. In reference to the role of the victims' rights movement in the increased tendency of victims speaking during sentencing procedures, Rapping writes that this trend enables "sentimentality," a term that she argues

> gets at the heart of what is most frightening and dangerous about the movement for victims' rights and the media's complicity in furthering its goals. Sentimentality is generally understood to be a kind of false, excessive, insincere, and hypocritical form of emotion. It is what is meant by the term "crocodile tears," the often inappropriately excessive and insincere display of grief and sorrow by those who presumably have some other motive or agenda that the display of grief serves to mask.³⁷

"Sentimental," "excessive," and "insincere" are all words often used to describe soap opera as well, of course. But the emphasis on the victim's story, to which Rapping rightly points, draws the court's attention to the personal, rather than the bigger picture, the problems with the system itself. And when court cases are televised, the cycle perpetuates itself, encouraging television viewers to adopt a personal, rather than political, stance on the problems plaguing the criminal justice system. An emphasis on punishing the perpetrator for the sake of making the victim feel better (even if the victim is already dead) reaffirms the dominance of the system.

Paul Wright maintains that since many of the more heavily funded of victims' rights groups are bankrolled by organizations affiliated with law enforcement, "these groups tend to parrot the party line of more police, more prisons, more punishment, more draconian laws."³⁸ And, since the facts show that more and more people who "fall into the categories of the powerless— the poor, the sexually 'different,' the non-white, and certainly the female" are being incarcerated, the politics of the victims' rights movement are self-defeating, and in fact work to maintain the power of the U.S. legal system and the oppression of minority groups.³⁹ Wright likewise states that "for now, victims continue to be defined as the white, middle- and upper-class person who is killed, raped, robbed, or assaulted by a stranger."⁴⁰

Rapping argues that placing women in the role of the helpless victim in need of protection perpetuates faith in a largely inadequate legal system, which punishes the "other" and is predicated upon an unjust definition of who is considered a victim. And yet women and the powerless become victims on TV crime drama again and again, and those who defend the voiceless, like the figure of the female M.E., become advocates for victims' rights, rather than political activists interested in reforming a problematic system. At the same time, the histrionics of the victims' rights movement suggest a feminized irrationality, which simultaneously relies upon emotion as a motivating force for justice and reaffirms the control of a fundamentally unjust system. This self-defeating paradox lies, too, at the heart of melodrama, which is associated with eliciting emotion, with sentimentality, and with femininity.[41] In a crime drama, the injection of melodrama allows television to address serious issues on a case-by-case, personal level, thereby removing much of the ideological weight of the issues themselves.

If Alexx is defined primarily by her motherhood, and Jordan primarily by her past victimhood, then obviously the narrative is underlining the emotional resonance possible when each is confronted by the evils of crime. One of the ways in which this is accomplished is by invoking the binary of "personal" versus "professional," which is a common trope for crime shows, especially when it comes to women. The melodramatic tendency of framing an issue in "personal terms" is a method by which a televisual figure can be devalued, or kept in check. "Making it personal" suggests melodrama, or femininity, while "keeping it professional" suggests a zero-degree, male subjectivity. Alexx on *CSI: Miami* deals with this constantly. While she has adopted a method of communicating with corpses that is based upon her caring and investment in reading the message of the body, the series also shows her struggling with professionalism. This is most often associated with her motherhood.

The episode I mentioned above, "Broken," in which Alexx must tamp down her emotions while she autopsies the body of a little girl, is one such example, but this becomes even more clear in the fourth season episode "Deviant," where she becomes implicated in a murder investigation because she put posters up informing her neighbors that a convicted child molester has moved into the area. After neighborhood fathers chase down and beat the man up, Alexx's decision to publicize the man's whereabouts is called into question. She defends herself: "I just wanted the parents to be informed so the parents could protect their children."[42] Her children, too, play in the park where the man was found, and by putting up posters, she looks after her own children and others who live in the neighborhood. For her maternal troubles, however, the chief medical examiner (male) strongly urges her to switch to the night shift, to preserve her chances for job advancement. While she decides to take the risk and stay on the day shift, the chief's obvious disapproval is her reward for letting her role as mother come in contact with her career. And interestingly, the reason she cites for staying with the day shift CSI team reveals emotions as well: she insists that "this team treats me like family."[43]

Jordan represents the victims' rights movement even more clearly than Alexx does, and the ease with which she begins to identify with a victim, and "makes it personal," contains the power she has as a medical examiner. Jordan has a tendency to go vigilante and has a tough, take-no-prisoners persona, but this is largely a smokescreen. She gets emotionally attached frequently. It's worth mentioning that a secondary character on *Crossing Jordan*, Lily (Kathryn Hahn), the grief counselor, is far more overtly sentimental than Jordan, and arguably functions to deflect accusations of "making it personal" away from Jordan. Lily cries easily and is caring and maternal. But the show presents Jordan as too personal and not professional enough, and her willingness to ally herself with the victim and break rules to help people is highly feminized. Again, her past victimhood informs her tendency to make things personal. In the episode "Family Ties," her tenacity in finding the baby girl's father after the mother's death relates to the loss of her own mother. She insists to her boss and friend Dr. Macy (Miguel Ferrer) that "someday this little girl is going to need to know what happened to her mother, not just who shot whom."[44] Dr. Macy calls her out on her personal connection and asks, "Whose mother are we talking about?" then insists, "Give it to the police, Jordan."[45] Someone accuses Jordan of "making it personal" and going after criminals with a vengeance basically every other episode, and it is also significant that at the start of the series, she has been fired from her previous job in Los Angeles for exactly this sort of behavior.

The show also defines Jordan by her empathy, particularly her ability to put herself in the victim's shoes. She often uses a role-playing game to find answers in a given case during the show's first two seasons. With a partner (usually her father, but also Woody and other secondary characters), she reenacts the crime in the hopes of discovering clues she might have missed. The manner in which scenes like this are filmed shows the way in which Jordan can insinuate herself into another's body, to see through someone else's eyes. As Jordan narrates, she and her partner flash back to the scene of the crime, taking the place of the original participants. By walking in the victim's or killer's shoes, Jordan personalizes a crime and draws it close enough to understand it. This suggests the way in which Jordan's approach to crime-solving is distinctly empathetic, over-the-top, and feminized. Again, it is difficult to separate Jordan's performance of autopsies from her investigation, since she has an expanded job description and rarely restricts herself solely to conducting autopsies.

Although women mediate between the past subjecthood of the corpse and the reduction of the corpse to a thing, a victim, which justifies a criminal prosecution, their vital role as the bearers of information must be contained and managed in a televisual narrative. A tendency to "make it personal" and let emotions overcome rationality functions in the narratives of both shows to deflect power away from the female M.E. Another way the female M.E.'s power is controlled, however, is more obvious—she is supervised. In keeping with the conservative trend in crime TV that Rapping describes, TV's depiction of autonomous autopsies performed by women are largely a thing of the past. While shows in the early 1990s like *The X-Files* allowed the female forensic pathologist to conduct autopsies alone, as the first and final word on cause of death and the process of dissection, *CSI: Miami* and *Crossing Jordan* rarely depict Alexx and Jordan completing autopsies by themselves. On *Crossing Jordan*, Jordan tends to work either in a group or with someone watching her, most often a man. Her boss, Dr. Macy, is male, as are her two partners. She briefly worked under a Black female supervisor during the second season, but for the most part she has a male supervisor in the room with her at all times. Jordan's actions are sometimes, but not always, recorded by either a video monitor or an audio recording device of some kind. Alexx's autopsy bay is even more interesting in this context: as the behind-the-scenes extras on the DVD for season one of *CSI: Miami* indicate, Alexx works in a teaching theater.[46] Her actions are monitored on up to four video monitors at any given time, and observers can also stand in the balcony area, which resembles the audience area of a teaching hospital. In addition, she is often watched by at least one person, usually her boss, Horatio Caine (David Caruso), who stands on the floor with her or up in the balcony, staring at her down in the theater and speaking through a voice-of-God-like microphone. This means that in a given autopsy scene, Alexx's movements are multiply mediated: by the monitors recording her, by Horatio's gaze, by Horatio's gaze on the monitors, by the camera's gaze, and by the audience's gaze on the TV screen. That's a lot of supervisory mediation.

To be fair, the tendency of these shows to avoid solo autopsies may also be a result of the "CSI Effect," the movement (named after the TV show) towards juries in criminal trials becoming savvier about the collection and interpretation of evidence, and often demanding more complicated and precise tests like DNA matching. A forensic pathologist whose actions are recorded and/or watched risks less criticism for missing evidence or performing an autopsy incorrectly. Mediation and supervision, in the real world, allow an M.E. to cover his or her bases. The video of an autopsy, like any widely seen video in today's culture, becomes evidence of competence or wrongdoing, and takes on a life of its own. One has only to consider cell phone videos or Facebook live streaming used as evidence in court cases—or in the court of public opinion—to see how important documentation becomes in an age of victims' rights.

Conclusion

Rapping emphasizes the importance of discussing how the voices and experiences of the powerless are heard, described, or dramatized, and although she's talking specifically about courtroom dramas, her insight applies to the crime genre as a whole. Alexx and Jordan, responsible worriers, ally themselves with helpless and subjectless victims to give them a voice, to translate in order that justice can be served. The emphasis both narratives place on the pathologists' melodramatic tendencies suggests that they *should* be observed—their positions are powerful, and emotional mistakes would have severe repercussions. Viewers, too, are another level of observation—we gaze at Alexx and Jordan as they gaze at corpses, and in the process, the horrors of the corpse are mitigated. But even as the female M.E.'s emotional filters make it easier for us to look at the abject object of the corpse, those filters deny her narrative credibility; the same charges leveled at soap opera narratives threaten to undermine her power. In the context of the victims' rights movement, this emphasis on the sentimentality of the female M.E., and the maternal relationship between the pathologist and the corpse, reproduces the tendency of melodrama to distract from broader social and political forces in favor of localized, personalized stories with tidy conclusions. The female gaze, then—the authoritative, medical female gaze—becomes a site of comfort, but only if the agency she wields is subjected to scrutiny, and prevented from becoming a threat to the dominant order.

Notes

1. Tim Kring, "Pilot," *Crossing Jordan*, season 1, episode 1, directed by Allan Arkush, aired September 24, 2001, on NBC.

2. Tim Kring (creator), *Crossing Jordan* (NBC: 2001–2007).

3. Anthony E. Zuiker, Ann Donahue, and Carol Mendelsohn (creators), *CSI: Miami* (CBS: 2002–2012).

4. Patricia Cornwell, *Postmortem* (New York: Scribner, 1990); David E. Kelley (creator), *Picket Fences* (CBS: 1992–1996); Chris Carter (creator), *The X-Files* (Fox: 1993–2002); Hart Hanson (creator), *Bones* (Fox: 2005–2017).

5. Elayne Rapping, *Law and Justice as Seen on TV* (New York: New York University Press, 2003), 5.

6. See Rapping, *Law and Justice*, 243–247, as well as Lauren Berlant, *The Queen of America Goes to Washington City: Essays on Sex and Citizenship* (Durham: Duke University Press, 1997), and, for a more recent and specific analysis of the role of racial politics in victims' rights discourse, see Julie A. Beck, "Victims' Rights and Public Safety? Unmasking Racial Politics in Crime Discourses Surrounding Parole Revocation for 'Lifers' in California," *Western Criminology Review* 11, no. 1 (2010): 20–36.

7. Eileen McNamara, "Revenging Angels," *Boston Globe Magazine*, February 23, 1992, 12.

8. Rapping, *Law and Justice*, 239.

9. Interestingly, one of the other female forensic pathologists on *Crossing Jordan*, Dr. Elaine Duchamps, whose role only lasted a season, also restricts herself to finding out the reason of death, and refrains from additional criminal investigation. Her opinion on the

matter is laid out in the episode "Family Ties" (Kathy McCormick, "Family Ties," *Crossing Jordan*, season 2, episode 11, directed by Ian Toynton, aired January 13, 2003, on NBC). Elaine, like Alexx, is a black woman—this may be a reach, but the restriction of the "expanded job description" so common in crime investigation shows today would seem to have some sort of containing function.

10. Elizabeth Klaver, *Sites of Autopsy in Contemporary Culture* (Albany: SUNY Press, 2005), 71.
11. *Ibid.*, 72.
12. Barbara Creed, *The Monstrous-Feminine: Film, Feminism, Psychoanalysis* (New York: Routledge, 1993), 9.
13. *Ibid.*
14. Klaver, *Sites of Autopsy*, 141.
15. *Ibid.*
16. See, in particular, Elizabeth Sarnoff, "Scared Straight," *Crossing Jordan*, season 2, episode 7, directed by Arvin Brown, aired November 18, 2002, on NBC. Although this is a topic for another essay, Jordan's possible bisexuality is addressed repeatedly when she develops a close relationship with a famous lesbian talk-show host played by Mariel Hemingway.
17. Creed, *The Monstrous-Feminine*, 13.
18. *Ibid.*, 13.
19. *Ibid.*, 14.
20. Elizabeth Devine and John Haynes, "Freaks and Tweaks," *CSI: Miami*, season 1, episode 23, directed by Deran Serafian, aired May 12, 2003, on CBS.
21. Steven Maeda, "Spring Break," *CSI: Miami*, season 1, episode 21, directed by Deran Serafian, aired April 28, 2003, on CBS.
22. Ian Biderman, "Bombs Away," *Crossing Jordan*, season 2, episode 2, directed by Ian Toynton, aired September 30, 2002, on NBC.
23. Mark Israel, "Ashes to Ashes," *CSI: Miami*, season 1, episode 5, directed by Bryan Spicer, aired October 21, 2002, on CBS; Elizabeth Sarnoff, "Secrets & Lies Part 1," *Crossing Jordan*, season 1, episode 22, directed by Michael Gershman, aired May 6, 2002, on NBC.
24. Klaver, *Sites of Autopsy*, 80.
25. Janice Radway, "Romance and the Work of Fantasy: Struggles Over Feminine Sexuality and Subjectivity at Century's End," in Jon Cruz and Justin Lewis, *Viewing, Reading, Listening: Audiences and Cultural Reception* (Boulder: Westview, 1994), 214, qtd. in Charlotte Brunsdon, *The Feminist, the Housewife, and the Soap Opera* (New York: Oxford University Press, 2000), 39.
26. Ildy Modrovich and Laurence Walsh, "Broken," *CSI: Miami*, season 1, episode 6, aired October 28, 2002, on CBS.
27. *Ibid.*
28. Mark Dube, "A Rock and a Hard Place," *CSI: Miami*, season 6, episode 19, directed by Gina Lamar, aired May 5, 2008, on CBS.
29. *Ibid.*
30. Barbara Ellis Nance, "Someone to Count On," *Crossing Jordan*, season 1, episode 21, directed by Nick Gomez, aired April 28, 2002, on NBC.
31. McCormick, "Family Ties."
32. Rapping, *Law and Justice*, 252.
33. Robin Nelson, *TV Drama in Transition: Forms, Values, and Cultural Change* (New York: St. Martin's Press, 1997), 23.
34. *Ibid.*, 46.
35. Nelson writes, "Seeing the face closely, the Close-Up implies, is to know the person: truth is identifiable in the felt human experience[....] Even though viewers may be aware of the convention, it nevertheless has an emotive power" (*ibid.*, 46–7).
36. Glen Creeber, *Serial Television: Big Drama on the Small Screen* (London: BFI Publishing, 2004), 12.
37. Rapping, *Law and Justice*, 244–245.
38. Paul Wright, "'Victims' Rights' as a Stalking Horse for State Repression," in *Prison*

Nation: The Warehousing of America's Poor, eds. Tara Herivel and Paul Wright (New York: Routledge, 2003), 63.

39. Rapping, *Law and Justice*, 167.
40. Wright, "Victims' Rights," 64.
41. Lynne Joyrich writes that televisual depictions of crime and social crises turn to melodrama to present narratives, often framing them in "personal terms as a way of avoiding the larger institutional, political, and ideological issues they raise." Lynne Joyrich, *Re-Viewing Reception: Television, Gender, and Postmodern Culture* (Bloomington: Indiana University Press, 1996), 49.
42. Krystal Houghton, "Deviant," *CSI: Miami*, season 4, episode 16, directed by Scott Lautanen, aired February 27, 2006, on CBS.
43. Ibid.
44. McCormick, "Family Ties."
45. Ibid.
46. "The Autopsy Theater Tour," *CSI: Miami: The Complete First Season on DVD* (Hollywood, CA: Paramount, 2004), DVD.

WORKS CITED

"The Autopsy Theater Tour." *CSI: Miami: The Complete First Season on DVD*. Hollywood: Paramount, 2004. DVD.
Beck, Julie A. "Victims' Rights and Public Safety? Unmasking Racial Politics in Crime Discourses Surrounding Parole Revocation for 'Lifers' in California." *Western Criminology Review* 11, no. 1 (2010): 20–36.
Berlant, Lauren. *The Queen of America Goes to Washington City: Essays on Sex and Citizenship*. Durham: Duke University Press, 1997.
Biderman, Ian. "Bombs Away." *Crossing Jordan*, season 2, episode 2. Directed by Ian Toynton. Aired September 30, 2002, on NBC.
Brunsdon, Charlotte. *The Feminist, the Housewife, and the Soap Opera*. New York: Oxford University Press, 2000.
Carter, Chris. *The X-Files*. Fox, 1993–2002.
Cornwell, Patricia. *Postmortem*. New York: Scribner's, 1990
Creeber, Glen. *Serial Television: Big Drama on the Small Screen*. London: BFI Publishing, 2004.
Creed, Barbara. *The Monstrous-Feminine: Film, Feminism, Psychoanalysis*. New York: Routledge, 1993.
Devine, Elizabeth, and John Haynes. "Spring Break." *CSI: Miami*, season 1, episode 23. Directed by Deran Serafian. Aired April 23, 2003, on CBS.
Dube, Mark. "A Rock and a Hard Place." *CSI: Miami*, season 6, episode 19. Directed by Gina Lamar. Aired May 5, 2008, on CBS.
Hanson, Hart. *Bones*. Fox, 2005–2017.
Houghton, Krystal. "Deviant." *CSI: Miami*, season 4, episode 16. Directed by Scott Lautanen. Aired February 27, 2006, on CBS.
Isreal, Mark. "Ashes to Ashes." *CSI: Miami*, season 1, episode 5. Directed by Bryan Spicer. Aired October 21, 2002, on CBS.
Joyrich, Lynne. *Re-Viewing Reception: Television, Gender and Postmodern Culture*. Bloomington: Indiana University Press, 1996.
Kelley, David. *Picket Fences*. CBS, 1992–1996.
Klaver, Elizabeth. *Sites of Autopsy in Contemporary Culture*. Albany: SUNY Press, 2005.
Kring, Tim. *Crossing Jordan*. NBC, 2001–2007.
Kring, Tim. "Pilot." *Crossing Jordan*, season 1, episode 1. Directed by Allan Arkush. Aired September 24, 2001, on NBC.
Maeda, Steven. "Spring Break." *CSI: Miami*, season 1, episode 21. Directed by Deran Serafian. Aired April 28, 2003, on CBS.
McCormick, Kathy. "Family Ties," *Crossing Jordan*, season 2, episode 11. Directed by Ian Toynton. Aired January 13, 2003, on NBC.

McNamara, Eileen. "Revenging Angles." *Boston Globe Magazine*, February 23, 1992. 12.
Modrovich, Ildy, and Laurence Walsh. "Broken." *CSI: Miami*, season 1, episode 6. Aired October 28, 2002, on CBS.
Nance, Barbara. "Someone to Count On." *Crossing Jordan*, season 1, episode 21. Directed by Nick Gomez. Aired April 28, 2002, on NBC.
Nelson, Robin. *TV Drama in Transition: Forms, Values, and Cultural Change*. New York: St. Martin's Press, 1997.
Rapping, Elayne. *Law and Justice as Seen on TV*. New York: New York University Press, 2003.
Sarnoff, Elizabeth. "Secrets and Lies Part 1." *Crossing Jordan*, season 1, episode 22. Directed by Michael Gershman. Aired May 6, 2002, on NBC.
Sarnoff, Elizabeth. "Scared Straight." *Crossing Jordan*, season 2, episode 7. Directed by Arvin Brown. Aired November 18, 2002, on NBC.
Wright, Paul. "Victims' Rights' as a Stalking Horse for State Repression." In *Prison Nation: The Warehousing of America's Poor*, edited by Tara Herivel and Paul Wright, 60–64. New York: Routledge, 2003.
Zuiker, Anthony E., Ann Donahue, and Carol Mendelsohn. *CSI: Miami*. CBS, 2002–2012.

A Woman in a Man's (Fictional) World

Considering the Importance of Dr. Molly Hooper in the BBC's Modern Adaptation of Sherlock

JENNIFER PHILLIPS

The character of Sherlock Holmes has made an indelible impact on English literature since his first appearance in Arthur Conan Doyle's novel *A Study in Scarlet*, published in 1887.[1] In the 130 years since, Holmes has returned not only in Conan Doyle's novels and stories, but in numerous Holmes "pastiche" novels, as well as over 200 portrayals in films and television, the latest and (arguably) greatest of which is the BBC adaptation, *Sherlock* (2010–present), where Sherlock Holmes (Benedict Cumberbatch) and his companion John Watson (Martin Freeman) have been lifted out of their late–Victorian context and placed in modern-day London, fit with mobile phones, online blogs, and blood-thirsty British paparazzi.[2]

When viewers are first introduced to Sherlock Holmes, he is shown in a way that not only references the original text, but also revises all prior conceptions of the character.[3] In a scene mentioned only in passing in *A Study in Scarlet*, yet rarely depicted on screen, Sherlock is shown repeatedly whipping a corpse with a riding crop—hardly the traditional heroic introduction. In this same scene, viewers are also introduced to another character: a small, mousey, shy woman in a lab coat who has a (not so) secret crush on the titular detective. As witness to the detective's gruesome display, this woman is not disturbed at all. In fact, mere moments after he finishes whipping the corpse, she asks him out for coffee. Sherlock answers with an order—"white with two sugars, thanks"—a sign of his obliviousness when it comes to the opposite sex. Her response to the mix-up is only to utter a meek "okay," and to proceed to make the detective his requested beverage.

This woman is Dr. Molly Hooper (played by Louise Brealey), Specialist Registrar at Saint Bartholomew's Hospital in London and the only recurring character in Mark Gatiss and Steven Moffat's adaptation who was not created by Arthur Conan Doyle himself. As they have stated on numerous occasions, Moffat and Gatiss originally set a rule only to include recurring characters who originated in Doyle's stories. However, because of Molly's impact in her first scene, aided by the skill of Brealey's performance, they soon found themselves breaking their rule.[4] As an original creation, *Sherlock*'s writers have complete creative freedom over the development of Molly Hooper's character, and as such, she is, arguably, one of the more developed characters in the series despite her limited screen-time.

In season one, Molly is shown as a one-note character—the girl with the hopeless crush. In season two, she not only stands up to Sherlock when he ruthlessly rejects and ridicules her in front of all of their friends, but she is later shown as the one person Sherlock relies on when he thinks everyone else (including John) has turned against him. By the third season, we learn that Molly was the one who made it possible for Sherlock to fake his own death and, in the season's concluding episode, we see that she is the only one who is willing to (literally and metaphorically) slap sense into the drug-addicted detective.

For a series where the majority of the online fan focus is on the implicit homoerotic subtext in the relationship between Holmes and his best friend John Watson, the figure of Molly Hooper has nevertheless garnered a rather large online following over the course of the series' first three seasons. Not only have the producers created a paratextual appendix to her character—a fictional online blog existing alongside Holmes' and Watson's own fictional websites[5]—but she has also been the focus of memes and Twitter campaigns, and online defenses in situations such as when producer Mark Gatiss made comments that minimized her character's role, or her most recent exclusion from the 2017 official *Sherlock* calendar. Much of the reaction to Molly, especially from season two onwards, focuses on her strength and resilience as well as the development of her relationship with Sherlock, from hopeless crush to "the one person that mattered most," as Sherlock himself declares.[6]

In this essay, I will analyze the progression of the depiction of Dr. Molly Hooper throughout the series, and the increasing importance she has in Sherlock's professional as well as private life. I will also analyze fan responses to the character, as well as consider the role of the creators' comments. Finally, I will highlight the way Molly Hooper functions as a role model for women in an otherwise male-dominated profession and as one of the few female characters in an otherwise almost entirely homosocial textual universe, arguing that she is key to the adaptation of Conan Doyle's stories into our modern world.

Homosocial Holmes

Very few female characters appear in the original Sherlock Holmes canon. Of those who do appear, none are shown to have interest in the detective beyond his skills at solving crimes. Moreover, women in Doyle's stories are less like characters and more frequently utilized as plot devices. For example, Mrs. Barclay's husband is found dead in "The Adventure of the Crooked Man" and Holmes investigates because he doesn't agree with the police's assumption that Mrs. Barclay was responsible.[7] However, this is not based on any analysis of her character or depth of interaction with her. Similarly, the character of Elise Cubitt is the source of the mystery in "The Adventure of the Dancing Men," even though it is her husband who approaches Holmes for assistance before his untimely death.[8] Although the character of Helen Stoner is the stereotypical damsel in distress in "The Adventure of the Speckled Band," her main plot function is to inform Holmes of the backstory of why she suspects her stepfather is plotting to kill her.[9] Once the exposition is dispensed with, she fails to feature. While all three women, among others within the Doyle canon, are seen interacting with the detective, they rarely if ever express their opinions of him, his methods, his actions, or even his personality. Instead, all impressions of Holmes in the original stories are filtered through John Watson's first-person narration, and although Watson does highlight some of Holmes' more idiosyncratic techniques, habits, and personality traits, there is very little indication of other characters' opinions of him, as Moffat himself has observed.[10]

Similarly, in the BBC adaptation, there are few characters whose opinions of Sherlock Holmes are shown. One of John's girlfriends expresses her unhappiness at John's willingness to let Sherlock get in the way of his friend's romantic entanglements.[11] Similarly, Journalist Kitty Reilly is more than willing to believe and publish Moriarty's lies about the detective.[12] In contrast to these characters, Molly's interactions with the detective present a more complete picture of a complex, intriguing, and often amusing relationship between the two characters. Her reaction to him in the "flogging" scene indicates a level of infatuation, if not attraction.[13] However, when he unceremoniously informs Molly that her boyfriend Jim (later revealed to be none other than villain Jim Moriarty himself) is gay, Molly doesn't hide her hurt, nor does she minimize the detective's role in creating it, asking irately why he has to "spoil" her relationship with Jim.[14] Similarly, when Sherlock accidentally deduces in front of all of their friends that Molly has "looooove" on her mind, unaware that those feelings are directed towards him, Molly tells him that he "always" says "such horrible things."[15] In the second season finale, Molly's honesty with Sherlock is taken one step further, as she reveals to the detective that she can see he is sad, even when he is attempting to hide it from John.[16] Thus, as creator Stephen Moffat himself has noted, Molly provides an additional perspective on the detective—that of a woman who can truly see him, and does not always appreciate what it is she sees.

There is a larger purpose for the character of Molly Hooper than merely refracting an additional aspect of Sherlock than that which is revealed by John Watson. As Moffat also has observed, Molly is, from season two onwards, frequently shown as "beating" Sherlock by coming out on top in almost every conversation they have.[17] Moffat cites the scene in "A Scandal in Belgravia" as a turning point: after Molly accuses him of saying "horrible things" he apologizes for his behavior for the first time.[18] Sherlock's apology shocks even his best friend; Watson visibly does a double take at the unprecedented behavior.

Much has been written criticizing the ending of "A Scandal in Belgravia,"[19] an adaptation of the well-known Conan Doyle story "A Scandal in Bohemia." In the original tale, Holmes is defeated by Irene Adler, a rare failure for the detective and the only time in Conan Doyle's canon where he is bested by someone of the opposite sex. Yet, when adapted in the BBC version, Irene Adler is transformed into a damsel in distress to be saved by a *deus ex machina* of Sherlock being in the right place at the right time to stop her execution. While this reversion to stale, misogynistic hero-tropes is an unfortunate direction for the series, when the episode is read with Molly Hooper in mind, and in light of the scene where she makes him apologize and admit he was wrong, there is a scant glimmer of empowered womanhood—at least there is one woman in the BBC series who does beat Holmes, even if it is not the same woman as in Conan Doyle's original version. Molly's continued ability to thwart, surprise, and even beat the detective is something that co-creator Steven Moffat is particularly fond of.[20]

In addition to Irene Adler, the other two main recurring female characters from Conan Doyle's canon included in the BBC adaptation are Sherlock and John's landlady Mrs. Hudson and John's wife, Mary Watson. Both of these characters have been modernized somewhat from their original incarnations. There are ongoing jokes about Mrs. Hudson's use of medicinal marijuana and her past as an exotic dancer in her deceased husband's drug cartel. Likewise, Mary is more than a mere housewife who tolerates her husband's exploits with his eccentric friend. In this version, she is revealed to have a past life as a CIA assassin gone rogue. Apart from this, both characters are nothing other than supportive, loving, and unquestioningly loyal to Sherlock. While the same is true of Molly, we have seen that she is also willing to question Sherlock, challenge him, and correct him when necessary, something no other character in the series, male or female, is given the ability to do. Even Moffat and Gatiss have noticed that the unintentional consequence of adding of Molly is to place Sherlock in the contemporary context.[21]

The role of Molly Hooper in the modernization of Sherlock Holmes is not only revealed in her agency and power over the detective, something rare within the original context, but her very role as a female doctor would be almost unthinkable in Conan Doyle's time. The modern qualities of Molly's character are evident in the way she was transformed in the 2015 Christmas Special "The Abominable Bride,"[22] where Holmes and Watson are transported back to their original Victorian setting through the plot device of Sherlock's drug-addled mind. As Steven Moffat noted at a promotional event months before the special aired, such a tampering with the timeframe caused problems for the characterization of Molly Hooper.[23] In order for Molly Hooper to exist in the Victorian era, the creators came up with an ingenious workaround: Molly would indeed appear as a pathologist, but one who hides her gender, dressing and acting like a man. So successful is her charade that even Holmes himself is fooled (although not Watson, as it is soon revealed).

Thus, when compared to the minor roles of women in the original canon, as well as the characterization of women in the BBC series, Molly provides a chance to see a larger perspective on the character of Holmes. She also functions to modernize the detective and the world in which he lives and works. However, if the function of Molly was merely to reveal aspects of the detective, and to remind the viewers that they are watching a modern version of his exploits, she would not be as powerful a character as many fans have taken her to be.

Molly in the Morgue

More than being inserted as a figure of modernity and a potential foil to Sherlock, Molly is also a skilled pathologist with an increasingly important professional role in assisting the detective in his work. After completing an experiment, Sherlock tells her "I need to know what bruises form in the next twenty minutes, a man's alibi depends on it, text me."[24] The phrase "text me" implies not only that Sherlock trusts Molly to provide him with accurate data via text, but that she has done so before. He doesn't have to give her his phone number; she already has it stored in her phone. Moreover, the stakes of the data are quite high: "a man's alibi depends on it."[25] This again demonstrates the high level of trust the detective has in Molly's professional skills.

However, Molly's role in Sherlock's investigations is not without its problematic elements. In another episode, Molly provides Sherlock access to the evidence he needs, but only after he manipulates her into allowing him to see a corpse that she has already autopsied.[26] He does this by complimenting Molly's hairstyle. While it is unfortunate that Molly is shown to be so easily manipulated by Sherlock in this instance, in a deleted line of dialogue from a later episode[7] there is an indication that Molly is aware that Sherlock has been playing on her feelings for him in order to get favors and access to the lab; she knows how he uses his "big, dark eyes and deep, deep voice" to coerce her into helping him.[28] However, it is not clear from this admittedly scrapped bit of dialogue that Molly was so self-aware in the earlier episode, set 3–4 years earlier. Nevertheless, it shows that Sherlock knows he can go to Molly to get access to important information for his cases, while Molly is more than happy to help.

So important has this aspect of Molly's character been that there was criticism leveled at the creators for the most recent use (or misuse) of Molly in the season four opener, "The Six Thatchers."[29] Instead of showing Molly's skillset as a pathologist or her ability to assist Sherlock in his investigations, Molly's role in the episode was to fill more "traditional" feminized roles as godmother at the Christening of baby Rosemond Watson, as on-call babysitter who fills in when the Watsons are off solving crimes with Sherlock, and, more tragically, as the one left literally and figuratively "holding the baby" at the end of the episode after Mary is shot and killed protecting Sherlock. Fans of Molly took to Tumblr to register their displeasure at her portrayal in the episode, with one fan asking, "why the fuck is it Molly—pathologist and therefore the most highly trained and professionally busy person in the entire show […] who gets left holding the baby."[30] In fact, if a viewer had just tuned into the latest episode, without any prior knowledge of the series, there is nothing to indicate that Molly is a highly educated and capable doctor. Her skill-set, as it appears in "The Six Thatchers," is limited to babysitting.

Sherlock co-creator Steven Moffat has frequently faced criticism for his portrayal of female characters, not only on *Sherlock* but also in the other series he runs, *Doctor Who*. Where this depiction of Molly isn't as problematic as the repeated Moffat trope of girl-to-woman-to-love-interest pattern noted in the latter,[31] this portrayal of Molly, removed from her professional setting and shoe-horned into traditionally "maternal" roles of godmother and babysitter, is especially troubling considering the same episode took the series' most empowered female character to date, former super-spy Mary Watson, and had her killed protecting Sherlock. This type of death of a female character is a continuation of a pattern originally identified in comic books, but which has more recently been seen as manifesting on popular television.[32] Mary's death, in what is essentially a glorified plot device to create angst for the central male characters (or, what many feminist critics call "stuffed in the fridge" in order to create "man pain"), rings a troubling note for the development of not only Molly as a character, but the series as a whole.[33]

Molly's Minions

From their reactions, it is clear that fans would much rather see Molly in her professional role than in any other incarnation in the series. This may be because the latest episode flies in the face of the development of Molly's character over the course of the series, which has depicted a broadening of her skills from assisting in minor experiments to attending to Sherlock's personal needs, to ultimately saving the detective's life. Moreover, Molly is shown as growing as a character, refusing to allow herself to be manipulated by Sherlock and literally slapping sense into him after his fall back into drug use.[34] As a reflection of Molly's growing importance in the work of the titular detective, fans have begun to reflect on her as a role model for young women, congregating around the Twitter and Tumblr hashtag #mollymatters to express their feelings for her character. Brealey was so moved by the posts that she took to Twitter to thank her fans for their response to Molly.[35]

Molly is so powerful in the eyes of some fans, particularly in her interactions with the male characters in the series, that a meme called BAMF!Molly was created. BAMF is an acronym for Badass Motherfucker, or, in other words, someone not to be messed with. A screen-capture from the scene in which Molly causes Sherlock to apologize for the first time is the basis of the meme. The image of Molly from that scene is accompanied by simple explanations of why she is such a BAMF. These include, "dated London's most notorious criminal—and then dumped his ass," "Deduced the crap out of Sherlock so much she made him stammer," and "tells off Sherlock for being so nasty."[36] Despite this meme, not all fans read Molly as a representative of female empowerment. In a Tumblr conversation accompanying the images, one critic claims that Molly has no backbone, while another lists five times she stands up to Sherlock (one for every episode in which she had appeared to that point).[37]

It seems that fans of her character are primarily responding to Molly's strength and skill. However, there is another element of her characterization that has also gained significant online fan attention: her relationship with the detective himself. As we have seen, in addition to establishing Molly firmly as a necessary assistant in Sherlock's cases, her introduction in the first episode foregrounds her feelings for the titular detective. In this way, Molly is similar to other characters who have been created in Sherlock Holmes pastiche fiction, whose roles highlight what was left implicit (or ignored) in Conan Doyle's original creation: the question of Sherlock Holmes' sexuality.

Yet, instead of developing a romantic relationship between the two characters (as occurs in Laurie R. King's *Mary Russel* series), Molly Hooper has been read alternatively as revealing Holmes as asexual, homosexual, or heterosexual.

In their commentary on the character, creators Moffat and Gatiss highlight that their intention for the character was for her only to appear in the original scene in which she asks Sherlock out for coffee, revealing how the concept of dating wouldn't even cross his mind, thus underscoring his asexuality or, at least, his disinterest in romantic relationships.[38] As Moffat observed, despite the fact that Molly was written as being "in love" with Sherlock, Sherlock clearly "didn't notice" her affections; romance just simply wasn't on his radar.[39]

Yet, despite the creators' intentions that this scene establishes Holmes as asexual, aromantic, or perhaps even naïve when it came to relationships, fans have made other readings of Molly's role in the opening scene. In one reading, often performed by fans who read a homosexual subtext in the Holmes/Watson relationship, Sherlock's disinterest in Molly Hooper is contrasted with his desire to impress John Watson in the next scene, which depicts the first meeting of the legendary pair. Sherlock's cool dismissal of Molly is juxtaposed with the way he appears to be pulling out all the stops in leaving an impression on Watson, by deducing that he is an injured veteran from the Afghanistan war and offering that the two move in together after only being in each other's presence for mere minutes.[40]

When read in isolation, it would seem that Molly's character was indeed intended only to establish the impossibility of Holmes as a sexual being, or at least hint strongly that this is not to be a version of Holmes who pursues such things. Yet, as the series progresses and Molly's role is expanded, a third possibility is raised, with many scenes in season three hinting at a possible future romantic link between the two. The season three opening episode begins with a "fantasy" version of how Sherlock survived the plunge off the roof of Saint Bartholemew's Hospital, which occurred in the cliffhanger ending of season two.[41] In this version, full of action movie tropes, Sherlock is shown not only utilizing a bungee cord and a hypnotist to pull of his ruse, but also smashing through a window and shocking a waiting Molly Hooper, whom he grabs and kisses soundly before continuing his retreat out of the hospital. Just like the introduction to Molly's character, this scene can be read in multiple ways. In the episode, Detective Lestrade (Rupert Graves), the character hearing this theory from the lips of fellow police officer-turned-Holmes-fanatic Philip Anderson (Jonathan Aris), calls it "bollocks" (a crude British colloquialism denoting disbelief). Yet, this very scene demonstrates the existence of sexual tension between the characters, something that is developed throughout season three.

Later in that same episode, there seems to be some degree of awkward hesitation when Sherlock asks Molly to "solve crimes" with him. The request is preceded by all the nerves of a man about to ask a woman out on a first date. While Molly first misinterprets the request, thinking that Sherlock is asking her out to dinner, at the end of the day their roles are reversed. As they leave their final job, Sherlock does indeed ask out Molly for dinner, a request she implicitly rejects. Confused by the day's events and her role as John's temporary "replacement," Molly asks what Sherlock's motives were, to which he replies that he is attempting to say thank you because Molly was the one person Moriarty thought didn't matter to Sherlock, and was, in fact, "the one person that matters the most."[42] Sherlock adds that Molly made his death and resurrection possible. When Sherlock notes that he sees that Molly is now engaged, he concedes that not all the men Molly falls for can turn out to be sociopaths, a reference not only to her feelings for him, but also her ill-fated relationship with villain Jim Moriarty. After wishing her future happiness, Sherlock smiles a small, sad smile before kissing Molly on the cheek. Slow, emotional music accompanies the scene to its conclusion, where Sherlock and Molly exit the building and separate, literally and figuratively taking different paths.

The scene is uncharacteristically full of emotion, particularly from the often-emotionless detective, and sits in odd contrast to the fact that the relationship between Molly and her fiancé is unceremoniously concluded (off-screen) in two episodes' time. For a series with precious little screen time, it seems peculiar that this sub-plot would be included at all. Fan theories about the role of Molly's fiancé included Tom acting as a secret bodyguard placed by Mycroft, Tom as one of the snipers who were threatening Sherlock's friends in the conclusion to season two, and the more obvious reading that he was only included as a joke due to his resemblance to Sherlock.[43] Yet, as one fan observed, the inclusion, and later conclusion, of Molly's short-lived engagement, while containing the potential to erase any future relationship between the detective and the pathologist, now leaves that option open for the writers should they choose to take it.[44]

Another small scene in the season three finale also strongly implies a connection between the two characters.[45] When a critically injured Sherlock goes missing from the hospital, John and Mary try to find out where he can be. In a scene that is shot in such a way as to obscure the identity of the person talking to Molly, Molly admits, almost to camera, that Sherlock sometimes sleeps in her spare bedroom, although soon corrects it to "my bedroom," adding that "we agreed he needs the space."[46] The meaning of this scene remains ambiguous. For one, the audience has no idea who Molly is talking to. Secondly, Molly's slip of the tongue, first reporting that Sherlock uses her spare bedroom before settling on her bedroom, adds a layer of confusion, and thirdly, Molly looks away, taking an awkward sip of her coffee cup after the admission and leaving the viewer to consider what it is she may be hiding. So confusing is the meaning of this short scene that some fans have dedicated thousands of words to deciphering it.[47]

The implicit relationship, or potential relationship revealed in these scenes is in contrast to the producers' and actors' own comments about Molly and Sherlock. Louise Brealey, the actress who plays Molly, encourages fans in their desires to see a romantic relationship between her character and the detective. Brealey has been known to post links to fan-made manipulated graphics depicting Sherlock and Molly in romantic embraces.[48] When the "fantasy" kiss between Molly and Sherlock aired, Brealey was inundated with thousands of new Twitter followers in mere minutes, with Brealey lightly mocking fans for watching the kiss on repeat.[49] Later, when the definition of "shipping" (a verb, meaning to actively support a romantic relationship between two fictional characters) was added to the *Oxford English Dictionary* along with the sample sentence, "I will always ship Sherlock and Molly," Brealey excitedly shared the news with her Twitter followers. Brealey even added, in a tweet she later deleted, that she had texted co-star Benedict Cumberbatch to let him know the news.[50] Yet, despite her excitement for a possible Sherlock/Molly coupling, Brealey also admits that she doesn't think that Molly is Sherlock's "type," adding that she's not sure what his type actually is.[51]

Brealey's ambivalence towards the romantic pairing of the characters is echoed in the comments of the series' producers. In 2013, before season three aired, Steven Moffat commented that he didn't "think" that Sherlock and Molly would end up dating, but admitted that the two share a "proper friendship."[52] In the same interview, co-producer Sue Vertue added that Sherlock and Molly's relationship certainly wouldn't look much like fandom imaginings evident on Tumblr, the online forum where many Sherlock fans congregate.[53] In a later interview Steven Moffat stated that while Sherlock might indeed love and adore Molly, he doesn't believe that Molly is willing to end up with Sherlock, despite the fact she is "fascinated" by him.[54] In light of the developments of their relationship throughout season three, and despite any rejections of the possibility from the actors and producers of the show, many fans spent the long hiatus between seasons three and four writing fan fiction depicting a possible romance between the pair. In addition to the relationship elements within these stories, many focus on the strength in Molly's character and her power as one of the few characters in the series who stands up to Sherlock when he is in the wrong.

In the relationship between Sherlock and Molly there is room for numerous readings, as completely platonic, as building towards a romantic entanglement, or as a rejection of any possible romance between Holmes and any female character. Yet, to limit Molly to mere (potential) love interest is to overlook her role in the series, and the impact her character has on the fans. When faced with criticism from other parts of the fandom for only wanting to see Molly and Sherlock together as some form of audience surrogate, fans have highlighted opposing readings of the pairing. One Tumblr user, citing frequent criticism that "people only ship Sherlolly [a portmanteau relationship name for Sherlock and Molly] because they are in love with Sherlock and living vicariously through Molly," responded by saying, "Joke's on you, my friend. I'm actually in love with Molly Hooper and living vicariously through Sherlock."[55] Or, as another blogger put it, "Sherlolly was never about Sherlock. Sherlolly is all about Molly. Molly Hooper, the sane, loving, lovable, quirky, capable, intelligent woman that any man would be lucky enough to have. The way the girl blossomed into a woman throughout the series (with a lot of corpses thrown along the way), and how she ultimately humanizes Sherlock unlike any other character."[56] Where there are undoubtedly some within the Sherlolly fandom who are attracted to the pairing because of the sexuality and charisma of Benedict Cumberbatch's portrayal, there is a large and vocal section of fans who are inspired and encouraged by the characterization of Molly herself.

Minimizing Molly

Treating Molly as mere audience-surrogate, or as anything less than the strong character they believe her to be, is something many Molly fans will not stand for. On several occasions when Molly's role in the series has been overlooked or minimized, fans reacted with a fury not unlike Molly's own when faced with Sherlock's drug relapse. In 2014, co-creator Mark Gatiss made an offhand comment about how Molly is only "moving wallpaper" in Sherlock's eyes.[57] This lead to a Tumblr riot where Molly's fans reclaimed the term, and formed what was called, tongue-in-cheek, the "wallpaper conspiracy." Images where manipulated, stories written, and meta-analyses performed wherein fans went to sometimes extreme and humorous lengths to stretch the interpretation of Gatiss' comment in a way that maximized, rather than minimized, Molly's role in the series.[58] One such satirical post posited that because Molly is "wallpaper," and Sherlock has been shown to vent his frustration by shooting his pistol into said wallpaper, then *clearly* "the bullets, with their phallic shape, penetrate into the willing wallpaper in an act symbolizing Sherlock and Molly's desired [*sic*] to go at it like rabbits."[59]

More recently, tensions, which are always high within the *Sherlock* fan community on blogging platform Tumblr, ran over when the largest group in the fandom, those who believe the show is implicitly encoding a romance story between Holmes and Watson (known colloquially as the portmanteau

"Johnlock"), mocked fans of Molly, particularly those who would like to see a romantic relationship develop between the detective and his pathologist. This criticism took the form of an attack on the character of Molly herself, minimizing her importance in the series by asserting that she had only appeared in a total of 8 minutes of screen-time over the 10 episodes which had aired until that point, and concluding that her function is as a mere "plot device" rather than a character.[60]

A rebuttal post was quickly published, showing that Molly not only had almost three times that amount of screen-time, including 21 minutes of interactions with Sherlock, but also that the trend was to increase the role of Molly throughout the series, implying a growth in the importance of her character, rather than a minimization.[61] More than merely responding with facts, Molly's fans rallied in creative ways, using images, stories, and theories to retake the concept of "eight minutes" and find ways to paint Molly (and often Sherlock) in various (often sexual) eight-minute scenarios.[62]

Finally, when it was revealed that Molly's character would be excluded from the official 2017 *Sherlock* calendar, some of Molly's fans voiced their willingness to produce their own fan-made version, while one fan, who is also a woman working in a STEM field, wrote this impassioned response:

> I am a woman in a STEM field. I work in a lab as a laboratory assistant. Without going into superfluous detail, it has taken me a long time and years of very hard work and setbacks to get where I am now. Molly Hooper has been a huge influence in keeping me strong when I wanted to give up. Her presence was enough to make me struggle just those few extra months when I wanted to throw it all in and accept my life as an exceptional retail associate. I saw her and what she did for a profession and it reminded me every damn day that it is possible and it is important to go after the work that I want to do in laboratory sciences. This character is important, to me and to a lot of people. And they couldn't find a single month to feature her. In. An. Episode. About. Ignoring. Women.[63]

There is indeed an irony that while Molly is shown as leading a group of women fighting for women's rights in the Victorian Era in the 2015 Christmas special, in 2017 her voice and narrative have been erased in the calendar based on that very episode. Thankfully, due to the popularity of online forums like Tumblr, such silences don't remain for long, and fans of Molly can find a place to celebrate her role in the series.

The functions of Molly Hooper in the BBC adaptation of *Sherlock* are numerous and oftentimes able to be read in contradictory ways. Where she was meant to appear only once, now she is a fan-favorite, as well as a favorite of co-creator Steven Moffat. Where she was meant to reveal Sherlock's disinterest in romantic entanglements, not only has she been read as evidence of Sherlock's homosexuality, but also, and increasingly, the series seems to point towards a development of an emotional, if not romantic connection between herself and Sherlock. More than a mere insertion of a token woman into the overwhelmingly homosocial textual world of Conan Doyle's stories, Molly is, in the BBC adaptation, more like "the Woman," Irene Adler, in that she is the only woman to beat Sherlock, and she does so more successfully than the series' characterization of Adler herself. Moreover, as the series develops, Molly is shown giving more and more professional and personal assistance to Sherlock in his investigations as well as his life. The depth of fan reactions to Molly attest to this. Molly Hooper is a well-rounded, engaging, non-stereotypical female character in a male-dominated fictional world, and an example to both women in STEM and all female fans of the series.

Notes

1. Arthur Conan Doyle, *A Study in Scarlet* (London: Ward Lock, 1886).
2. Mark Gatiss and Steven Moffat (creators), *Sherlock* (BBC: 2010–present).
3. Steven Moffat, "A Study in Pink," *Sherlock*, season 1, episode 1, directed by Paul McGuigan, aired July 25, 2010, on BBC One.
4. Mayer Nissim, "Sherlock Showrunner Steven Moffat: 'Molly Broke Our First Rule,'" *Digital Spy*, December 9, 2013.
5. *Molly Hooper* (blog), accessed November 1, 2016; *The Personal Blog of Dr. John H. Watson* (blog), accessed November 1, 2016; *The Science of Deduction* (blog), accessed November 1, 2016.
6. Mark Gatiss, "The Empty Hearse," *Sherlock*, season 3, episode 1, directed by Jeremy Lovering, aired January 1, 2014, on BBC One.
7. Arthur Conan Doyle, *The Memoirs of Sherlock Holmes* (London: Ward Lock, 1893).
8. Arthur Conan Doyle, *The Return of Sherlock Holmes* (London: Ward Lock, 1903).
9. Arthur Conan Doyle, *The Adventures of Sherlock Holmes* (London: Ward Lock, 1892).
10. "Even Benedict Cumberbatch Fangirls Like Molly," *Metro*, December 9, 2013.
11. Steven Moffat, "A Scandal in Belgravia," *Sherlock*, season 2, episode 1, directed by Paul McGuigan, aired January 1, 2012, on BBC One.
12. Stephen Thompson, "The Reichenbach Fall," *Sherlock*, season 2, episode 3, directed by Toby Haynes, aired January 15, 2012, on BBC One.
13. Moffat, "A Study in Pink."
14. Mark Gatiss,"The Great Game," *Sherlock*, season 1, episode 3, directed by Paul McGuigan, aired August 8, 2010, on BBC One.
15. Moffat, "A Scandal in Belgravia."
16. Thompson, "The Reichenbach Fall."
17. Nissim, "Sherlock Showrunner Steven Moffat."
18. *Ibid.*
19. For example, see Jane Clare Jones, "Is Sherlock Sexist? Steven Moffat's Wanton Women," *The Guardian*, January 3, 2012; Erin Derwin, "Irene Adler: Forever Feminist," *The Artifice*, April 22, 2014; Aja Romano, "Why Does the Man Behind 'Doctor Who' and 'Sherlock' Still Have a Job?" *The Daily Dot*, December 12, 2015.
20. "Even Benedict Cumberbatch Fangirls Like Molly."
21. Christina Radish, "Steven Moffat on New Stories, Moriarty, Lestrade's Ideal Date, and Much More," *Collider*, July 12, 2015.
22. Steven Moffat and Mark Gatiss, "The Abominable Bride," *Sherlock*, Christmas Special, directed by Douglas Mackinnon, aired January 1, 2016, on BBC One.
23. Flicks in the City, "Sherlock Comic Con 2015 Panel," *YouTube* video, posted July 9, 2015.
24. Moffat, "A Study in Pink."

25. Ibid.
26. Stephen Thompson, "The Blind Banker," *Sherlock*, season 1, episode 2, directed by Euros Lyn, aired August 1, 2010, on BBC One.
27. Steven Moffat, "His Last Vow," *Sherlock*, season 3, episode 3, directed by Nick Hurran, aired January 12, 2014, on BBC One.
28. you-keep-me-right-jw, "Deleted Scenes," *You Keep Me Right!* (Tumblr blog), November 7, 2014.
29. Mark Gatiss, "The Six Thatchers", *Sherlock*, season 4, episode 1, directed by Rachel Talalay, aired January 1, 2017, on BBC One.
30. camillo1978, "Question: Why the Fuck...," *Cam* (Tumblr Blog), accessed January 4, 2017.
31. Ted B. Kissell, "Doctor Who's Girl-Women Weirdness," *The Atlantic*, March 28, 2013.
32. Daniel Feinberg, "Critic's Notebook: Why Did So Many Female Characters Die on TV Last Week?," *The Hollywood Reporter*, April 11, 2016.
33. "Stuffed into the Fridge," *TV Tropes*, accessed January 4, 2017; Sam Maggs, "If You Want to Get Angry, Watch This 'Women in Fridges' Supercut," *The Mary Sue*, August 6, 2014.
34. Moffat, "His Last Vow."
35. Kate Willis, "Sherlock Star Louise Brealey on What It's Like to Win an Army of Fans," *Independent*, November 14, 2014.
36. strawberrypatty, "Why Molly Hooper Is the Biggest BAMF in Sherlock," *Strawberry Patty* (Tumblr blog), 2013, accessed January 4, 2017.
37. The original post is lost. An image of it is cached at https://s-media-cache-ak0.pinimg.com/564x/29/6a/a7/296aa78b9c4cdccefb13da55027be3e0.jpg, accessed January 4, 2017.
38. Radish, "Steven Moffat on New Stories."
39. Ibid.
40. Rebekah TJLC Explained, "TJLC Explained: Episode 15—Molly Hooper," *YouTube* Video, posted May 15, 2016.
41. Gatiss, "The Empty Hearse."
42. Ibid.
43. Many such discussions took place online, but one collection can be seen in the reddit thread, "Sherlock sizing up Molly's Boyfriend," reddit.com, accessed January 1, 2017.
44. "Series Three: A Study in Relationships," Sherlolly.com, accessed November 1, 2016.
45. Moffat, "His Last Vow."
46. Ibid.
47. cheshiregrimmjow, "In Which I Overanalyze Mollys Bedroom Comment in His Last Vow," *Cheshiregrimmjow* (Tumblr blog), January 14, 2014.
48. Cate Sevilla, "28 Reasons to Worship Louise Brealey, AKA Molly from 'Sherlock,'" *Buzzfeed*, January 14, 2014.
49. Alistair McGeorge, "Louise Brealey: Benedict Cumberbatch Kiss in Sherlock Gave Me 7,000 Twitter Followers in 5 Minutes," *Mirror*, June 25, 2014; Sevilla, "28 Reasons to Worship Louise Brealey."
50. Emma Daly, "Sherlock Makes the Dictionary in New Definition of 'Ship,'" *Radio Times*, May 20, 2014.
51. Elizabeth Day, "Louise Brealey: I Don't Think Molly is Really Sherlock's Type," *The Guardian*, January 22, 2012.
52. Flicks in the City, "Sherlock Comic Con 2015 Panel."
53. Ibid.
54. Denise Martin, "What's Next on *Sherlock*? Steven Moffat Answers Our Lingering Questions About Season 3," *Vulture*, February 3, 2014.
55. doctor_molly_hooper_holmes, "People Only Ship Sherlolly Because...," *You Can See Me...* (Tumblr blog), April 15, 2016.
56. rosamundi, "What some people fail to realize...," *Rose of the World* (Tumblr blog), December 28, 2016.

57. doctor_molly_hooper_holmes, "Several Months Ago...," *You Can See Me...* (Tumblr blog), October 16, 2014.

58. thewallpaperconspiracy, "Mollpaper photobombs Mycroft," *The Wallpaper Conspiracy* (Tumblr blog), April 7, 2014; Fanfics are archived at http://archiveofourown.org/tags/The%20Wallpaper%20Conspiracy, accessed November 1, 2016.

59. cecylc, "Sherlolly Meta as Supported by the Wallpaper Conspiracy," *Shine Bright Like a Diamond* (Tumblr blog), March 17, 2014.

60. The "eight minute" post has since been deleted. Another Johnlock post asserting that the minutes of screen time are the main measurement of Molly's importance is alltheroadsleadtotjlc's post, "Molly Hooper Meta," *fuck it* (Tumblr blog), September 19, 2016.

61. strawberrypatty, "You want to know what's SUPER fun?" *Strawberry Patty* (Tumblr blog), December 31, 2016.

62. Many of these response posts are archived at *Eight Minute Molly* (Tumblr blog).

63. astraceaeblue, "guys, i am tired," *Fishing for lake trout* (Tumblr blog), November 20, 2016.

WORKS CITED

alltheroadsleadtotjlc. "Molly Hooper Meta." *fuck it* (Tumblr blog), September 19, 2016. http://alltheroadsleadtotjlc.tumblr.com/post/150646317930/molly-hooper-meta.
astraceaeblue. "guys, i am tired." *Fishing for lake trout* (Tumblr blog), November 20, 2016. http://asteraceaeblue.tumblr.com/post/153441144198/guys-i-am-tired-i-am-so-tired-i-have-been-for-a.
camillo1978. "Question: Why the Fuck..." *Cam* (Tumblr Blog). Accessed January 4, 2017. https://camillo1978.tumblr.com/post/155266614704/question-why-the-fuck-is-it-molly-pathologist.
cecylc. "Sherlolly Meta as Supported by the Wallpaper Conspiracy." *Shine Bright Like a Diamond* (Tumblr blog), March 17, 2014. http://cecylc.tumblr.com/post/79844418285/sherlolly-meta-as-supported-by-the-wallpaper.
cheshiregrimmjow. "In Which I Overanalyze Mollys Bedroom Comment in His Last Vow." *Cheshiregrimmjow* (Tumblr blog), January 14, 2014. http://cheshiregrimmjow.tumblr.com/post/73321707005/in-which-i-overanalyze-mollys-bedroom-comment-in.
Conan Doyle, Arthur. *The Adventures of Sherlock Holmes*. London: Ward Lock, 1892.
_____. *The Memoirs of Sherlock Holmes*. London: Ward Lock, 1893.
_____. *The Return of Sherlock Holmes*. London: Ward Lock, 1903.
_____. *A Study in Scarlet*. London: Ward Lock, 1886.
Daly, Emma. "Sherlock Makes the Dictionary in New Definition of 'Ship.'" *Radio Times*, May 20, 2014. http://www.radiotimes.com/news/2014-05-20/sherlock-makes-the-dictionary-in-new-definition-of-ship.
Day, Elizabeth. "Louise Brealey: I Don't Think Molly Is Really Sherlock's Type." *The Guardian*, January 22, 2012. https://www.theguardian.com/theobserver/2012/jan/22/louise-brealey-molly-sherlock-interview.
Derwin, Erin. "Irene Adler: Forever Feminist." *The Artifice*, April 22, 2014. http://the-artifice.com/irene-adler-forever-feminist/.
doctor_molly_hooper_holmes. "People Only Ship Sherlolly Because..." *You Can See Me...* (Tumblr blog), April 15, 2016. http://doctor-molly-hooper-holmes.tumblr.com/post/142874010962/people-only-ship-sherlolly-because-they-are-in/.
_____. "Several Months Ago..." *You Can See Me...* (Tumblr blog), October 16, 2014. http://doctor-molly-hooper-holmes.tumblr.com/post/100137516637/what-is-the-wallpaper-conspiracy.
Eight Minute Molly (Tumblr blog). Accessed January 4, 2017. http://www.eightminutemolly.tumblr.com.
"Even Benedict Cumberbatch Fangirls Like Molly." *Metro*, December 9, 2013. http://metro.co.uk/2013/12/09/sherlock-writer-mark-gatiss-even-benedict-cumberbatch-fangirls-like-molly-4223394/#ixzz4PlSaVTvZ.

Feinberg, Daniel. "Critic's Notebook: Why Did So Many Female Characters Die on TV Last Week?" *The Hollywood Reporter*, April 11, 2016. http://www.hollywoodreporter.com/fien-print/critics-notebook-why-did-female-882659.
Flicks in the City. "Sherlock Comic Con 2015 Panel." *YouTube* video, posted July 9, 2015. https://www.youtube.com/watch?v=TtWPTMZRgzY.
Gatiss, Mark. "The Empty Hearse." *Sherlock*, season 3, episode 1. Directed by Jeremy Lovering. Aired January 1, 2014, on BBC One.
_____. "The Great Game." *Sherlock*, season 1, episode 3. Directed by Paul McGuigan. Aired August 8, 2010, on BBC One.
_____. "The Six Thatchers." *Sherlock,* season 4, episode 1. Directed by Rachel Talalay. Aired January 1, 2017, on BBC One.
Gatiss, Mark, and Steven Moffat. *Sherlock*. BBC, 2010–present.
Jones, Jane Clare. "Is Sherlock Sexist? Steven Moffat's Wanton Women." *The Guardian*, January 3, 2012. https://www.theguardian.com/commentisfree/2012/jan/03/sherlock-sexist-steven-moffat/.
Kissell, Ted B. "Doctor Who's Girl-Women Weirdness." *The Atlantic*, March 28, 2013. http://www.theatlantic.com/entertainment/archive/2013/03/-i-doctor-who-i-s-girl-women-weirdness/274453/.
Maggs, Sam. "If You Want to Get Angry, Watch This 'Women in Fridges' Supercut." *The Mary Sue*, August 6, 2014. http://www.themarysue.com/fridging-supercut/.
Martin, Denise. "What's Next on *Sherlock*? Steven Moffat Answers Our Lingering Questions About Season 3." *Vulture*, February 3, 2014. http://www.vulture.com/2014/01/sherlock-finale-postmortem-steven-moffat-interview.html.
McGeorge, Alistair. "Louise Brealey: Benedict Cumberbatch Kiss in Sherlock Gave Me 7,000 Twitter Followers in 5 Minutes." *Mirror*, June 25, 2014. http://www.mirror.co.uk/tv/tv-news/louise-brealey-benedict-cumberbatch-kiss-3762001.
Moffat, Steven. "His Last Vow." *Sherlock*, season 3, episode 3. Directed by Nick Hurran. Aired January 12, 2014, on BBC One.
_____. "A Scandal in Belgravia." *Sherlock*, season 2, episode 1. Directed by Paul McGuigan. Aired January 1, 2012, on BBC One.
_____. "A Study in Pink." *Sherlock*, season 1, episode 1. Directed by Paul McGuigan. Aired July 25, 2010, on BBC One.
Moffat, Steven, and Mark Gatiss. "The Abominable Bride." *Sherlock*, Christmas Special. Directed by Douglas Mackinnon. Aired January 1, 2016, on BBC One.
Molly Hooper (blog). Accessed November 1, 2016. http://www.mollyhooper.co.uk/.
Nissim, Mayer. "Sherlock Showrunner Steven Moffat: 'Molly Broke Our First Rule.'" *Digital Spy*, December 9, 2013. http://www.digitalspy.com/tv/sherlock/news/a536572/sherlock-showrunner-steven-moffat-molly-broke-our-first-rule/.
The Personal Blog of Dr. John H. Watson (blog). Accessed November 1, 2016. http://www.johnwatsonblog.co.uk/.
Radish, Christina. "Steven Moffat on New Stories, Moriarty, Lestrade's Ideal Date, and Much More." *Collider*, July 12, 2015. http://collider.com/sherlock-steven-moffat-on-new-stories-moriarty-lestrades-ideal-date-and-much-more/.
Rebekah TJLC Explained. "TJLC Explained: Episode 15—Molly Hooper." *YouTube* Video, posted May 15, 2016. https://www.youtube.com/watch?v=q9dDEwoBpFc.
Romano, Aja. "Why Does the Man Behind 'Doctor Who' and 'Sherlock' Still Have a Job?" *The Daily Dot*, December 12, 2015. http://www.dailydot.com/via/steven-moffat-sexism-sherlock-doctor-who/.
rosamundi. "What some people fail to realize..." *Rose of the World* (Tumblr blog), December 28, 2016. http://rosamundi.tumblr.com/post/155053284160/what-some-people-fail-to-realize-is-that-sherlolly.
The Science of Deduction (blog). Accessed November 1, 2016. http://www.thescienceofdeduction.co.uk/.
"Series Three: A Study in Relationships." Sherlolly.com. Accessed November 1, 2016. http://www.sherlolly.com/meta/series-three-a-study-in-relationships/.
Sevilla, Cate. "28 Reasons to Worship Louise Brealey, AKA Molly from 'Sherlock.'" *Buzzfeed*,

January 14, 2014. https://www.buzzfeed.com/catesevilla/28-reasons-to-worship-louise-brealey-aka-molly-from-sherlock.

"Sherlock sizing up Molly's Boyfriend." Reddit.com. Accessed January 1, 2017. https://www.reddit.com/r/Sherlock/comments/1ufqr1/sherlock_sizing_up_mollys_boyfriend/.

strawberrypatty. "Why Molly Hooper Is the Biggest BAMF in Sherlock." *Strawberry Patty* (Tumblr blog), 2013. Accessed January 4, 2017. http://strawberrypatty.tumblr.com/post/20762968892/i-needed-to-properly-convey-how-i-feel-about-this.

_____. "You want to know what's SUPER fun?" *Strawberry Patty* (Tumblr blog), December 31, 2016. http://strawberrypatty.tumblr.com/post/155174762627/you-want-to-know-whats-super-fun-numbers.

"Stuffed into the Fridge." *TV Tropes*. Accessed January 4, 2017. http://tvtropes.org/pmwiki/pmwiki.php/Main/StuffedIntoTheFridge.

Thompson, Stephen. "The Blind Banker." *Sherlock*, season 1, episode 2. Directed by Euros Lyn. Aired August 1, 2010, on BBC One.

_____. "The Reichenbach Fall." *Sherlock*, season 2, episode 3. Directed by Toby Haynes. Aired January 15, 2012, on BBC One.

thewallpaperconspiracy. "Mollpaper photobombs Mycroft." *The Wallpaper Conspiracy* (Tumblr blog), April 7, 2014. http://thewallpaperconspiracy.tumblr.com/post/81942859235/mollpaperphotobomb.

Willis, Kate. "Sherlock Star Louise Brealey on What It's Like to Win an Army of Fans." *Independent*, November 14, 2014. http://www.independent.co.uk/arts-entertainment/tv/features/sherlock-star-louise-brealey-interview-what-its-like-to-win-an-army-of-fans-9859892.html.

you-keep-me-right-jw. "Deleted Scenes." *You Keep Me Right!* (Tumblr blog), November 7, 2014. http://you-keep-me-right-jw.tumblr.com/post/102024038830/06-deleted-scenes-from-the-sherlock-chronicles.

The River, the Rock, the Relative and the Returned

Depictions of Women Scientists in Doctor Who's Moffat Era

KRISTINE LARSEN

The titular character of the long-running BBC series *Doctor Who* has always been accompanied by inquisitive and adventurous women on his journeys through time and space.[1] Some pass in and out of the alien Time Lord's millennia-long life in the space of a single episode, while others travel beside him for a season or more as an official companion. One of the most famous of the long-running female companions, Sarah Jane Smith (Elisabeth Sladen), even became the star of her own spinoff series, *The Sarah Jane Adventures*.[2]

After an impressive run from 1963 until 1989, the series went into hiatus, with the exception of a made-for-television movie in 1996. The so-called "New Who" series began (in the same canonical universe) in 2005 under the supervision of producer and head writer Russell T. Davies. Lynnette Porter argues that while Davies' revisioning "revitalized the television series, the companions who graced the TARDIS between 2005 and 2009 also should be credited with increasing the series' appeal to a wider audience."[3] Chief among these new companions were Rose Tyler (Billie Piper), Dr. Martha Jones (Freema Agyeman), and Donna Noble (Catherine Tate). The transition from Davies' tenure at the helm to the Steven Moffat Era (2010–present) was concomitant with the introduction of a controversial female companion, Amy Pond (Karen Gillan). Porter summarizes the controversy as a backlash against Amy's uncharacteristically "fierce self-determination and ability to get what she wants by force of personality," traits that make her "seem far more controlling and manipulative than previous companions."[4]

Amy and long-time boyfriend Rory Williams (Arthur Darvill) conceive a daughter on their wedding night while on board the TARDIS (the Doctor's time machine), a child whom her mother names Melody Pond and who is born with Time Lord–like regenerative powers.[5] The infant is kidnapped, raised, and brainwashed by a rebellious sect of the religious order the Silence (led by Madame Kovarian [Frances Barber]), and turned into an assassin who kills the Doctor on two occasions (albeit temporarily). After realizing that Kovarian's hatred of the Doctor is misplaced, Melody, whose name has been mistranslated and changed to River Song (Alex Kingston), becomes an archaeologist and eventually the wife of the Doctor. She is revealed to have inherited many of her mother's bolder traits, including a heightened sexuality, and, like her mother before her, has had both her fans and detractors. The controversy over female characters in the Moffat Era has been fueled, in part, by a rather vociferous debate among fans and scholars as to whether or not Steven Moffat's writing (especially of female characters) reflects an inherently misogynist viewpoint.[6] For his part, Moffat has vehemently denied such claims, but that has done little to quell the controversy.[7]

While River Song's role as the Doctor's wife certainly makes her an important character in the series, her role as a scientist also is worthy of analysis. In her 2010 Ph.D. thesis *Enlightenment was the Choice:* Doctor Who *and the Democratisation of Science*, Lindy Orthia analyzes non-recurring (i.e., non-companion) scientists in episodes of the BBC series broadcast between 1963 and 2008. Roslynn Haynes' 2003 paper lists seven common stereotypes in Western literature: the Faustian "evil alchemist"; the heroic "noble scientist"; the absent-minded "foolish scientist"; the Frankensteinian "inhuman researcher"; the Indiana Jones–like "scientist as adventurer"; the "mad, bad, dangerous scientist" perhaps best represented by H.G. Wells' Doctor Moreau; and the "helpless scientist" whose work cannot be controlled.[8] Since Orthia finds no examples of Haynes' "scientific adventurer" type in *Doctor Who* through 2008, she instead groups all "good" scientists into the "noble scientist" category and adds a new category, "scientist victim," those who are "not free to make ethical choices," usually due to the control of others.[9] Only 21.5 percent of these non-recurring scientist characters are female, and there are far more female "noble scientists" than female "mad scientists" or female "inhumane researchers" (making up 54.3 percent as opposed to 8.6 percent and 20 percent, respectively).[10]

She furthermore finds that "female scientist characters in *Doctor Who* were more likely than their male counterparts to fulfill the role of scientist only tokenistically, with a narrative function that moved them away from science and away from specialization, if indeed women were present at all."[11] As only River Song's first two appearances in the series are included in Orthia's study, previous analysis of her character as a scientist is rudimentary at best, and with the hindsight gleaned from now having viewed the entire televised arc of the character's rather tangled timeline, Professor River Song's role as a scientist deserves to be reassessed. In addition, three more significant female scientists have appeared in the series during the Moffat Era, geologist Nasreen Chaudhry (Meera Syal), UNIT Chief Scientist Kate Lethbridge-Stewart (Jemma Redgrave), and UNIT scientist Petronella Osgood (Ingrid Oliver).[12]

It is also interesting to note that since Orthia analyzes both male and female scientists, she chooses not to utilize Eva Flicker's six stereotypes of women scientists found in feature films: the old maid who is married to her work (until she abandons her science and reclaims her femininity through her love for a man); the male woman (a middling, asexual scientist who relies on her assertiveness to survive in an all-male environment); the naïve expert (ethical, good-looking, but ineffective); the evil plotter (an attractive, self-absorbed vixen with questionable morals who wields her sexuality as a weapon); the daughter/assistant (whose character is defined only through her relationship with a male scientist); and the lonely heroine (a strong, competent, ethical scientist and who can simultaneously be feminine but who still requires a male mentor to be successful).[13] Flicker's system is not only germane to this essay, but will be shown to be quite useful. This essay will therefore analyze for the first time the three above-mentioned female scientists, as well as reevaluate River Song, utilizing the systems of Orthia, Haynes, and Flicker, in order to situate their portrayal within the larger debate of Steven Moffat's characterization of women in *Doctor Who*. The majority of the female scientists of the Moffat Era are complex, fully developed characters rather than simple stereotypes, and as such provide both largely positive representations of female scientists as well as potential role models for young fans of the series.

The Rock: Geologist Dr. Nasreen Chaudhry

In the year 2020, geologist Dr. Nasreen Chaudhry leads a project to drill deeper into the Earth than has ever been accomplished before.[14] Not only is her penetration of Mother Earth fraught with sexual innuendo, but as noted by portraying actress Meera Syal, Nasreen is "quite a tomboy academic with no make-up, big Caterpillar boots and not afraid to get her hands dirty" who has succeeded in an all-male environment directing male subordinates.[15] Her practical work boots, stereotypical black-rimmed glasses, functional black pants, button down shirt, and comfortable black women's coat appear at first glance to paint her as an only slightly feminized version of the standard trope of scientist as nerd.[16] Nasreen's appearance largely confirms this stereotype, with the exception her jewelry (including an amethyst teardrop necklace) that feminizes her otherwise rather masculine attire.

As the drill site in a small Welsh village is plagued by unexplained earthquakes and the disappearance of several individuals into the ground, the Doctor (whose TARDIS has, as usual, inexplicably delivered him to these space-time coordinates at just this critical moment) immediately takes control of the situation. Although initially taken aback by the Doctor's rude manner, Nasreen quickly realizes that he knows more about the situation than she does, and acquiesces to all his commands. However, she remains curious rather than fearful; she meets the Doctor's rudeness with assertiveness and his compassion with enthusiastic agreement. When her assistant, Tony Mack (Robert Pugh), suggests they dissect a captured subterranean creature to look for its "weak points" the Doctor counters "No dissecting, no examining. We return their hostage, they return ours, nobody gets harmed.... You are decent, brilliant people. Nobody dies today. Understand?"[17] Swept up in the thrill of this rallying call to noble actions, Nasreen breaks into applause, and then sheepishly composes herself, a hint of tears in her eyes. She follows the Doctor into the TARDIS, demanding to be a part of this mission. She argues, "I have spent all my life excavating the layers of this planet, and now you want me to stand back while you head down into it? I don't think so."[18] Nasreen continues to self-confidently hold her own against the Doctor, going so far as to playfully pluck his suspenders, even as her sense of wonder grows concerning both his obviously alien lifestyle and the equally foreign subterranean world of the so-called Silurians, a reptilian species that considers the planet to be theirs.

Underground, Nasreen works to make peace with the Silurians, who are prepared to go to war with the humans. Nasreen not only agrees to destroy her equipment to preserve the peace and save the Silurians, she also decides to remain underground. This decision is partly motivated by a desire to be with Tony (who remains underground to await a future cure for his mutation-causing Silurian sting), but also due to her scientific curiosity. In her words, "I've got what I was digging for. I can't leave when I've only just found it."[19]

Nasreen's single-mindedness in pursuing scientific knowledge undeniably has dire consequences, leading to the death of at least two Silurians and nearly global war with the reptilian species.[20] While she is certainly not a mad scientist, it is fitting to label her as initially belonging to Haynes' category of the helpless scientist who cannot control her work. In terms of Flicker's stereotypes, at the onset Nasreen appears to fit the old maid trope, but as the arc evolves, so does she. Syal explains that Nasreen "has an intense curiosity and passion" which leads her to continue "learning all the time, even as far as romance is concerned."[21] More specifically, Nasreen appears completely surprised when Tony kisses her. When she tries to lamely protest, he offers,

"Like you didn't know."[22] She breaks the meek stereotype here, grabbing his face and kissing him back, before pulling back and adjusting her glasses and jacket. As she elects to remain beneath the earth with Tony, it is suggested that they will have a romantic relationship in the future, but given that her decision is also motivated by her scientific curiosity, she is not to be thought of as giving up her science for a man. Rather, she has found a way to have both her science and a meaningful relationship. Her willingness to compromise (including the willingness to sacrifice her drill site) also labels her as a noble scientist. Considered in totality, she therefore reflects an overall positive representation of a woman scientist. Blogger Derek of Crustula.com lists Nasreen as one of the characters who "should have become companions," based on the fact that she "was a scientist, she was witty, not easily flustered and was a capable 'woman of a certain age.'"[23] Since becoming a companion is considered a supreme honor in the universe of *Doctor Who*, this suggestion paints Nasreen as a complex, interesting character that has the potential to advance the plot of the series. In addition, since some companions become nearly as beloved to the fandom as the Doctor himself (e.g., Sarah Jane Smith), the idea that Nasreen has the "right stuff" to become a companion also signifies her potential as a positive role model for young viewers.

The Relative and the Returned: UNIT Scientists Kate Lethbridge-Stewart and Petronella Osgood

The ultimately diplomatic resolution of Nasreen's adventure reflects the Doctor's commitment to brokering peace between enemies. Yet, despite his commitment to pacifism wherever possible, the Doctor has had powerful friendships with military leaders, and perhaps none so deep as that with Brigadier Alastair Gordon Lethbridge-Stewart (Nicholas Courtney). Most of their time together was during the Doctor's third incarnation, when he was exiled to Earth and spent his time as scientific advisor to UNIT (United Nations—later Unified—Intelligence Taskforce), an organization set up to protect the earth against extraterrestrials. According to the character's official BBC biography, "Fiercely patriotic, the Brigadier never encountered an alien that he didn't attempt to shoot or blow up," a philosophy that put him at odds with the Doctor's more diplomatic approach.[24]

In the Moffat Era, the Doctor has found a different Stewart in charge of UNIT, the Brigadier's daughter Kate. When mysterious alien cubes appear all across the planet, Amy and Rory's front door is smashed in by over-zealous UNIT soldiers under Kate's command. After apologizing for the rough entrance, she introduces herself as the "head of scientific research at UNIT."[25] Note that she is not referred to as Dr. Stewart, and indeed her academic credentials are never explained in the series.[26] This is consistent with her larger role as leader of UNIT within the series but significantly downplays her role as a scientist. The Doctor is intrigued, asking "Since when did science run the military," to which she answers, "Since me."[27] She later explains that, despite the fact that she has dropped the Lethbridge from her name in order to earn her position in her own right rather than through nepotism, she has learned much from her father: "Science leads, he always told me. Said he'd learned that from an old friend."[28] The official BBC biography of the character notes that she is "intelligent, quick-witted and has a dry sense of humour. She is prone to moments of doubt and anguish when the odds seem overwhelming, and at one point the Doctor gently raised her morale."[29] Kate does, indeed, demonstrate a lack of confidence in nearly all of the six episodes in which she appears, and relies on the Doctor for guidance. For example, when all airplanes appear to be frozen in time midflight, Kate's first instinct is to call the Doctor, leading her to panic when he doesn't answer his phone.[30] Kate is also prone to blunders in judgment; for example in the 50th Anniversary Special "The Day of the Doctor" she has UNIT bring the TARDIS (via helicopter sky crane) to their HQ when it is found in London, not realizing that the Doctor and his companion are still inside.[31] She also often relies on others to save her, the most surprising case occurring when she is presumed dead in the crash of an airplane; her father, the Brigadier, his post-death consciousness housed in a Cyberman's robotic body, catches her mid-fall and safely returns her to earth.[32]

It is in the above-mentioned helicopter scene from "The Day of the Doctor" that viewers meet another female UNIT scientist, the delightfully nerdy Petronella Osgood. The consummate geek and Doctor groupie, she endears herself to the audience by donning bits of clothing copied from various incarnations of the Doctor, such as the Fourth Doctor's trademark scarf and the Eleventh Doctor's signature bowtie. Like Kate Stewart, she is never referred to as Dr. Osgood, so her precise scientific credentials are unknown. This is particularly unfortunate, for as a young woman, Osgood is already doubly marginalized as a scientist. Denying her earned academic credentials only adds to her marginal status. Despite this, Osgood quickly establishes herself as a central character and keen scientist. According to the character's official BBC biography, she is "a brilliant young UNIT scientist and massive fan of the Doctor."[33] Her demonstrated intellectual prowess (e.g., she is the first to understand the significance of a mysteriously large quantity of stone dust)[34] stands in contrast to her physical frailties (myopia that necessitates the stereotypical black rimmed glasses and asthma that requires the use of an inhaler). From their very first scene together, the differences between Osgood and

Kate are made crystal clear. Kate is not only the more (albeit, still questionably) confident as well as the senior scientist, but also far more feminine and fashionable. Tall, slender, and beautiful, the blonde Kate dresses in tight black trousers and heels with a fitted pea coat over an equally well-fitted black woman's suit jacket and feminine camisole, while the shorter and frumpier Osgood, her brunette hair pulled back into a severe ponytail, initially wears a white lab coat, practical shoes, and ill-fitted jeans along with the ridiculously long Fourth Doctor scarf. Another difference is the fact that Kate is often called by her first name, while the junior scientist is referred to by her last name only.[35] Both of these characteristics simultaneously downplay Osgood's gender at the same time that they accentuate her role as a stereotypical scientist (the reverse being true of Kate).

In the 50th anniversary special, the end of the world is only averted when the Doctor wipes the memories of Kate, Osgood, and the shape-shifting Zygon invaders masquerading as Kate and Osgood, and the quartet is forced to work together to establish a peace treaty. However, Osgood and her Zygon double are able to work out who is human and who is not (and realize that this must be kept secret from the others), again reflecting her (their) superior intelligence.[36] Osgood quickly became a fan favorite, with actress Ingrid Oliver not only noting that she has received countless enthusiastic messages from fans of the show, but pictures of fans cosplaying her character. In Oliver's words, "There's clearly mass appeal if 60-year-old men want to be a girl scientist."[37] Fans lamented Osgood's seemingly gratuitous demise in "Death in Heaven" at the hand of the Doctor's long-time nemesis the Master (here in a female regeneration called Missy), but rejoiced at her powerful return in the two-parter "The Zygon Invasion"/"The Zygon Inversion."[38] Here it is explained that during the events of the 50th anniversary special one of the shape-shifting alien Zygons had permanently taken on the form of Osgood, the dual Osgoods afterwards assuming the role of ultimate peacekeepers as part of Operation Double, the treaty between humanity and the 20 million Zygons now peacefully living on earth disguised in human form. Their refusal to see the other as alien—they proclaim that they are both Osgood—introduces a fascinating nuance to the usual stereotype of female scientist as Other.

Unfortunately, when one of the Osgoods dies, a rebel Zygon leader named Bonnie believes that her people are in danger and violates the treaty. Kate's initial impulse is to bomb the town, but the Doctor convinces her to postpone the attack. *Doctor Who TV* contributor Nathan Lobo uses this change of mind to laud the "fantastic Kate Stewart" for "her tendency to favour non-violent and scientific methods of sorting out issues than just going in guns blazing ... as her father preferred to do before he met the Doctor."[39] However, it is important to acknowledge that her first instinct is to violence, as it is in her original encounter with the Zygons where she threatens to destroy the planet rather than have secret technology fall into Zygon hands.[40] Kate again considers weapons of mutually assured mass destruction to stop the Zygon rebellion, when she and Bonnie both threaten to engage the two so-called Osgood boxes. Uncertain as to which button (if either) will cause the destruction of humans and which the genocide of the Zygons, Bonnie and Kate pause long enough for the Doctor to argue his case, and in the end it is Kate who eventually steps back from the brink of destruction first.[41] While she ultimately does choose peace, it is unclear how Lobo can justify his interpretation of her character. She clearly has hawkish tendencies, and while she certainly appeals to technology to solve problems, it is too often the technology of mass destruction. In addition, her connection to science never goes beyond calling herself the Chief Science Officer of UNIT, labeling her as an example of Orthia's contention that women in the series often only practice science in a tokenistic way. In contrast, Osgood is clearly represented as a real scientist, and frequently appeals not only to the scientific method, but also more broadly to logical thinking to solve problems.

In terms of both Haynes' and Flicker's categories of fictional women scientists, Kate Stewart is difficult to classify, since she really does nothing scientific at all. Osgood clearly begins her arc as one of Haynes' bumbling foolish scientists, but quickly establishes herself as both the intellectual and ethical centers of her storylines. Her role as a noble scientist is thus firmly established by the end of her first episodic appearance, in keeping with her increasingly positive (and complex) portrayal as a woman scientist. Like Kate, Osgood cannot be so clearly aligned with Flicker's tropes, unless one counts her as initially a daughter/assistant under the tutelage of a more "male"—i.e., more confident and powerful—scientist in Kate Stewart.

Josh Steer reflects upon the secret of Osgood's popularity, and attributes it to three specific factors: her construction as an obvious nod by Steven Moffat to the fans and their loyalty to the Doctor, her character development across the four episodes in which she appears, and her interactions with others, especially her pacifism.[42] Her development is most clearly reflected in her growing self-confidence; while in her first appearance she twice cowers and prays to herself that the Doctor will save her, by her return in season nine she not only is far more self-reliant, but also has no trouble bearing the responsibility for the safekeeping of the entire planet. Osgood is also a young woman who clearly values intelligence, empathy, and loyalty above the rather shallow, materialistic values that are stereotypically assigned to women in much of our modern media (e.g., an obsession with physical beauty and being part of the "in crowd"). Thus, she acts as an exceptionally positive role model for female viewers of all ages. In our last view of her, or rather them, they confidently walk away from the departing TARDIS after they both take a triumphant puff on their asthma inhalers. What was originally depicted as a sign of human frailty is, in the end, worn like a badge of honor. It is her battle cry, as she prepares to move forward with a new sister Osgood (signifying that she, herself, has literally been changed through this experience) in her renewed role as protector of the planet.

The River: Archaeologist Professor River Song

In her study, Orthia classifies River Song, an archaeologist, as among the noble scientists, strictly based on the character's first two episodes in the series, "Silence in the Library" and "Forest of the Dead" (episodes of the Davies Era written by Steven Moffat).[43] Due to the backwards nature of the character's timeline relative to the Doctor's, these episodes actually represent her *last* two meetings in the flesh with the Time Lord, as she dies near the end of "Forest of the Dead"[44] in order to save the lives of the Doctor and thousands of strangers.[45] Asher-Perrin notes that in their first episode together, River "has all the power: she is the one who calls the Doctor, she is the one who scolds him when he's being obstinate, she is the one who rallies the group and moves them along[....] It is she who grabs the Doctor's hand when the[y] first run together, not the other way around. She is taking *him* on as a companion in that first meeting."[46] While River Song is undoubtedly a powerful character in her first episodes, it is in her later adventures in which we come to realize that she is nothing less than a veritable force of nature, who utilizes equal parts intelligence and raw sexuality to manipulate both the laws of nature and the people around her (including the Doctor). Unfortunately, at first glance she becomes, in Orthia's terminology, only tokenistically a scientist in these later episodes. Or does she?

Asher-Perrin argues that the path that leads River to become "Professor Song" is deeply troubling from a feminist perspective in that the plot "is retconned so that it's all due to her obsession with a man who is *nearly a stranger* to her. Not because she adores history, or loves to explore, or needs to answer unanswerable questions. It's because she doesn't know her future boyfriend all that well, and textbooks are the easiest place to find him at the start."[47] River Song freely admits to the admissions committee of The Luna University that she wants to study archaeology because "I'm looking for a good man."[48] However, her answer is an interesting twist on the old trope in American culture of the woman (often from a well-off family) who is sent to college (usually to major in one of the humanities) in order to find a husband. Such a woman is said to be pursuing her "MRS degree."[49] In contrast, River Song not only earns a Ph.D., but is most often referred to as Doctor Song. Indeed, even the Doctor refers to her as "Doctor Song" after she has completed her degree (in her timeline) but before they become close (in his timeline).[50] In a curious juxtaposition, in "Flesh and Stone" we have characters referring to the Doctor and Doctor Song.[51] As he later explains to Clara Oswald (Jenna Coleman), the appellation "Doctor" is a name he chose, "like a promise you make," reflecting his dedication to helping those in need.[52] While his use of "Doctor" is honorific (or perhaps, better said, is aspirational), River's use of the term is certainly earned.

Ironically, the Doctor has an open disdain for archaeologists; for example, when he meets River for the first time (in his timeline), he notes, "I'm a time traveler. I point and laugh at archaeologists."[53] River, on the other hand, proudly proclaims her chosen profession. In one early encounter with the Silence, River impresses Rory with her ability to take out their enemy in an acrobatic hail of gunfire. Knowing well the Doctor's preference to avoid killing, River playfully asks Rory, "My old fellow didn't see that, did he? He gets ever so cross," to which an impressed Rory inquires, "So, what kind of doctor are you?" Without turning around, River fires behind her, killing a straggler, and without missing a beat, answers "Archaeology. Love a good tomb."[54]

McGeough suggests that there are two stereotypes of female archaeologists in popular culture: the beautiful "privileged women with a love of adventure" who are "unaware of or unwilling to acknowledge the male gaze," and the normally mousy-appearing "junior level scholars" who are suddenly revealed to be beautiful "when they take off their glasses and let down their hair."[55] Neither of these descriptions fit the fashion-conscious and sexually confident River Song, whom the Doctor succinctly describes to Winston Churchill as "Hell in high heels" (although she appears equally comfortable in battle fatigues or an evening gown).[56] Indeed, her favorite weapon to use against men (besides her sexuality itself) is hallucinogenic lipstick. One of the most important turning points in her life is when she kills the Doctor with poisoned lipstick, and, after observing the anguish of her parents, transfers all of her regeneration energy to the Doctor, restoring him to life. This is the moment that signals the metaphoric death of Melody Pond, a brainwashed assassin corrupted by the Silence, and the birth of River Song, child of the TARDIS and future wife of the Doctor.[57]

Given the strength of character and agency River Song displays throughout her time in the series, why has there been disappointment voiced concerning her character? Much of it concerns her early life as a pawn of the Silence. As Asher-Perrin reflects, River "spends her formative years with an existence that orbits around the Time Lord. She has no ambition of her own, no purpose beyond his destruction."[58] In addition, upon completing her Ph.D. she is again kidnapped again by the Silence and forced to assassinate the Doctor.[59] In perhaps her greatest display of power and autonomy, she utilizes her remaining TARDIS-born powers to literally shatter time: all moments in history occur at once. In this parallel universe River ridicules her nemesis, exclaiming "It was such a basic mistake, wasn't it, Madame Kovarian. Take a child, raise her into a perfect psychopath, introduce her to the Doctor. Who else was I going to fall in love with?"[60]

The climax of this episode is also the source of vociferous complaints by many fans. In particular, as Joanna Robinson describes, their "uncomfortable wedding scene" in "The Wedding of River Song" is "the pinnacle of a dysfunctional relationship."[61] In an interesting turnabout of the traditional shotgun wedding, the Doctor appears to marry River solely so that she will acquiesce and allow time to flow freely again. In the present, River appears to kill the Doctor, and the other characters mourn his loss. For her supposed crimes River is sentenced to 12,000 consecutive life sentences in an interstellar maximum-security prison, although she often escapes for undefined periods of time in order to have further adventures, including many romantic date nights with her husband (who is very much alive and living undercover).

In many of these adventures, River utilizes her archaeological training as well as her innate intelligence and mischievous spirit, although until her very last adventure her motives are suspiciously self-centered (or, at the very least, Doctor-centered). For example, in the first episodes in which Amy and Rory meet River she is on a consulting job to help procure a military weapon—a dangerous living statue called a Weeping Angel—from the debris of a starliner that had crashed into an archaeological site. River had conveniently left a personal SOS for the Doctor so that he would just happen to be at the right space-time coordinates to save her from the very same doomed craft, which allows her to offer her services as an archaeologist for hire in the first place.[62] In "The Pandorica Opens," frustrated that the Doctor hasn't returned her calls, River escapes from prison, buys a mini time machine through dubious means, and gets the Doctor's attention by carving a message for him into a cliff on the oldest planet in the universe. River's message (according to legend an undecipherable "message from the dawn of time") is her trademark salutation "Hello Sweetie" plus space-time coordinates. Not only has River cleverly used archaeological information (she travels back in time and creates the archaeological site), but she also selfishly brings the Doctor to Stonehenge in the time of the Roman Empire (where she is masquerading as Cleopatra).[63]

Mark A. Hall notes that female archaeologists tend to be portrayed in films as "determined, independent and intelligent (stock heroic requirements it has to be admitted)."[64] But in addition, he reflects that in a number of films it is seen that "women professionals are human too and subject to the foibles of greed, professional rivalry and psychotic, mad-scientist obsession."[65] Kevin McGeough draws attention to a particularly unrealistic aspect of depictions of archaeologists in popular culture, namely the Indiana Jones stereotype of archaeologist as treasure hunter, in which he or she "either splits the loot with private donors, or is paid a cash settlement by the museum or government agency that retained his services."[66] These stereotypes fit well with Haynes' category of the scientist as adventurer as well as Flicker's evil plotter.

Nowhere is this more clearly seen in the case of River Song than in her penultimate (in her timeline) adventure with the Doctor. In the 2015 Christmas special "The Husbands of River Song," she tricks the murderous cyborg potentate Hydroflax into marrying her so that she can retrieve the famous Halassi Androvar diamond that has become lodged in his head.[67] Not recognizing the Twelfth Doctor, she believes him to be a surgeon and coldly orders him to remove Hydroflax's head in order to access the stone. River explains, "I basically married the diamond. The Halassi want their diamond back, so they came to me."[68] When the Doctor asks why she was given the task, she retorts, "I'm an archaeologist," to which the Doctor adds, "Slash murderer slash thief."[69] Never one to back down from an insult, River offers (in a rather cavalier Indiana Jones way) that "an archaeologist is just a thief. With patience."[70] River recounts the king's crimes, and explains that the "murder of a creature like that wouldn't weigh heavily on my conscience, even if I had one."[71] But River has no intention of returning the diamond to its rightful owners. Instead, she intends to sell it to the highest bidder on board a starship full of murderers that she knows (through a previous archaeological dig) will actually crash after being hit in a meteorite storm. Her ultimate plan is to reclaim the diamond at the crash site in the future. Instead, after escaping in the meteorite storm, River and the Doctor spend their last night together, as legend had long held, at the Singing Towers of Darillium, where, fortunately for the star-crossed lovers, nights last 24 years. It is only River's realization that the Doctor truly does love her that softens her heart and turns her into the noble scientist that viewers first meet in 2008, a woman willing to allow a computer to burn out her brain in order to save 4000 strangers and prevent the Doctor from making that sacrifice himself.[72]

To return to Orthia's original assessment of her character, is River Song a marginalized (or even marginal) female scientist, or a powerful, complex character? She is the only person to whom the Doctor has told his true name, a name the audience is not privy to. She utilizes her archaeological knowledge and skills on numerous occasions. She saves his life more than once, ironic given the fact that she has been trained to take his life instead. She is unique in her ability to pilot the TARDIS, arguably even more masterfully than the Doctor himself. In her analysis, Orthia rates River Song as among the noble scientists, based on her selfless actions in the Library. After having seen the entirety of River Song's arc, it is apparent that this nobility has been achieved only at the end of a lengthy and often painful metamorphosis, which makes it that much more powerful. Her nobility is not a mere stereotype, but rather is won through blood, sweat, and countless tears. In her evolution from infant kidnapping victim and brainwashed assassin to noble scientist, I argue that River Song provides a strong role model of female agency and is the most complex character of the Moffat Era.

Looking to the Future, with One Eye to the Past

As we have seen, the four main female scientists of the Moffat Era of *Doctor Who* are, in their own ways, multi-faceted characters that defy simple classification into established tropes. All but one of these women come into their own over the course of their respective arcs, demonstrating significant character development while never losing their identities as scientists. The sole character to remain rather two-dimensional in many ways is interestingly also the woman who is the least scientific: Kate Lethbridge-Stewart. The Moffat years therefore seem to paint women scientists in a largely positive light.

It is instructive to remind ourselves that, for all its adult themes, *Doctor Who* was initially conceived to be a children's show. Therefore, negative stereotypes of women scientists reflected in science fiction media for children may, as I have suggested elsewhere, have a chilling effect on girls who might otherwise consider science as a career.[73] Conversely, positive depictions of women in science in children's science fiction and fantasy (for example, in the character of *Harry Potter*'s Hermione Granger) have the potential to fan the flames of budding scientists, of all genders.[74] It is therefore encouraging that in a 2016 study of scientific characters in *Doctor Who* through 2013, Orthia and Morgain find that there is no gender difference in the depicted scientific credibility of these characters. In addition, as they note, the relative percentage of female scientist characters has increased significantly over the show's tenure, from a low 15 percent in the 1960s to 42 percent in the 2000s, all positive findings for those interested in depictions of women in science.[75]

In her thesis, Orthia also points out that of the 36 humanoid (i.e., non-robotic) companions prior to the Moffat Era, while women make up 64 percent of the total companions, the relative percentage of scientist companions is gender neutral (approximately 30.5 percent of all companions, regardless of gender).[76] This equality is heartening, until one analyzes the relationships between the Doctor and his companions more closely. Based on this analysis, Orthia concludes that the role of true companion (i.e., traveling in the TARDIS long-term) is "largely unsuitable for scientists, particularly in the presence of messianic Doctors whose narrative function is to be brilliant and infallible."[77] However, she tempers this with the insight that during incarnations of a "fallible Doctor, scientist companions could maintain their scientific credibility, beat the Doctor at science, and receive the Doctor's blessing for it."[78] Since the Doctors of both the Davies and Moffat Eras have largely been flawed, fallible characters, this would explain why there have been successful strong female scientists in recent years, even if their numbers have been relatively low and they have not reached the status of long-term travel in the TARDIS (with the possible exception of River Song).

Given Osgood's popularity, fans have speculated online as to whether she would become the Twelfth Doctor's new companion (after the exit of Clara Oswald), especially given the fact that the Doctor teases one of the Osgoods with such a possibility before her untimely death.[79] Again, to be elevated to the role of companion is an honor within the canon of the series, for the Doctor is selective about whom he invites to accompany him on his journeys throughout all of time and space. Cassie Beyer argues that despite the popularity of Osgood, it would be nearly impossible for this scenario to work precisely because the character is a Mary Sue, and "the Doctor doesn't need a fangirl."[80] In addition, as Osgood herself notes after the end of the Zygon rebellion when the Doctor openly extends an invitation, while she wants to come "More than anything," she has to remain because she has "a world to keep safe."[81]

What about the Doctor being portrayed by a woman? When David Tennant announced he was leaving the series, the UK Resource Centre for Women in Science, Engineering and Technology (UKRC) argued for such a bold move, noting "that making a high profile sci-fi character with a following like Doctor Who female would help to raise the profile of women in science and bring the issue of the important contribution women can and should make to science in the public domain."[82] Similar calls were made when Tennant's successor Matt Smith voiced his intentions to leave the series.[83] Moffat explained that such a casting was impossible simply because he had already made up his mind to cast Peter Capaldi as the next Doctor.[84] Moffat does take credit for making a female Doctor possible in the future, claiming "It wasn't part of the fiction of the show until I wrote it. And I keep establishing it."[85] Here Moffat is referring to three *Doctor Who* episodes during his time at the helm in which it is established that Time Lords can change gender from one regeneration to the next.[86] Now, with Chris Chibnall taking over as the showrunner for the 2017 season, a female Doctor has been announced: Jodie Whittaker will be the first woman in the role.[87]

Regardless of the veracity of the charges of misogyny filed against him, Moffat opined in 2015, "We need better female role models and representation on screen. [...] We do need to do better. It's important to me that the little girls watching see Amy or Clara or Rose and want to be like them."[88] But perhaps Moffat is missing the point with this list of characters. I argue that it should be more important that little girls want to be Nasreen Chaudhry, River Song, or, perhaps best of all, Petronella Osgood. That would, indeed, be a powerful legacy for the Moffat Era of *Doctor Who*.

NOTES

1. Sydney Newman (creator), *Doctor Who* (BBC: 1963–1989; 2005–present).
2. Russell T. Davies (creator), *The Sarah Jane Adventures* (Sci-Fi Channel: 2007–2011).
3. Lynnette Porter, "Chasing Amy: The Evolution of the Doctor's Female Companion in the New *Who*," in *Doctor Who in Time and Space*, ed. Gillian I. Leitch (Jefferson, NC: McFarland, 2013), 253.
4. *Ibid.*, 257.
5. According to show canon, a Time Lord's body regenerates into a different physical form after his or her body is mortally wounded. This allows additional actors to play the lead character over time.
6. Aja Romano, "Why Does the Man Behind 'Doctor Who' and 'Sherlock Holmes' Still Have a Job?," *The Daily Dot*, January 13, 2014.
7. Chris Johnson, "Doctor Who Writer Steven Moffat Denies He Has Made Show More Misogynist," *The Guardian*, November 28, 2015.
8. Roslynn Haynes, "From Alchemy to Artificial Intelligence: Stereotypes of the Scientist in Western Literature," *Public Understanding of Science* 12 (2003): 244.
9. Lindy A. Orthia, *Enlightenment Was the Choice:* Doctor Who *and the Democratisation of Science* (Ph.D. Thesis, The Australian National University, 2010), 195–198.
10. *Ibid.*, 196–197.
11. *Ibid.*, 245.
12. Other female scientific characters have appeared in a single episode or have played background roles in two episodes and are not analyzed here.
13. Eva Flicker, "Between Brains and Breasts: Women Scientists in Fiction Films," *Public Understanding of Science* 12 (2003): 310–315.
14. Chris Chibnall, "The Hungry Earth," *Doctor Who*, season 5 episode 8, directed by Ashley Way, aired May 22, 2010, on BBC; Chris Chibnall, "Cold Blood," *Doctor Who*, season 5, episode 9, directed by Ashley Way, aired May 29, 2010, on BBC.
15. Catherine Jones, "As an Actor, You Regard Being in *Doctor Who* as Becoming Part of Television History," *Wales Online*, May 22, 2010.
16. The common stereotype of a scientist as a balding, middle-aged, Caucasian male dressed in a white lab coat and glasses is so pervasive in society that it is commonly reflected in the drawings of children. When asked to draw a female scientist, children's images vary little from this basic depiction. For example, a British study found that children tend to picture women scientists as being "thick glasses, flat shoes, big feet, judo types with muscular calves and sensible clothes," often referred to as the "flat chested flat heeled syndrome." Lynda Measor and Pat Sikes, *Gender and Schools* (London: Cassell, 1992), 74–75.
17. Chibnall, "The Hungry Earth."
18. *Ibid.*
19. Chibnall, "Cold Blood."
20. The wider racial and ethnic issues reflected in this episode are deconstructed by Rachel Morgain in "Mapping the Boundaries of Race in the Hungry Earth/Cold Blood," *Doctor Who and Race*, ed. Lindy Orthia (Bristol: Intellect Press, 2013), 252–267.
21. Jones, "As an Actor."
22. Chibnall, "The Hungry Earth."
23. Derek, "The Modern *Doctor Who* Characters That Should Have Become Companions," Crustula.com (blog), March 29, 2013.
24. "Brigadier Alastair Gordon Lethbridge-Stewart (Nicholas Courtney)," *Doctor Who*, BBC website, last modified September 24, 2014.

25. Chris Chibnall, "The Power of Three," *Doctor Who*, season 7, episode 4, directed by Douglas Mackinnon, aired September 22, 2012, on BBC.
26. Interestingly, she introduces herself to the Cyberman army in "Death in Heaven" as "Kate Stewart. Divorcee, mother of two, keen gardener, outstanding bridge player. Also Chief Scientific Officer, Unified Intelligence Taskforce, who currently have you surrounded." While this may be interpreted as her downplaying her status as a scientist, it is more likely an attempt at humor, something the Cybermen do not understand. Steven Moffat, "Death in Heaven," *Doctor Who*, season 8, episode 12, directed by Rachel Talalay, aired November 8, 2014, on BBC.
27. Chibnall, "The Power of Three."
28. *Ibid.*
29. "Kate Stewart," *Doctor Who*, BBC website, accessed September 15, 2016.
30. Steven Moffat, "The Magician's Apprentice," *Doctor Who*, season 9, episode 1, directed by Hettie Macdonald, aired September 19, 2015, on BBC.
31. Steven Moffat, "The Day of the Doctor," *Doctor Who*, 50th anniversary special, directed by Nick Hurran, aired November 23, 2013, on BBC.
32. Moffat, "Death in Heaven."
33. "Osgood," *Doctor Who*, BBC website, accessed September 15, 2016.
34. Moffat, "The Day of the Doctor."
35. In "The Zygon Inversion" the Doctor finally asks Osgood what her name is and is told "Petronella." Peter Hartness and Steven Moffat, "The Zygon Inversion," *Doctor Who*, season 9, episode 8, directed by Daniel Nettheim, aired November 7, 2015, on BBC.
36. Moffat, "The Day of the Doctor."
37. Kathryn Williams, "Look Who's Back from the Dead as Osgood Returns to *Doctor Who*," *Wales Online*, October 30, 2015.
38. Peter Hartness, "The Zygon Invasion," *Doctor Who*, season 9, episode 7, directed by Daniel Nettheim, aired on October 31, 2015, on BBC.
39. Nathan Lobo, "A Few Thoughts on Kate Stewart," *Doctor Who TV*, November 5, 2015.
40. Moffat, "The Day of the Doctor."
41. Hartness and Moffat, "The Zygon Inversion."
42. Josh Steer, "Why Osgood Is So Popular," *Doctor Who TV*, October 30, 2015.
43. Steven Moffat, "Silence in the Library," *Doctor Who*, season 4, episode 8 directed by Euros Lyn, aired May 31, 2008 on BBC; Steven Moffat, "Forest of the Dead," *Doctor Who*, series 4, episode 9, directed by Euros Lyn, aired June 7, 2008 on BBC.
44. Strictly speaking, while the first meeting of the Doctor and River Song in his timeline *is* their last physical meeting in *her* timeline (ending with her death), the remainder of their timelines connect in a much more nonlinear manner. For a brief summary, see Huw Fullerton, "River Song's Doctor Who Life in Order," *Radio Times*, December 25, 2015.
45. Given that the focus of this essay is on these four women as scientists, much of the controversy surrounding River Song's relationship with the Doctor falls out of the scope of this discussion. Interested readers are directed to Joanna Robinson, "How the *Doctor Who* Christmas Special Finally Gave River Song the Husband She Deserves," *Vanity Fair*, December 25, 2015; Emily Asher-Perrin, "The Problem with River Song," Tor.com, January 8, 2014.
46. Asher-Perrin, "The Problem with River Song."
47. *Ibid.*
48. Steven Moffat, "Let's Kill Hitler," *Doctor Who*, season 6, episode 8, directed by Richard Senior, aired August 27, 2011, on BBC.
49. Paul Mackendrick, "Education for the Art of Living," *The Journal of Higher Education* 23, no. 8 (1952): 427.
50. Steven Moffat, "The Impossible Astronaut," *Doctor Who*, season 6 episode 1, directed by Toby Haynes, aired April 23, 2011, on BBC.
51. Steven Moffat, "Flesh and Stone," *Doctor Who*, season 5, episode 5, directed by Adam Smith, aired May 1, 2010, on BBC.
52. Steven Moffat, "The Name of the Doctor," *Doctor Who*, special, directed by Saul Metzstein, aired May 18, 2013, on BBC.

53. Moffat, "The Impossible Astronaut."
54. Steven Moffat, "Day of the Moon," *Doctor Who*, season 6, episode 2, directed by Toby Haynes, aired April 30, 2011, on BBC.
55. Kevin McGeough, "Heroes, Mummies, and Treasure: Near Eastern Archaeology in the Movies," *Near Eastern Archaeology* 69, no. 3–4 (2006): 181–182.
56. Steven Moffat, "The Wedding of River Song," *Doctor Who*, season 6, episode 13, directed by Jeremy Webb, aired on October 1, 2011, on BBC.
57. Moffat, "Let's Kill Hitler."
58. Asher-Perrin, "The Problem with River Song."
59. Gareth Roberts, "Closing Time," *Doctor Who*, season 6 episode 12, directed by Steve Hughes, aired on September 24, 2011, on BBC.
60. Moffat, "The Wedding of River Song."
61. Robinson, "How the Doctor Who Christmas Special Finally Gave River Song the Husband She Deserves."
62. Steven Moffat, "The Time of Angels," *Doctor Who*, season 5, episode 4, directed by Adam Smith, aired April 24, 2010, on BBC; Steven Moffat, "Flesh and Stone," *Doctor Who*, season 5, episode 5, directed by Adam Smith, aired May 1, 2010 on BBC.
63. Steven Moffat, "The Pandorica Opens," *Doctor Who*, season 5, episode 12, directed by Toby Haynes, aired July 17, 2010, on BBC.
64. Mark A. Hall, "Romancing the Stones: Archaeology in Popular Cinema," *European Journal of Archaeology* 72, no. 2 (2004): 169.
65. Ibid.
66. McGeough, "Heroes, Mummies, and Treasure," 175.
67. Steven Moffat, "The Husbands of River Song," *Doctor Who*, special 17, directed by Douglas Mackinnon, aired December 25, 2015, on BBC.
68. Ibid.
69. Ibid.
70. Ibid.
71. Ibid.
72. Moffat, "Silence in the Library"; Moffat, "Forest of the Dead."
73. Kristine Larsen, "Toys, a T-Rex, and Trouble: Cautionary Tales of Time Travel in Children's Film," in *The Galaxy Is Rated G: Essays on Children's Science Fiction Film and Television*, eds. R.C. Neighbors and Sandy Rankin (Jefferson, NC: McFarland, 2011), 228–247.
74. Kristine Larsen, "Boy Wizards and Girl Scientists: Rowling's Contributions to Science Outreach," in *Teaching with Harry Potter*, ed. Valerie Estelle Frankel (Jefferson, NC: McFarland, 2013), 56–68.
75. Lindy A. Orthia and Rachel Morgain, "The Gendered Culture of Scientific Competence: A Study of Scientist Characters in Doctor Who 1963–2013," *Sex Roles* 75 (2016): 91.
76. Orthia, *Enlightenment Was the Choice*, 196–197.
77. Ibid., 258.
78. Ibid.
79. Moffat, "Death in Heaven."
80. Cassie Beyer, "Why Osgood Won't Be the New Doctor Who Companion," *History, Interrupted* (blog), November 11, 2015.
81. Hartness and Moffat, "The Zygon Inversion."
82. Graeme McMillan, "'Doctor Who Should be a Woman' Say Female Scientists," *Gizmodo Io9*, December 3, 2008.
83. Alison Pezanoski-Browne, "The Good Doctor: Four Arguments for Why 'Doctor Who' Should Get a Female Doctor," *Bitch Media*, April 12, 2013.
84. Sonia Saraiya, "Steven Moffat on Why He Hasn't Cast a Female Doctor Yet," *Salon*, August 9, 2015.
85. Ibid.
86. Steven Moffat, "Dark Water," *Doctor Who*, season 8, episode 11, directed by Rachel Talalay, aired November 1, 2014, on BBC; Steven Moffat, "Hell Bent," *Doctor Who*, season 9, episode 12, directed by Rachel Talalay, aired December 5, 2015, on BBC; Neil Gaiman, "The

Doctor's Wife," *Doctor Who*, season 6, episode 4, directed by Richard Clark, aired May 14, 2011, on BBC.

87. "Jodie Whittaker: Doctor Who's 13th Time Lord to Be a Woman," *BBC News*, July 16, 2017.

88. Patrick Mulkern, "Steven Moffat Talks Ratings, Misogyny, Casting Missy, Ashildr's End Game, the Next Companion and Leaving *Doctor Who*," *Radio Times*, December 2, 2015.

WORKS CITED

Asher-Perrin, Emily. "The Problem with River Song." Tor.com, January 8, 2014. http://www.tor.com/2014/01/08/the-problem-with-river-song-doctor-who/.

Beyer, Cassie. "Why Osgood Won't Be the New *Doctor Who* Companion." *History, Interrupted* (blog). November 11, 2015. http://blog.cnbeyer.com/tag/osgood/.

"Brigadier Alastair Gordon Lethbridge-Stewart (Nicholas Courtney)." *Doctor Who*, BBC website. Last modified September 24, 2014. http://www.bbc.co.uk/doctorwho/classic/episodeguide/companions/page14.shtml.

Chibnall, Chris. "Cold Blood." *Doctor Who*, season 5, episode 9. Directed by Ashley Way. Aired May 29, 2010, on BBC.

_____. "The Hungry Earth." *Doctor Who*, season 5 episode 8. Directed by Ashley Way. Aired May 22, 2010, on BBC.

_____. "The Power of Three." *Doctor Who*, season 7, episode 4. Directed by Douglas Mackinnon. Aired September 22, 2012, on BBC.

Davies, Russell T. *The Sarah Jane Adventures*. Sci-Fi Channel, 2007–2011.

Derek. "The Modern Doctor Who Characters That Should Have Become Companions." *Crustula* (blog), March 29, 2013. https://crustula.com/2013/03/29/the-modern-doctor-who-characters-that-should-have-become-companions/.

Flicker, Eva. "Between Brains and Breasts: Women Scientists in Fiction Films." *Public Understanding of Science* 12 (2003): 307–318.

Fullerton, Huw. "River Song's *Doctor Who* Life in Order." *Radio Times*, December 25, 2015. http://www.radiotimes.com/news/2015-12-25/river-songs-doctor-who-life-in-order.

Gaiman, Neil. "The Doctor's Wife." *Doctor Who*, season 6, episode 4. Directed by Richard Clark. Aired May 14, 2011, on BBC.

Hall, Mark A. "Romancing the Stones: Archaeology in Popular Cinema." *European Journal of Archaeology* 72, no. 2 (2004): 159–176.

Hartness, Peter. "The Zygon Invasion." *Doctor Who*, season 9, episode 7. Directed by Daniel Nettheim. Aired on October 31, 2015, on BBC.

Hartness, Peter, and Steven Moffat. "The Zygon Inversion," *Doctor Who*, season 9, episode 8. Directed by Daniel Nettheim. Aired November 7, 2015, on BBC.

Haynes, Roslynn. "From Alchemy to Artificial Intelligence: Stereotypes of the Scientist in Western Literature." *Public Understanding of Science* 12 (2003): 243–253.

"Jodie Whittaker: Doctor Who's 13th Time Lord to be a Woman." *BBC News*, July 16, 2017. http://www.bbc.com/news/entertainment-arts-40624288

Johnson, Chris. "*Doctor Who* Writer Steven Moffat Denies He Has Made Show More Misogynist." *The Guardian*, November 28, 2015. https://www.theguardian.com/media/2015/nov/28/doctor-who-writer-steven-moffat-denies-misogynist-claims.

Jones, Catherine. "As an Actor, You Regard Being in *Doctor Who* as Becoming Part of Television History." *Wales Online*, May 22, 2010. http://www.walesonline.co.uk/lifestyle/showbiz/actor-you-regard-being-doctor-1919273.

"Kate Stewart." *Doctor Who*, BBC website. Accessed September 15, 2016. http://www.bbc.co.uk/programmes/profiles/2h0xM8B6TJRYMwdhqmGcnj7/kate-stewart.

Larsen, Kristine. "Boy Wizards and Girl Scientists: Rowling's Contributions to Science Outreach." In *Teaching with Harry Potter*, edited by Valerie Estelle Frankel, 56–68. Jefferson, NC: McFarland, 2013.

_____. "Toys, a T-Rex, and Trouble: Cautionary Tales of Time Travel in Children's Film." In *The Galaxy is Rated G: Essays on Children's Science Fiction Film and Television*, edited by R.C. Neighbors and Sandy Rankin, 228–247. Jefferson, NC: McFarland, 2011.

Lobo, Nathan. "A Few Thoughts on Kate Stewart." *Doctor Who TV*, November 5, 2015. http://www.doctorwhotv.co.uk/a-few-thoughts-on-kate-stewart-77709.htm.
Mackendrick, Paul. "Education for the Art of Living." *The Journal of Higher Education* 23, no. 8 (1952): 423–428, 456.
McGeough, Kevin. "Heroes, Mummies, and Treasure: Near Eastern Archaeology in the Movies." *Near Eastern Archaeology* 69, no. 3–4 (2006): 174–185.
McMillan, Graeme. "'Doctor Who Should Be a Woman' Say Female Scientists." *Gizmodo Io9*, December 3, 2008. http://io9.gizmodo.com/5100908/new-doctor-should-be-female-say-female-scientists.
Measor, Lynda, and Pat Sikes. *Gender and Schools*. London: Cassell, 1992.
Moffat, Steven. "The Angels Take Manhattan." *Doctor Who*, season 7, episode 5. Directed by Nick Hurran. Aired September 29, 2012, on BBC.
_____. "Dark Water." *Doctor Who*, season 8, episode 11. Directed by Rachel Talalay. Aired November 1, 2014, on BBC.
_____. "The Day of the Doctor." *Doctor Who*, 50th anniversary special. Directed by Nick Hurran. Aired November 23, 2013, on BBC.
_____. "Day of the Moon." *Doctor Who*, season 6, episode 2. Directed by Toby Haynes. Aired April 30, 2011, on BBC.
_____. "Death in Heaven." *Doctor Who*, season 8, episode 12. Directed by Rachel Talalay. Aired November 8, 2014, on BBC.
_____. "Flesh and Stone." *Doctor Who*, season 5, episode 5. Directed by Adam Smith. Aired May 1, 2010, on BBC.
_____. "Forest of the Dead." *Doctor Who*, series 4, episode 9. Directed by Euros Lyn. Aired June 7, 2008, on BBC.
_____. "Hell Bent." *Doctor Who*, season 9, episode 12. Directed by Rachel Talalay. Aired December 5, 2015, on BBC.
_____. "The Husbands of River Song." special 17. Directed by Douglas Mackinnon. Aired December 25, 2015, on BBC.
_____. "The Impossible Astronaut." *Doctor Who*, season 6, episode 1. Directed by Toby Haynes. Aired April 23, 2011, on BBC.
_____. "Let's Kill Hitler." *Doctor Who*, season 6, episode 8. Directed by Richard Senior. Aired August 27, 2011, on BBC.
_____. "The Magician's Apprentice." *Doctor Who*, season 9, episode 1. Directed by Hettie Macdonald. Aired September 19, 2015, on BBC.
_____. "The Name of the Doctor." *Doctor Who*, special 13. Directed by Saul Metzstein. Aired May 18, 2013, on BBC.
_____. "The Pandorica Opens." *Doctor Who*, season 5, episode 12. Directed by Toby Haynes. Aired July 17, 2010, on BBC.
_____. "Silence in the Library." *Doctor Who*, season 4, episode 8. Directed by Euros Lyn. Aired May 31, 2008, on BBC.
_____. "The Time of Angels." *Doctor Who*, season 5, episode 4. Directed by Adam Smith. Aired April 24, 2010, on BBC.
_____. "The Wedding of River Song." *Doctor Who*, season 6, episode 13. Directed by Jeremy Webb. Aired on October 1, 2011, on BBC.
Morgain, Rachel. "Mapping the Boundaries of Race in *The Hungry Earth/Cold Blood*." In *Doctor Who and Race*, edited by Lindy Orthia, 252–67. Bristol: Intellect Press, 2013.
Mulkern, Patrick. "Steven Moffat Talks Ratings, Misogyny, Casting Missy, Ashildr's End Game, the Next Companion and Leaving *Doctor Who*." *Radio Times*, December 2, 2015. http://www.radiotimes.com/news/2015-12-02/steven-moffat-talks-ratings-misogyny-casting-missy-ashildrs-end-game-the-next-companion-and-leaving-doctor-who.
Newman, Sydney. *Doctor Who*. BBC: 1963–1989; 2005–present.
Orthia, Lindy A. *Enlightenment Was the Choice*: Doctor Who *and the Democratisation of Science*. Ph.D. diss., the Australian National University, 2010.
Orthia, Lindy A., and Rachel Morgain. "The Gendered Culture of Scientific Competence: A Study of Scientist Characters in *Doctor Who* 1963–2013." *Sex Roles* 75 (2016): 79–94.

"Osgood." *Doctor Who*, BBC website. Accessed September 15, 2016. http://www.bbc.co.uk/programmes/profiles/nb0PrNpn29JsBkggCkrytT/osgood.
Pezanoski-Browne, Alison. "The Good Doctor: Four Arguments for Why *Doctor Who* Should Get a Female Doctor." *Bitch Media*, April 12, 2013. https://bitchmedia.org/post/the-good-doctor-four-arguments-for-why-doctor-who-should-get-a-female-doctor.
Porter, Lynnette. "Chasing Amy: The Evolution of the Doctor's Female Companion in the New *Who*." In *Doctor Who in Time and Space*, edited by Gillian I. Leitch, 253–267. Jefferson, NC: McFarland 2013.
Roberts, Gareth. "Closing Time." *Doctor Who*, season 6, episode 12. Directed by Steve Hughes. Aired September 24, 2011, on BBC.
Robinson, Joanna. "How the *Doctor Who* Christmas Special Finally Gave River Song the Husband She Deserves." *Vanity Fair*, December 25, 2015. http://www.vanityfair.com/hollywood/2015/12/doctor-who-river-song-final-episode-christmas-special.
Romano, Aja. "Why Does the Man Behind 'Doctor Who' and 'Sherlock Holmes' Still Have a Job?" *The Daily Dot*, January 13, 2014. http://www.dailydot.com/via/steven-moffat-sexism-sherlock-doctor-who/.
Saraiya, Sonia. "Steven Moffat on Why He Hasn't Cast a Female Doctor Yet" *Salon*, August 9, 2015. http://www.salon.com/2015/08/09/steven_moffat_on_why_he_hasnt_cast_a_female_doctor_yet_i_think_it_would_have_been_a_disaster/.
Steer, Josh. "Why Osgood Is So Popular." *Doctor Who TV*, October 30, 2015. http://www.doctorwhotv.co.uk/why-osgood-is-so-popular-77484.htm.
Williams, Katheryn. "Look Who's Back from the Dead as Osgood Returns to *Doctor Who*." *Wales Online*, October 30, 2015. http://www.walesonline.co.uk/whats-on/film-news/look-whos-back-dead-osgood-10361135.

About the Contributors

Bridget M. **Blodgett** is an associate professor of simulation and game design at the University of Baltimore. She researches technology within Internet culture, the social impact of virtual worlds and Internet culture on offline life, and the online gaming community.

Ashley Lynn **Carlson** is an associate professor of English at the University of Montana Western. She researches 19th- and 20th-century women's literature, science and literature, television and popular culture. She edited *Genius on Television* and has published on contemporary television and 19th century women's writing.

Hope J. **Crowell** is pursuing a bachelor of arts in English with a minor in professional communications at the University of Montana Western. Her research interests include Victorian literature and contemporary dystopian fiction.

Cary M.J. **Elza** is an assistant professor of media studies at University of Wisconsin–Stevens Point. She received her Ph.D. from Northwestern University. She has published on children's and teen media, science fiction and fantasy series, new media and fandom, and early animation.

Laura **Foster** completed her Ph.D. at Cardiff University in 2014. Her research focuses on the workhouse in 19th-century culture. She also researches crime fiction, gender studies and visual culture. Her publications include articles in *Victorian Network* and the *Journal of Victorian Culture*.

Natalie **Krikowa** researches and teaches media, audience engagement, genre studies and Australian cultural histories of lesbian and queer media. She holds a doctorate in creative arts in media and cultural studies from the University of Technology Sydney. She is also the creative director of Zenowa Media.

Kristine **Larsen** is a professor of astronomy at Central Connecticut State University. She researches and teaches the intersections between science and gender, science and popular culture, and the history of science. She is the author or coeditor of multiple books.

JZ **Long** is an assistant professor of communications at Wilson College. In addition to publications on popular themes in cinema and television, his research analyzes the field of media regulation, particularly issues involving the First Amendment and the FCC.

Helen **McKenzie** is a doctoral candidate at Cardiff University in Wales. Her thesis is on professional authors in the mid–19th century, particularly the rise of the female writer. Her research interests include the Victorian periodical press, women's studies and popular culture.

Erin **Nicholes** holds a bachelor's degree in print journalism from the University of Montana and is pursuing a second in English and secondary education at the University of Montana Western. Her research interests include women writers and their histories.

Lisa K. **Perdigao** is the humanities program chair and a professor of English at the Florida Institute of Technology. Her research and teaching interests are American literature, film, television, comics and YA literature. She has published two books and numerous articles on films and television series.

Jennifer **Phillips** is a researcher in literature and culture at the University of Wollongong and honorary co-director of the Australian Studies Centre at Wuhan University in China. Her interests include literature, gender, cultural identity and adaptation theory. She has published works on various TV shows and novels.

Anastasia **Salter** is an assistant professor of digital media at the University of Central Florida. She is the author of *Jane Jensen* and *What Is Your Quest?* She is a member of the Electronic Literature Organization board of directors and the Modern Language Association Committee on the Status of Women in the Profession.

Lauren Riccelli **Zwicky** holds a Ph.D. in English from the University of Miami and is faculty co-appointed in literature and gender studies at Metropolitan State University. Her research examines intersections of gender and sexuality in contemporary American literature and culture. She has published work in *Assuming Gender* as well as several edited collections.

Index

ABC 103
Adventure Time 3, 20–25, 30–32
Agent Carter 102–116
Amazon 9, 16
Anderson, Gillian 78, 79
Annedroids 9, 11–16
anti-feminism 37, 41
archaeology 195–199
Arrow 37, 39, 42–43, 48
Athena SWAN 147

BBC 134, 170–174, 181–182, 187, 188, 191–192
biology 2, 9, 13, 21, 22, 87, 95, 96, 113, 122
Blindspot 120–131
Bones 4, 36–39, 43–45, 48–49, 78, 148n23, 152
Buffy the Vampire Slayer 78, 79
Butler, Judith 57

Captain America: The First Avenger 102, 103, 105
Captain America: The Winter Soldier 102
CBS 67, 120
chemistry 9, 10, 22
Clinton, Hillary 25
computer science 1–2, 7, 9, 21–22, 36, 45–48, 73–74, 77, 115–116, 121–122, 126
Creed, Barbara 155–157
Criminal Minds 4, 37, 39, 45–49
Crossing Jordan 4, 152, 154, 157–161, 163–166, 166–167n9
CSI: Crime Scene Investigation 120, 122, 153
"CSI Effect" 49, 165
CSI: Miami 152–154, 157–166
Curie, Marie 38, 109, 110
The CW 72, 73

de Certeau, Michel 155
desexualization *see* sexualization
disability 66, 73, 80, 146
discrimination 158; and gender 2, 36, 59, 127, 130; in hiring 2, 127; in the workplace 2, 86, 130; *see also* misogyny; sexual harassment
Doctor Who 4, 175, 187–201

engineering 1–5, 7, 9, 11–16, 25–32, 36, 48, 56–67, 77–80, 109

Facebook 165; *see also* social media
fandom *see* fans
fans 4, 28, 42–43, 44–45, 48, 78, 171–172, 174, 175–182, 188, 189, 191, 193, 194, 197, 200
femininity 4, 10–13, 26, 30, 62–67, 78, 88, 91–94, 106, 111, 122–125, 127, 129–131, 136–137, 139, 141, 143, 145–146, 158–161, 163, 189, 193; *see also* sexuality
feminism 4, 86–99, 104, 109, 114, 115, 154, 159, 175–176, 195
forensic pathology 4, 39, 77, 134–166, 174–175
Foucault, Michel *see* panopticism
Freudian psychology 156–157
Friedan, Betty 104–105, 111, 113
Fringe 78

Gatiss, Mark 171, 174, 177, 180
geology 189–191
Girl Scouts of America 8, 11
Girls Who Code 3, 86

Harry Potter 199
HBO 3
high school 2, 3, 9–11, 48; *see also* teenagers
Hulu 79, 115

isolation (of women in STEM) 3–4, 8, 11–12, 15, 20, 21–32, 62, 144
ITV 135, 150n65

Jessica Jones 87

Kristeva, Julia 155–156

Index

The L Word 93
Law and Order 153
loneliness *see* isolation

MacGyver 67
Mad Max: Fury Road 87
Marvel 102–116
Marvel's Agents of S.H.I.E.L.D. 79, 115
masculinity 13, 25, 57–67, 91–93, 106, 109, 122–123, 129, 139–140, 145; *see also* sexuality
mathematics 1–3, 7–8, 13, 15, 16, 36, 59, 67, 77, 123
McKellar, Danica 15
medical examiners *see* forensic pathology
mentoring 2, 3, 8–9, 13–15, 25, 28, 141, 189
Microsoft 3
misogyny 20, 113, 137, 141, 144, 173, 188, 200; *see also* discrimination; sexual harassment
Moffat, Steven 4, 171–182, 187–189, 191, 194, 195, 199–201

National Girls Collaborative Project 3
National Math + Science Initiative 1
National Science Foundation 17, 36
NBC 120, 152
NCIS 4, 37, 39–41, 48, 120
Netflix 3, 9, 16, 79, 87, 115
Nielsen Company 3

objectification (of women) 63, 74, 92, 104, 138, 143, 156; *see also* sexualization
The 100 4, 56, 64–67, 71–80
Orphan Black 4, 86–99

panopticism 92, 138
patriarchy 4, 86–88, 93–99, 109, 111, 113–114, 135–6, 159
PBS 9, 13, 15–16
performativity 57
Phineas and Ferb 31–32
Prime Suspect 135, 147, 148
Project Mc^2 9–16

Quantico 79

race 8, 10, 12, 14, 57–59, 66–67, 71–80, 108–109, 121–122, 154, 160, 162, 165, 167, 201; African American 8, 10, 14, 108–109, 160; Asian American 14, 64; Blacks 12, 57, 122, 154, 165, 167; Caucasians 8, 14, 58, 75, 79, 93, 122, 153, 154, 162, 201; and diversity 10, 12, 14, 67, 79; Hispanics 8, 10, 58, 72; Latino/as, 14, 72, 74–80, 121–122; minorities 10, 66, 71–72, 76, 80, 162; white-savior trope 62; *see also* stereotypes
Radway, Janice 154, 159
Rizzoli and Isles 78
role models 4, 8–9, 10, 14, 16, 25, 31, 56, 60, 78, 79, 99, 121–131, 137, 147, 171, 176, 189, 191, 194, 199, 200

The Sarah Jane Adventures 187
Scientific American 56
SciGirls 9, 13–17
Scorpion 4, 56, 64–67
"Scully Effect" 79, 80
sexual harassment 2, 11, 41; *see also* discrimination; misogyny
sexual orientation 61, 90, 162; *see also* sexuality
sexuality = 26, 29, 31, 37, 40, 41, 43, 74, 86, 90, 92–93, 95–96, 108, 111, 122–123 156, 176, 180, 188, 189, 195, 196; asexuality 177, 189; bisexuality 93, 167n16; heterosexuality 89, 92, 95–96, 123, 177; homosexuality 92, 122, 177, 181; *see also* sexual orientation
sexualization (of women) 4, 40, 43, 49, 92–93, 109, 142, 154–157, 159; *see also* objectification
Sherlock 4, 170–182
Showtime 60
Silent Witness 134–147
soap operas 43, 154, 159, 161–162, 166
social media 9, 86, 165, 170, 171, 175–176, 179–181
Star Trek: The Original Series 37, 47, 57
Star Trek: Voyager 4, 56–67
Stargate SG-1 4, 56, 60–64, 78
stereotype threat 8, 16; *see also* stereotypes
stereotypes 37–39, 48–49, 71–72, 124, 199; and gender 2–3, 8, 10–11, 16, 20–21, 32, 37, 39–41, 43, 48–49, 58–60, 65, 67, 71, 74–79, 89–91, 121, 123, 125, 129–131, 135–136, 141, 143–144, 146, 148, 150, 189–191, 196, 199; and race 58, 60, 66, 72, 74–78, 79; of scientists 20, 21, 32, 37, 43, 45, 48–49, 67, 125, 136, 146, 188–190, 193, 196, 198, 199, 201n16; *see also* stereotype threat
Steven Universe 3–4, 20–22, 25–32

Tales of Suspense 103, 104
teenagers 3, 7–16, 21, 31, 65–67, 71–80, 112, 122–123, 126, 141
Transparent 93
Tumblr 175–176, 179–181; *see also* social media
Twitter 171, 176; *see also* social media

UK Resource Centre for Women in Science, Engineering, and Techonlogy (UKRC) 147, 150n68, 200

victims' rights 153–154, 161–166, 166n6

The X-Files 78–79, 152, 165
Xena: Warrior Princess 78, 79

www.ingramcontent.com/pod-product-compliance
Lightning Source LLC
Chambersburg PA
CBHW032055300426
44116CB00007B/754